# Teaching Literature in the A Level Modern Languages Classroom

This book provides essential support and advice on using literature in the A level modern languages classroom, addressing key concerns such as ways to approach this task and how to maximise the benefit to students. There are strategies for understanding works of different genres as well as ways to analyse plot, characterisation, themes and style, all presented in a logical way that allows existing teaching methods to be built upon.

Including a step-by-step approach to all aspects of planning, resourcing and teaching literature in modern languages at advanced levels, this book covers essential topics such as:

- Why teaching and studying literature is important
- How to choose the text
- Preparing and introducing the literary text
- Understanding the characters, themes, style and structure
- Writing examination essays
- Ways to spark creative language use before and beyond the set text

Based on the latest A level modern languages syllabus, this practical book will help both new and experienced teachers approach teaching literature with more confidence, which will enrich their students' language learning and inspire their creativity beyond examination requirements.

**Katherine Raithby** formerly taught French and German to A level in Cambridgeshire. She then led the Modern Languages PGCE programme at the University of Bath, UK, and its affiliated training providers for many years. Her PhD research focused on giftedness in Modern Languages education.

**Alison Taylor** is a freelance language specialist, with a range of teaching experience at secondary level. She subsequently worked in Secondary Teacher Education at the University of the West of England, UK.

# Teaching Literature in the A Level Modern Languages Classroom

## A Teacher's Guide to Success

*Katherine Raithby
and Alison Taylor*

Routledge
Taylor & Francis Group

LONDON AND NEW YORK

First published 2020
by Routledge
2 Park Square, Milton Park, Abingdon, Oxon, OX14 4RN

and by Routledge
52 Vanderbilt Avenue, New York, NY 10017

*Routledge is an imprint of the Taylor & Francis Group, an informa business*

*British Library Cataloguing-in-Publication Data*
A catalogue record for this book is available from the British Library

*Library of Congress Cataloging-in-Publication Data*
A catalog record has been requested for this book

ISBN: 978-1-138-30350-8 (hbk)
ISBN: 978-1-138-30351-5 (pbk)
ISBN: 978-0-203-73102-4 (ebk)

Typeset in Optima
by Swales & Willis, Exeter, Devon, UK

# Contents

# Acknowledgements

The authors wish to acknowledge and thank people they have worked with who have inspired their thinking and thereby contributed to the book.
Particular thanks are due to:
Jean-Yves Faou for his advice and help in checking the French;
John Clare for his advice and help in checking the German;
María del Mar Sánchez Bermúdez for her invaluable help in checking the Spanish;
Dr Carol Morgan for her advice and encouragement;
Les Green for many happy literature lessons in the 1980s;
Paul for limitless love, support and cups of tea over the last 30 years.

# 1 | Introduction

## Introduction

We have both taught A level Modern Foreign Languages (MFL) in the UK and know the joy and satisfaction of working with motivated language students as they develop their linguistic competence and cultural understanding through the two-year examination course. The progress of many students is remarkable as they make the transition from GCSE (see Notes at the end of this chapter) to become confident communicators and enthusiastic enquirers into the language and culture of the target language country.

As teacher educators, we understand, however, that the picture is often more complex. To achieve this transformation, considerable demands are placed upon the beginning teacher, and the high-stakes A level examination can appear a daunting prospect. Teaching the literature component of the syllabus can seem particularly challenging. The purpose of our book is to support teachers to approach these lessons with well-informed confidence and to widen the choices and strategies available to them to help their students to gain enjoyment and examination success from their A level literature study.

In this introductory chapter we shall discuss the context and scope of the book and outline the organisation of the chapters.

## The aims of the book

The book seeks

- to provide beginning teachers and those new to teaching literature with a **structured guide** to approaching this aspect of the syllabus to help students to achieve **examination success**;

- to encourage all teachers to develop a **positive approach** to teaching literature and a **framework** within which to work;

- to offer **practical suggestions for classroom and independent activities** which can be **adapted** for a variety of texts and languages;

- to help teachers to consider the benefits of using literary texts to **enrich language learning** and inspire students' **creativity beyond examination** requirements and in the years **before A level**.

## Who is this book for?

Many teachers will bring years of experience to literature teaching and be comfortable in sharing enthusiastic and innovative practices with students and colleagues alike. Hopefully this book can offer some additional and inspiring ideas and materials.

However, this book primarily has the novice literature teacher in mind. Our experience of working as PGCE tutors has shown us that many teachers feel personally and professionally unprepared for teaching literature, with teacher education programmes often only having limited space to devote to A level as a whole, and far less to literature teaching in particular. This sense of unpreparedness may be exacerbated if the teachers themselves have had little experience of foreign literature as MFL degree courses may not have included any cultural perspective on language that can be accessed through literature (Gieve and Cunico 2012). Literature may be seen as a distraction from a primary linguistic purpose (Pachler *et al.* 2007) and there may be questions about the value of teaching literature and its compulsory insertion into an already crowded syllabus.

It is important to see how the study of literature can actually *enrich* the language syllabus. A substantial first section of the book invites teachers to address the question of the purpose of literature study and what this means for their teaching approach, before planning a single lesson. What the teacher believes about literature study will inevitably affect how lessons are planned and this will in turn influence students' own perceptions, positive or negative, of literary study and how they learn (discussion in Bloemert *et al.* 2017).

The book itself is timely due to the change in A level examinations from 2018, which requires students to study at least one work of foreign literature and sit a written examination in the target language at the end of their course. The linguistic and conceptual challenge posed by this change may seem quite daunting for new teachers and students alike and it is hoped that this book can provide them with valuable support.

# The wider picture

## *Professional development*

An important aspect of a teacher's role is revisiting and extending one's own knowledge and skills. The budgets for professional development continue to be squeezed in schools and much training now takes place on-site and in-house. Many MFL Faculties already find it useful to share ideas on teaching and this book offers suggestions around different aspects of the process of teaching literature, and ideas for materials and activities.

It can also be helpful to talk to colleagues in the English Faculty to test ideas and to start a conversation about teaching literature and encouraging reading for pleasure in the foreign language. This opportunity for interdepartmental collaboration could generate wider discussions about a coherent languages curriculum and be mutually beneficial (e.g. Pomphrey 2004; Hagger-Vaughan 2016).

Many teachers nowadays are actively engaged in investigating their practice both routinely in their own classroom and for further accreditation. The references to other books and academic research papers are included for the benefit of those beginning and established teachers who may have chosen to write their academic assignments for PGCE or Masters study on this topic. The actions at the end of each chapter summarise its recommendations and these could be used as a starting point for discussions within teaching teams.

## *Teachers of English to speakers of other languages (TESOL)*

Teaching literature has been embedded in much TESOL practice across the world for decades and may also offer new ideas for MFL teachers. Surprisingly little on the other hand has been written on teaching literature in the MFL context. Many of the sources consulted and referenced in writing this book come from the TESOL world (see Gilroy and Parkinson 2008) but have been made relevant to contemporary UK A level practice. It is hoped that TESOL professionals may also find some of the approaches, questions and suggestions in the book informative as there is no reason why they should not be used in their context.

Similarly, teachers of foreign languages in other countries, e.g. in North America, Australia and Europe, who are preparing students for comparable examinations, will find ideas which are transferable to their own context.

# How to use the book

Whatever the teacher's starting point, the intention of this book is to act as a guide through different aspects of preparing and teaching literature lessons. The approach is primarily practical and aims to illustrate the steps suggested with usable activities. A more theoretical discussion is also included where appropriate to help teachers reflect on practice and their own goals.

The book is underpinned by the examination requirements and prescribed texts of the new A level syllabi for French, German and Spanish (the most commonly taught languages at A level). Providing detailed notes on how to teach any particular work of literature falls outside the scope of this book and other materials are available for this purpose. The approaches are designed to be adapted to any language or literary text as choice or necessity dictate. We have, however, made reference to books taken from the current A level lists of prescribed texts to illustrate some of our discussions. A full list of the texts mentioned may be found at the end of the book.

Other adaptations may be necessary as the classroom situations in which literature (and A level) is taught may vary greatly and teachers will choose what works for them. Some exercises and activities, for example, may work best in schools with a significant number of A level language students, but it is hoped that ideas may be adapted for work with individual students where necessary and provide a spark for teachers' own ideas tailored to their students and situation. Similarly, it is clear that the study of literature can be a means of providing stretch and challenge for gifted linguists, whilst some students will need more support, both linguistically and in how to respond intellectually to the texts and the questions posed about them. Ideas for differentiated challenge are included, but teachers know their own students best.

This book cannot answer all the questions teachers may have, but by discussing overall principles as well as specific examples, the answers can emerge from each teacher's professional knowledge of his or her own context and will of course need to take practical considerations into account.

Whilst the principal focus of this book is on teaching literature at A level, it can undoubtedly be useful to introduce literature earlier in the school and as part of the GCSE syllabus. Perhaps the best preparation for A level is that students have been routinely exposed to a range of literary reading throughout their language learning (Chambers 1991; Turner 1999). It is possible to adapt some of the activities for use with younger learners, if they are given greater linguistic support.

A final note concerns the study of **foreign film**. This is a permissible alternative to a literary text for one of the two examination essays, and early evidence shows that trainee teachers often feel confident in film studies and have seen the culture of their chosen language, literally, through this lens. Many of the analytical skills they possess to critique this medium are transferable to literature, e.g. evaluating character, plot, meaning and cultural references. Similarly, the strategies that the director or writer use to influence the audience or reader can be considered both on screen and on paper. This expertise can be useful, and some activities may prompt comparisons between the two media.

# Chapters

The book is structured to help new teachers, or teachers new to teaching literature, to plan and deliver lessons with confidence. Each chapter guides the teacher through different aspects of this process and concludes with a list of suggested actions. There are also suggestions on target language usage, supporting students of different abilities, integrating literature with other aspects of the syllabus, incorporating the skills of listening and speaking alongside reading and writing, developing students' analytical skills and maintaining student enthusiasm and engagement.

**Chapter 2** tackles the question of why teach (or study) literature at all and reflects the complexities of the new situation for A level teachers. Understanding the 'why' helps teachers to make decisions about the 'how', and underpins the methodological approach discussed in subsequent chapters. This will enable teachers to plan their learning goals positively and effectively.

**Chapters 3 and 4** support teachers in choosing the 'right' literary text for them and their students and guide them through the initial stages of preparation for teaching it. This includes gathering useful information, long-term planning and consideration of how to encourage independent and collaborative working.

**Chapter 5** looks at the preliminary or pre-teaching activities which can be used as an introduction to literature with a class.

**Chapter 6** considers the challenges associated with studying a novel and offers strategies to support students' reading competence, balancing independent and whole-class tasks. Teaching short stories is also considered.

**Chapter 7** examines the particular characteristics of studying a play.

**Chapters 8 and 9** focus on areas of characterisation, theme, structure and style with reference to the types of question which may be expected in the final examination.

**Chapter 10** looks specifically at preparing students to draw together all they have learnt to write essays about the texts in the target language.

**Chapter 11** offers ideas for using literature earlier in the school curriculum and suggests suitable texts in French, Spanish and German. It also discusses ways of exploiting literature as a spark for students' own creative output beyond simply the demands of the examination.

**Appendix 1** suggests sources of support for teachers to assist in their teaching.

**Appendix 2** gives examples of language useful for discussion of literature in French, German and Spanish.

**Appendix 3** includes a model for students to complete as a record of their own reading in French, German and Spanish.

**Appendix 4** suggests exemplar activities for a text which can be used post-GCSE and pre-A level.

## Notes

The General Certificate of Education Advanced level (**A level**) is an optional examination studied by 16–18 year olds in the UK (except in Scotland). It is a Level 3 qualification completed at the end of secondary schooling. Students usually study 3 or 4 subjects. Places for undergraduate study at university are typically dependent upon grades achieved in A levels. A level students would be described as 'intermediate' level language learners. The Advanced Subsidiary (**AS**) examination may currently be taken by students at the end of the first year of their A level study as a stand-alone qualification.

The General Certificate of Secondary Education (**GCSE**) is the main qualification taken by 14–16 year olds in England in a range of subjects.

The Postgraduate Certificate in Education (**PGCE**) is a one-year graduate teaching qualification in the UK.

The **examination boards** offering the new A level qualifications in French, Spanish and German in England are the Assessment and Qualifications Alliance (AQA); Edexcel, part of Pearson qualifications, and Eduqas, the English arm of WJEC which offers qualifications in Wales. The Council for the Curriculum, Examinations and Assessment (CCEA) sets examinations in Northern Ireland. Scotland has a different system of examinations.

## References

Bloemert, J., Paran, A., Jansen, E. and van de Grift, W., 2017. Students' perspective on the benefits of EFL literature education. *The Language Learning Journal*. DOI:10.1080/09571736.2017.1298149

Chambers, G., 1991. A-level literature in the 90s: a fresh start. *The Language Learning Journal*, 3, pp.34–40.

Gieve, S. and Cunico, S., 2012. Language and content in the modern foreign languages degree: a students' perspective. *The Language Learning Journal*, 40(3), pp.273–291.

Gilroy, M. and Parkinson, B., 2008. Teaching literature in a foreign language. *Language Teaching*, 29(4), pp.213–225.

Hagger-Vaughan, L., 2016. Towards 'languages for all' in England: the state of the debate. *The Language Learning Journal*, 44(3), pp.358–375.

Pachler, N., Evans, M. and Lawes, S., 2007. *Modern Foreign Languages: Teaching School Subjects 11-19*. Abingdon: Routledge.

Pomphrey, C., 2004. Professional development through collaborative curriculum planning in English and modern languages. *Language Learning Journal*, 29(1), pp.12–17.

Turner, K., 1999. Working with literature. In: N. Pachler, ed. *Teaching Modern Foreign Languages at Advanced Level*. London: Routledge, pp.209–229.

# 2 Why teach (or study) literature?

## Introduction

The place of literature within the teaching of Modern Foreign Languages in UK schools and universities has been debated over many decades. This has also been the case in English Language Teaching courses (*e.g.* Kramsch and Kramsch 2000). As literature returns as a compulsory element in the UK A level MFL syllabus, teachers may hold differing views about the desirability of this change, especially during a period when the viability of post-16 MFL courses is threatened in many schools, colleges and universities (Tinsley and Board 2017; Vidal Rodeiro 2017).

Teaching literature may be seen as somewhat different from teaching the other components of the MFL syllabus. This is in part because of the lack of recent advice available compared with the array of methodological theories on teaching communication skills, grammar and vocabulary. However, some more fundamentally personal questions which teachers have about what constitutes literature and its usefulness in a crowded language curriculum may also be involved. Furthermore, literature is usually an area of personal preference and individual interpretation and negotiating and developing these skills with students may represent a new challenge for teachers.

It is certainly easier for teachers to embrace this new challenge if they develop a clear rationale for the **benefits** that literature can offer to their students (Bloemert *et al.* 2016). Indeed, evidence also shows a clear link between teachers' perceptions of the **purpose of literature** study (influenced by their own personal and professional learning histories) and their **pedagogical approach** in the classroom. The **'why'** (teachers' beliefs) undoubtedly influences the **'how'** (teachers' behaviour) (Borg 2003; Carroli 2008). This in turn affects how *students* perceive the purpose of study and their engagement with it (Bloemert *et al.* 2017). It is therefore worth spending some time to unpick **why** we should teach (or study) literature. Simply stating that it is currently an examination requirement will not suffice in response to the question posed. After all, for some teachers, teaching literature is merely an official edict, whereas for others it is a *sine qua non* of language teaching. Whatever one's point of view, formulating the benefits of literature for learners will influence how teachers approach the task of preparing to teach it.

This chapter considers how literature can be beneficial in the second language learning process. **Benefits** will include **linguistic skill development, intercultural understanding, personal development** and wider **transferable skills**. These areas are also pursued in later chapters with practical advice.

It is also useful to consider adopting an **integrated (and interactive) approach** to teaching literature, where literature is seen as part of, rather than separate from, other aspects of the syllabus and hopefully thus ensuring better examination success. In this process the **student perspective** is of course of considerable importance.

## The current climate

It is already accepted by many language educators, university researchers, business leaders and government departments that language learning is an essential component of developing a linguistically and interculturally competent workforce for the economic and diplomatic health of the country in our globalised world (*e.g.* British Academy 2011). Successive educational reforms in the UK, however, have sent out both positive *and* negative messages to students about the value of studying languages and increasing concern has been expressed about falling rates of participation in post-compulsory language courses at Advanced and undergraduate level. Other worrying trends which have been noted include the gender and socio-economic disparity revealed by the disproportionate number of undergraduate linguists who are female and drawn from independent schools, higher socio-economic groups and particular national regions (British Academy 2011; LCLC 2015; Tinsley and Board 2017). These issues prompt the following questions: Is language study then for a privileged elite? How relevant is it in today's world?

In this challenging climate, the way in which A level MFL study is seen by the public (*i.e.* through subject content requirements *e.g.* DfE 2015a) can usefully be analysed. Closely following the recommendations of the A Level Content Advisory Board (ALCAB 2014), the first aim of the Department for Education subject content for MFL is that the syllabus will allow students to

> [i] enhance their linguistic skills and [ii] promote and develop their capacity for critical thinking on the basis of their knowledge and

understanding of the language, culture and society of the country or countries where the language is spoken. (DfE 2015a p.3 *our numerical additions*)

Here then the key features are all aims to which the study of literature can contribute. The stated opportunity for students

to engage critically with intellectually stimulating texts, films and other materials in the original language, developing an appreciation of sophisticated and creative uses of the language and understanding them within their cultural and social context. (DfE 2015a p.3)

associates these three objectives specifically with literature and film study and these can help to answer the question 'why teach (or study) literature?'

## The historical perspective

However, as literature has been absent from the compulsory A level syllabus for some years, it is worth including some historical perspective here. Since the 1990s there have been several changes in the syllabus both pre- and post-16. Some of the changes (*e.g.* removing the requirement to study literature and emphasising a 'Languages for All' policy which required all students to study an approved European language until the age of 16 (DES/WO 1990)) suggest a determination to help MFL to shed its elite, academic image, an impression which had been reinforced by its literary component.

The literature which had been studied at A level mirrored what was being taught in university language courses. These followed the classical tradition of studying a high culture **canon of literature** which was capable of cultivating both intellect and moral character (*e.g.* Racine, Corneille, Goethe, Schiller and Cervantes), but often felt remote from students' cultural and linguistic experience. Thus, in the 1980s and earlier, A level Modern Languages courses required the study of four or five 'worthy' texts (including more modern classics such as Camus, Sartre, Dürrenmatt, Brecht or Lorca) which were chosen due to their literary and intellectual merit in their own linguistic canon but were examined in English. In many ways, this mirrored the English literature examination, only in translation.

Top-down and bottom-up pressures combined to bring about change to this model in the 1980s. At university level, the teaching of modern languages had to be justified in economic terms and literature became a *tool* for language development and analysis, and for learning about culture. A more inclusive, popular view of culture itself also resulted in work by more contemporary, female and non-metropolitan authors being included on the syllabus. This change at university could be seen as an attempt to make literature more relevant for students and similar pressures were also felt at A level. Concerns about falling examination entries, student disaffection and perceptions of difficulty which persist today (Tinsley and Board 2017) prompted action. In 1984 the Joint Matriculation Board's proposal to 'relegate' literature to a coursework option was both welcomed and decried (Bayley 1994).

With the advent of GCSE and the emphasis on communicative methodology (Littlewood 1981) and teaching in the target language, the University of Oxford Delegacy of Local Examinations also addressed the issue of who decides which literature is worthy of study. In the new syllabus, specific texts were not prescribed and, in French for example, teachers could choose to study (for assessment in the target language) either two French novels, two French plays, the presentation of childhood or adolescence or women in French literature (University of Oxford Delegacy 1996). Writing in the target language reflected the linguistic purpose of literature study but raised concerns that only superficial responses would be possible (Chambers 1990).

After the 'Curriculum 2000' reforms, the A level syllabus of the new millennium included 'cultural topics' where literature became one option among similar expressions of the target language people's nationhood and identity, alongside film, history, geography and art. The choice of text was still open-ended and the questions posed in the written examination were necessarily highly generalised as any work of literature may be used to answer them. The specific assessment objective to demonstrate knowledge of the target language society was eventually dropped from the A level mark scheme.

In the most recent reforms of the examination syllabi, both at GCSE and A level, the familiar political aim of 'raising standards' may be detected. Certain changes both at GCSE and A level, including the compulsory inclusion of literature in the language syllabus may seem like a return to earlier principles (Long 2017). ALCAB (2014 p.2) particularly noted disapprovingly the removal of 'direct engagement with material relating to the society of the countries where the language of study is spoken' in the previous syllabus. The new syllabus emphasises culturally rich content anchored in the culture of the target language countries rather than generalised ('uninspiring') lifestyle topics. It has restored the assessment objective (worth 20%) linked to 'knowledge and understanding of [...] different aspects of the culture and society of countries/communities where the language is spoken'. The return to prescribed texts means that once again, examination questions can be set which address the texts specifically and can therefore require answers which probe texts in greater depth. Interestingly, after pressure from teachers, these answers are required to be in the target language rather than English as originally proposed.

# What is literature?

Contemporary definitions of 'literature' span a broad spectrum of cultural discourse which may be scientific, political or technical (Pountain 2017) rather than the traditionally 'literary'. Within 'fictional' or 'creative' literature, the range also extends between the tradition of high 'culture' and popular bestsellers. For the present purposes, literature encompasses the prescribed texts on the UK A level syllabi and reflects this breadth. It is clear that some texts are taken from the traditional literary canon (e.g. *Le Tartuffe* which appears on all A level French syllabi) and many have been popular examination texts over decades. Others are modern texts which have been bestsellers in their country or internationally and tell engaging stories which capture the imagination or illuminate life in a particular period. Some offer fine examples of the language in use, others have the power to speak to a modern audience directly either about contemporary problems or enduring dilemmas. All embody some 'notion of value', which is linked to the aims and requirements of the particular examination and classroom context (Parkinson and Reid Thomas 2000 p.24). Therefore, the choice of a particular work of literature to teach will depend upon what the teacher wishes to achieve with his or her students.

The purpose of literature according to Brumfit (2001 p.89) is to 'enrich our imaginative, metaphorical and symbolic needs, not to provide us with information'. It can affect the reader at a deeper level and 'Classic' literature even has the 'capacity for sustained, complex, and sophisticated contribution to our understanding of the human condition' – *i.e.* something which offers insight into the more universal essence of humanity (*ibid.* p.91). For an examination which seeks to develop understanding of another culture, critical thinking about the world and perhaps oneself, then literature has a role to play.

# Concerns about teaching (studying) literature

The ALCAB proposals to include literature in the new MFL A level syllabus were met with concern and dismay in some quarters however (DfE 2015b). One argument against the inclusion of literature in the syllabus was a perceived **unattractiveness** to students, (and particularly those whose primary interest lies in science-based subjects (DfE 2015b)) who simply wanted to learn to communicate. The assertion that students want to learn to communicate rather than read old books encapsulates the language versus content debate and the role of cultural knowledge in language learning.

Literature has also gained the reputation of being **difficult** and therefore perhaps better suited to undergraduate study (Chambers 1991; Turner 1999). This rather exclusive stance stems from the inherent challenge of reading extended material in the target language whilst also grappling with culturally unfamiliar or challenging ideas. The dominance of classic texts using archaic or highly literary language and the fact that there had been no graded progression in reading material has added to this problem. The 'remote' language and socio-historical contexts may make literature seem inaccessible and unappealing. Indeed, literature could be seen as exacerbating the 'curricular discontinuity' between GCSE and A level (Stables and Stables 1996 p.52).

From a teacher's perspective, combating this area of difficulty may be seen as detracting from the **time available** to teach more functional language. Furthermore, due to the challenge of ensuring students' understanding of both language and ideas, teachers may feel forced into a more **didactic**, English-based, mode of teaching (Parkinson and Reid Thomas 2000). This has the double disadvantage of potentially threatening active student engagement *and* their exposure to the target language. Another layer of complexity is added when students are required not only to read and discuss, but also to *write* analytically about the texts in the **target language**, which is surely a logical extension of using literature within a modern foreign languages syllabus. Students have the opportunity to demonstrate higher levels of both thought and language through this analysis but handling the language with the necessary confidence requires significant commitment from both teachers and students.

The rest of this chapter will offer teachers a rationale for combating these concerns and show that reading fiction can be pleasurable and beneficial not only to a student's linguistic but also personal and intercultural development.

# The case for literature

The aforementioned difficulties remind teachers of the need to think carefully about how to overcome these potential pitfalls, and what makes literature teaching worth the effort. Second language educators have categorised the benefits of literature study in different ways over time (Bloemert *et al.* 2016 provide a useful overview of these categorisations). Bloemert and colleagues' (2016 pp.173–176) own theorisation of these categories is dependent upon a fundamental division in how literature teaching is conceived: is the primary purpose the *study of literature*, in which case, they argue, the focus is on the literary text itself and teaching emphasises the formal literary elements of the novel or play (the **text approach**) and the historical and biographical context of the text (the **context** approach). This resembles mother tongue literature lessons and traditional undergraduate syllabi.

The alternative position is the *use of literature as a resource*. Here the focus is on the students and how literature may be used to develop their self-awareness and critical thinking (the **reader** approach) and language proficiency (the **language** approach). So, the purpose of literature study can be seen as helping to develop students' literary knowledge, their cultural awareness, their wider critical or linguistic skills. According to the study's findings (*ibid.*) whichever purpose teachers prioritise will affect how they approach their teaching and the experience of their students. Being aware of this can help teachers to reflect on their practice and experiment to be more inclusive in the range of approaches used.

Indeed, many teachers at A level may feel that using literature as a *resource* most closely meets their overall language and personal development aims for their students but recognise that examination success also requires knowledge of both text *and* context.

## Linguistic skill development

For many advocates of teaching literature, especially within the second language English teaching community, the benefits of literature study are primarily **linguistic**. Duff and Maley (2007 p.8) are clear that their approach is to use literary texts 'as a resource to teach language', a resource which can in Chambers' words (1990 p.35) 'influence the quality of [students'] linguistic competence'. Bloemert *et al.*'s (2017) study of Dutch secondary school students reported that the majority of students themselves also saw the benefits of literature in relation to their language development. However, teachers need to examine *how* exactly literature can contribute to language study in order to capitalise upon this fully. This is an important way in which to integrate literature study into the wider teaching programme in order to work effectively within the inevitable time pressures of the syllabus. A good starting point is to look at how literature may aid the development of the four language skills of reading and writing, listening and speaking.

### Reading

Reading literature has a particular role to play in developing the important **skill of reading**. This skill is regularly practised both explicitly and incidentally in class with a wide range of factual material, but it may be argued that non-factual material offers a **complementary reading experience**.

- A novel or short story provides **extended reading material** which offers the potential for a more immersive experience in both language and ideas. Grellet (1981) sees extensive reading as a **fluency activity** which encourages learners' facility with the language.

- The study of literature also offers **intensive reading practice. Interest** in the story may help students both to persevere and internalise the language.

- Literature also offers a different type of **authentic material**: prose, drama or poetry written for a native speaker audience and which addresses issues which the author found significant. To deny learners access to literature, reduces the range of their authentic reading experience (Chambers 1991).

- The use of literature is cited as a means of demonstrating to learners that the language can **communicate** something 'important, interesting and meaningful', which is a key element in successful and engaging MFL pedagogy (TSC 2016 p.13). Literature can offer A level students access to substantial themes and **meaningful content**, in line with their intellectual maturity.

- It can hook students and set them on a lifelong **fascination** with language, culture and country (see political aide, journalist and broadcaster, Alastair Campbell's essay on 'Madame Bovary' 2018).

- Chambers (1991) talks of the authentic task of **reading for pleasure** which can complement other forms of texts. If the literary text (at an accessible level) can generate interest and enjoyment in the reader, then this can be a motivating factor and make the language itself more memorable and therefore reproducible by the student (Collie and Slater 1987).

It is important to acknowledge however that in *teaching* the text, we may alter the 'authentic' reading experience as experienced by readers in their native tongue (Parkinson and Reid Thomas 2000). Literature is not, after all, written primarily to be analysed by foreign language students for an examination! Practical considerations of understanding the text remain uppermost in the teacher's mind, but it is worth remembering that questions and exercises which 'pre-package' the text unduly, may deprive students of a more spontaneous reading experience (Carroli 2008 p.12–13).

Whilst all the factors listed help to support the students' general **decoding ability**, a different type of reading is also possible with literature, one which invites the reader to move beyond simple factual extraction, to a **greater personal involvement** with the text. To illustrate this, a distinction is drawn between efferent reading and aesthetic reading.

**Efferent reading** is essentially functional and principally concerned with gathering key information from a passage. This clearly has a role to play in following the plot, but may also be associated with a pedagogical approach in which a particular 'correct' **interpretation** by the teacher about the text is transmitted to students. In this case the focus is on what the students 'take away' from the text, rather than what they bring to it themselves (Nguyen 2016).

**Aesthetic reading** on the other hand requires the reader to take a much more active role in the construction of meaning and be conscious of his or her own responses to the text. Aesthetic reading encourages the reader to experience the text through the filter of his or her own individual experience and personality (Nguyen 2016). This requires a much more personal relationship with the text and develops both the reader's emotions and critical faculties. This approach celebrates the particular ability of literature to be both 'specific and universal; individual and "collective"' (Carroli 2008 p.7), that is to say that the voice of the individual author can speak to each reader on an individual level.

Kramsch (1993 p.140) explains the difference between reading for information (efferently) and reading as an experience (aesthetically) as the eye scanning the page for gist and detail, and the eye, in turns, reading the text and looking inward to the reader for her response as 'students read and pause, read and pause, letting their mind make associations, evoke prior texts, assess the effect of the choice of a word or phrase'. This may well be a different way of reading for students which will need to be discussed explicitly in class. The pedagogical implications also require the teacher to allow space so that students can consider their **personal response** to their reading, and discuss them with others to explore and negotiate these meanings. This may be seen as an 'interactive approach' (Nguyen 2016) and draws on reader-response theories. This can help students to offer personal responses to the characters' dilemmas which is sometimes required in the examination questions.

*Reader-response theory*

**Reader-response** theory has been influential in recent years in how teaching literature is approached. This theory challenges traditional notions that the meaning of literature is an objective entity which is transmitted from the author to the reader via the text. If this were the case, in a classroom context, 'what the text means' could simply be taught in a similar way to a grammatical construction and then the 'correct' interpretation assessed by examination. The opposite of this approach sees literary meaning to be entirely subjective and determined by the reader alone. More realistically, it is in fact a combination of both author and reader who join together to create meaning (Bredella 2000). The author chooses to tell his or her story in a particular way (rather than another) with the intention of affecting the reader. Understanding the context of the author and the work is therefore relevant. How the reader interprets this work, how he or she is affected by it, completes the other side of the equation, and may be influenced by the reader's own context including personal experiences, socio-historical norms, beliefs etc. This stance can be particularly helpful within school literature lessons as it teaches students that there is no one correct interpretation and to express opinions freely, without the fear of being wrong (Carroli 2008).

By encouraging learners to interact personally with the text, readers become aware of the need to look beyond the surface information of a text. Students are encouraged to develop their **interpretive abilities** by recognising the difference between the literal meaning of words and phrases and the deeper ideas which the language conveys. Teachers can help them to move from a literal to **inferential understanding** of a text (Lazar 1993). It may be through this type of approach that literature can help learners to go beyond the purely *linguistic* benefit of reading literature and begin to develop broader critical and personal skills and lay the foundations for intercultural communicative competence.

## Reading: as language input

Reading input nourishes linguistic output; it encourages language acquisition and expands language awareness (Lazar 1993). Indeed, the view that literary language can provide learners with a **good model** to emulate corresponds with the traditional view of the value of studying canonical texts. Literature provides examples of the language 'in use' and the standardised form of a language (as found in dictionaries) has often been drawn from literary usage (Pountain 2017). Depending upon the text chosen, some language patterns may appear remote from the A level student's linguistic toolkit, but other patterns may be contemporary and transferable. With the most able students, Pountain's (2017 p.268) claim that 'artistry provokes reflection on the language in so many ways' may even be in evidence. Analysis of how sophisticated language is constructed may also sensitise students to different ways of writing.

A literary text can offer a wide range of examples of **registers** and types of language. Different **genres** (e.g. poetry or prose) can develop different language skills. Readers can see examples of less common **grammatical structures in context**, and teachers can exploit these as part of their grammatical teaching programme, thus allowing integration with other areas of the syllabus (Pountain 2017). Texts also support vocabulary learning, offering a memorable context (i.e. poetry) which might help retention. Indeed, the same online tools (e.g. www.textivate.com; www.memrise.com) which are used to practise generalist vocabulary and constructions are also useful here. Similarly, the skills of text manipulation and translation can be practised with literary excerpts. Of course, literary study encompasses not only the language found in the texts, but also the language with which the texts are discussed and written about (Parkinson and Reid Thomas 2000).

# *Writing*

For many, the desired consequence of reading literature is to improve students' own **writing**, and the A level mark scheme at the higher levels clearly rewards fluency and accuracy, and a variety of vocabulary and syntax. Thinking of literature as a catalyst for **creative writing** is also very important. The models given may boost students to attain 'a higher linguistic gear' (Morgan 1996 p.45). For Duff and Maley (2007 p.9), literature becomes a vehicle for discussion, production and for the expression of 'the world of personal experience which every student carries within'. Pountain (2017) argues that creative response to literature has a place in undergraduate assessment schemes, and there is no reason why this should not be the case with younger students. This creative response may also heighten the reader's connection with the text (Nguyen 2016). Examples of how literature can be used to fire students' creative writing may be found in Chapter 11. Using literature as a springboard for one's own writing articulates the process of **aesthetic reading** and response and can be enjoyable, satisfying, stimulating and liberating. Indeed Hermann (cited in Morgan 1996) argues that the act of using a *foreign* language in this way releases a *stronger* and less conventional personal response, as students are freed to inhabit a different skin.

## Speaking and listening

Advocates for literature have argued for many years that literature can also be a vehicle for genuine communication. Watching and enacting plays, listening to and reading aloud short stories and poetry offer an obvious way in which to interact with the spoken language, developing one's own pronunciation, intonation and speech patterns.

An 'interactive' approach to teaching literature (Nguyen 2016) requires meaningful dialogue between students. Students' oral skills developed throughout the course are put to work here. The literary text, its themes, characters, plot and style form the basis for discussion, where, in the best communicative traditions, there is a genuine information gap as students offer and receive opinions on meaningful topics. Indeed, one might argue that it is through open discussion with classmates, that students begin to understand the values, beliefs and intentions of a text rather than simply its content, form and structure.

## Literary competence

Even though this is not a primary aim of current A level literature study, Lazar (1993 p.13) makes the point that there is also scope to develop the 'conventions of interpretation' regarding different literary genres through literature study. For some students this may usefully build upon knowledge from their first language studies, for others it may give them new skills, attitudes and abilities to talk about any literature (Brumfit 1985; Carter 2007).

## (Inter)cultural understanding

A compelling reason for the study of languages is the view they allow access to other cultures. The aims of the A level syllabus declare it to be 'conceived as an integrated study with a focus on language and culture and society' (DfE 2015a p.4). Language and culture (including literature) exist symbiotically as any society expresses itself through its language, and its language is both shaped by and embodies a society and its culture. Kramsch (1993) argues that literature offers access to a particular culture on a personal level, through the direct dialogue between writer and reader. This connection forms the basis of the aesthetic reading experience and can activate a student's engagement with the foreign culture beyond the classroom walls. It can bring the culture to life.

What does literature contribute to cultural knowledge for second language learners? One may argue for the intrinsic interest to be found in new stories in new settings. One can learn about specific cultural practices through descriptive passages in literature (Morgan 1994). Indeed, learning about another culture may represent the *primary* motivation for language study for some students (LCLC 2015) and research amongst university undergraduates has shown that whereas 'enjoyable literature' in a student's mother tongue has to be entertaining and aesthetically pleasing, knowledge of the second language culture and society is what makes reading enjoyable in a second language (Carroli 2008 p.41). Students *expect* to learn about the country in this way.

Beyond enjoyment and knowledge *about* certain unfamiliar practices however, teachers and politicians ascribe a greater purpose to learning about other cultures. Linguistic proficiency alone is insufficient to meet the diplomatic and economic needs of the country in a globalised world (British Academy 2011) and for citizenship in the 21st century, **intercultural communicative competence** is needed (e.g. Byram 2008; UNESCO 2013). This **intercultural literacy** is not a question of content as such, rather the development of an open and respectful disposition towards otherness and a set of attitudes and behaviours which allow understanding of other cultures to take place (see Byram's set of five *savoirs* 1997).

This cannot be achieved however without the ability to reflect critically on one's own culture, and literature once again provides a space to explore new ways of seeing the familiar. We see that there are different ways of being and doing. This may encompass the celebration of festivals on one hand through to the organisation of government and the law, from religious conventions to those of social politeness. This geographical, cultural and perhaps historical difference encourages critical reflection on *both* societies. This **reflexivity** is at the heart of intercultural competence and can be encouraged in the literature classroom.

Teachers can also guide their students to see that literature is not an objective or necessarily representative view of the target language culture. This is one cultural insider shining a spotlight on individual and collective aspects of their society in the name of fiction: the text is selective and written for a particular purpose which reflects a particular perspective. Discussions around these perspectives encourage students to challenge stereotypes and question author motives and reader assumptions. Protagonists' actions invariably reveal that, just as in the UK, not everyone within a culture will think the same way (*cf.* the varying and ambiguous responses to the reunification of Germany explored in König's *Ich fühl mich so fifty-fifty*) or share one single cultural identity.

Through discussion, students can learn that culture (including their own) is a negotiated, dynamic entity, not something fixed which can translate directly from one language or one nation to another. This active engagement with understanding new language and culture helps the student to become more self-aware (Carter 2007). Literature often seeks to challenge how we think about things and can hold a mirror up to our own society and beliefs as much as to those of the original audience. This provides an excellent springboard for teachers and students to conduct substantive discussions exploring a wide range of topics and can lead to personal growth beyond the language classroom.

## Personal development: transferable skills

### Critical thinking

The new A level syllabus places significant emphasis on the importance of languages in developing **critical thinking skills** and is a specific element of the literature component. Analytical writing at AS and particularly A level is required to access the highest grades. Definitions of critical thinking vary, but essential components include both the ability and disposition to analyse what is said, judge the information given, evaluate arguments and inferences, form well-reasoned decisions and judgements and express these through coherent argument (Lai 2011; Cambridge Assessment undated). As already established, reading literature requires the ability to interpret and read for meaning on several levels.

These skills encompass both interpretation and argumentation. In order to write a successful essay, learners need to be able to marshal ideas and demonstrate logical thought processes and measured conclusions, illustrating multiple viewpoints. This criticality extends to oral discussion, where the ability to share, reflect on and modify one's opinions is developed through the study of literature. Collaborative working skills are enhanced.

### Empathy and self-awareness

Through the development of intercultural skills, the reader is invited to adopt a different perspective on the familiar and be receptive to the unfamiliar. Seeing through the eyes of multiple protagonists encourages empathy for different viewpoints and may be particularly useful for teenagers. Encouragement to relate the experiences of fictional characters to their own contexts and emotions may also prompt greater self-awareness and reflexivity.

## *Cognitive challenge and motivation*

The study of literature offers considerable cognitive **challenge** for all students and ready-made extension opportunities for gifted linguists. The challenge can be found across all the aspects discussed to date: language, content and the demands for an affective and creative response. Literature is an intellectual, but also a cultural and personal challenge and can contribute to the interest of the subject (ALCAB 2014) through both its content and the sense of achievement of tackling something difficult. Given that **motivation** is a key factor in language participation and success (Phillips and Lindsay 2006; Ehrman 2008), literature can add a desirable new dimension to language studies.

# An integrated approach and the student perspective

Literature study can encompass all these different benefits for students but how we package our teaching will consciously or subconsciously affect the message they receive about their value: do tasks predominantly focus on language, literary form, background facts or students' personal response?

Bloemert *et al.* (2016, 2017 p.2) make a strong case for the intersection of all four of their approaches (text, context, reader and language) in what they call a 'Comprehensive Approach to FL Literature Learning'. This describes

> a classroom where the teacher deals with all these areas, bringing together a focus on the text itself and information about the context, and encouraging the learners to make connections with the text, all the time ensuring that support is being given to language learning. (Bloemert *et al.* 2017 p.2)

Their research with Dutch secondary school teachers showed that teachers' use of the four approaches varied significantly and that the particular emphasis used by the teacher affected the students' experience and learning from literature. Dissatisfaction arose where teachers had not explained to students the purpose of their integrated approach and students resented activities which did not seem to be fully focussed on linguistic development. Nguyen (2016) also found that an emphasis on student response and discussion may be uncomfortable for some students who would prefer prepackaged transmission of text and context information. This emphasises the importance of talking to students about their expectations of literature study so that teachers and students can jointly shape how they work towards their goals (and examination success) in a constructive manner. The use of the target language as the medium of response in the examination strengthens the case for such an integrated approach in a way that would have been undermined by the original English-based proposals.

Joseph Joffo's *Un sac de billes*
  Students will:

a)  gain the confidence to read and understand a novel in French;

b)  learn techniques to support their independent reading;

c)  gain an understanding of the wartime context for Jews in France;

d)  explore their own responses to childhood and to the experiences of Joseph and Maurice and the emotions they evoke;

e)  appreciate how Joffo captures a child's view of what is happening;

f)  practise [a specific area of grammar];

g)  develop their critical and interpretive skills through peer discussion and collaborative working;

h)  learn how to organise their thoughts and write a formal essay.

*Figure 2.1* Aims for studying Joffo's *Un Sac de billes*.

A balanced approach can start by setting out one's objectives. Of course, examination success is a given, but what else will the students develop through this area of the A level course? Deciding on these aims may help to clarify both the choice of text, and the structure of the teaching programme and the activities undertaken. Figure 2.1 suggests some possible aims for Joffo's *Un sac de billes*.

## Conclusions

Given the potential linguistic, cultural and wider personal benefits of literary study, especially when combined in an integrated programme, it is hoped that any concerns teachers may have about the re-introduction of compulsory literature study into the A level examination may be lessened. Many of the set books address themes which overlap with other A level topics and the critical and interpretive skills developed through the study of literature should assist students in their understanding and discussion of non-literary texts and intercultural practices. Lessons can be designed to ensure that students develop their oral and written competence and that the language of the text is not a barrier for students to the benefits which the study of literature can bring. Indeed, this process should enhance students' self-esteem and sense of achievement as a result of accessing the literature through the medium of the foreign language.

This book provides suggestions of how these goals may be achieved.

# Further reading

Gilroy and Parkinson (2008) offer a **historical overview** of teaching literature in a foreign language and different schools of thought about pedagogy.

Chambers (1991) offers a clear discussion of the role of literature within the **A level** syllabus at the start of the 1990s.

Kramsch (1993), Bredella (2000) and Nguyen (2016) discuss **reader-response theory** and **aesthetic reading** in greater depth.

Gonçalves Matos (2005) provides a useful exploration of **intercultural reading**.

Bloemert *et al.* illustrate how to research the use of different **teaching approaches** in lessons (2016) and the effect of these on student perceptions of literature (2017).

# Implications for teaching

Chapters 3 and 4 consider how to prepare for teaching literature. Before embarking upon these practical next steps, take some time to reflect and act on the following:

- Examine your own professional and personal history and beliefs with regards to literary study and their influence on your current perspective.

- Develop a personal (and positive) rationale for how the study of literature will benefit your students and be able to explain this to them.

- Set out your aims for what you hope students will learn from the study – encompass linguistic, cultural and personal goals and be explicit about what these are.

- Consider the implications of each of these goals for your teaching approach – how will you achieve them? This may encompass target language usage, classroom organisation, the role of discussion and independent learning.

- Consider ways of integrating the literature element into the broader aims of your teaching programme.

- Be aware that how you 'package' literature will influence students' response to literature and its purpose.

- Remember that meaning is both co-created and individual and allow opportunities for discussion and personal responses.

- Elicit and act on students' own perspectives of literature study and develop a programme which both supports and, where necessary, challenges their thinking.

# References

The A Level Content Advisory Board (ALCAB), 2014. *Report of the ALCAB Panel for Modern Foreign and Classical Languages*. Accessed March 2018 https://alevelcon tent.files.wordpress.com/2014/07/alcab-report-of-panel-on-modern-foreign-and-classical-languages-july-2014.pdf.

Bayley, S., 1994. Literature in the modern languages curriculum of British Universities. *The Language Learning Journal*, 9, pp.41–45.

Bloemert, J., Jansen, E. and van de Grift, W., 2016. Exploring EFL literature approaches in Dutch secondary education. *Language, Culture and Curriculum*, 29(2), pp.169–188.

Bloemert, J., Paran, A., Jansen, E. and van de Grift, W., 2017. Students' perspective on the benefits of EFL literature education. *The Language Learning Journal*. DOI:10.1080/09571736.2017.1298149.

Borg, S., 2003. Teacher cognition in language teaching: a review of research on what language teachers think, know, believe, and do. *Language Teaching*, 36, pp.81–109.

Bredella, L., 2000. Literary texts. In: M. Byram, ed. *Routledge Encyclopaedia of Language Teaching and Learning*. London: Routledge, pp.375–382.

British Academy, 2011. *A Position Paper: Language Matters More and More*. London: British Academy. Accessed March 2018 www.britac.ac.uk/publications/language-matters-more-and-more.

Brumfit, C., 1985. *Language and Literature Teaching: From Practice to Principle*. Oxford: Pergamon.

Brumfit, C., 2001. *Individual Freedom in Language Teaching*. Oxford: Oxford University Press.

Byram, M., 1997. *Teaching and Assessing Intercultural Communicative Competence*. Clevedon: Multilingual Matters.

Byram, M., 2008. *From Foreign Language Education to Education for Intercultural Citizenship: Essays and Reflections*. Clevedon, UK: Multilingual Matters.

Cambridge Assessment, (undated). *Critical Thinking Factsheet 1. Deriving the Definition*. Accessed April 2018 www.cambridgeassessment.org.uk/images/126126-critical-thinking-factsheet-1.pdf.

Campbell, A. 2018. *'Madame Bovary' The Essay, The Book that Changed Me*. BBC Radio 3 Broadcast 5 April 2018.

Carroli, P., 2008. *Literature in Second Language Education*. London: Continuum.

Carter, R., 2007. Literature and language teaching 1986–2006: a review. *International Journal of Applied Linguistics*, 17(1), pp.3–13.

Chambers, G., 1990. Wer die Wahl hat, hat die Qual: choosing an appropriate A-level syllabus. *The Language Learning Journal*, 2, pp.39–41.

Chambers, G., 1991. A-level literature in the 90s: a fresh start. *The Language Learning Journal*, 3, pp.34–40.

Collie, J. and Slater, S., 1987. *Literature in the Language Classroom: A Resource Book of Ideas and Activities*. Cambridge: Cambridge University Press.

Department for Education (DfE), 2015a. *Modern Foreign Languages GCE AS and A Level Subject Content*. London: DfE.

Department for Education (DfE), 2015b. *Reformed GCSE and A Level Subject Content Consultation Government Response*. London: DfE. Accessed March 2018 www.gov.uk/government/uploads/system/uploads/attachment_data/file/397672/Reformed_GCSE_and_A_level_subject_content_Government_Response.pdf.

Department of Education and Science/Welsh Office (DES/WO), 1990. *Modern Foreign Languages for Ages 11–16 National Curriculum*. London: HMSO.

Duff, A. and Maley, A., 2007. *Literature*. 2nd ed. Oxford: Oxford University Press.

Ehrman, M., 2008. Personality and good language learners. In: C. Griffiths, ed.. *Lessons from Good Language Learners*. Cambridge: Cambridge University Press, pp.61–72.

Gilroy, M. and Parkinson, B., 2008. Teaching literature in a foreign language. *Language Teaching*, 29(4), pp.213–225.

Gonçalves Matos, A., 2005. Literary texts: a passage to intercultural reading in foreign language education. *Language and Intercultural Communication*, 5(1), pp.57–71.

Grellet, F., 1981. *Developing Reading Skills: A Practical Guide to Reading Comprehension Exercises*. Cambridge: Cambridge University Press.

Kramsch, C., 1993. *Context and Culture in Language Teaching*. Oxford: Oxford University Press.

Kramsch, C., and Kramsch, O., 2000. The avatars of literature in language study. *Modern Language Journal*, 84, pp.533–573.

Lai, E., 2011. Critical Thinking: A Literature Review. Pearson Assessments. Accessed April 2018 https://images.pearsonassessments.com/images/tmrs/CriticalThinkingReviewFINAL.pdf.

Lazar, G., 1993. *Literature and Language Teaching: A Guide for Teachers and Trainers*. Cambridge: Cambridge University Press.

Littlewood, W., 1981. *Communicative Language Teaching. An Introduction*. Cambridge: Cambridge University Press.

The London Centre for Languages and Cultures (LCLC), 2015. 'A future for languages in schools?' Report on Proceedings. Accessed March 2018 www.ucml.ac.uk/sites/default/files/pages/161/LCLC%20Colloquium%20Report_October2015.pdf.

Long, R., 2017. *Briefing Paper Number 06962, GCSE, AS and A Level Reform (England)*. London: House of Commons Library.

Morgan, C., 1994. They think differently from us. *The Language Learning Journal*, 9, pp.4–6.

Morgan, C., 1996. Creative writing in foreign language teaching. In: L. Thompson, ed. *The Teaching of Poetry: European Perspectives*. London: Cassell, pp.44–54.

Nguyen, H.T.T., 2016. How does an interactive approach to literary texts work in an English as a foreign language context? Learners' perspectives in close-up. *Innovation in Language Learning and Teaching*, 10(3), pp.171–189.

Parkinson, B. and Reid Thomas, H., 2000. *Teaching Literature in a Second Language*. Edinburgh: Edinburgh University Press.

Phillips, N. and Lindsay, G., 2006. Motivation in gifted students. *High Ability Studies*, 17(1), pp.57–73.

Pountain, C. J., 2017. The three Ls of modern foreign languages: language, linguistics, literature. *Hispanic Research Journal*, 18, pp.253–271.

Stables, A. and Stables, S., 1996. Modern languages at A-level: the danger of curricular discontinuity. *The Language Learning Journal*, 14, pp.50–52.

Teaching Schools Council (TSC), 2016. *Modern Foreign Languages Pedagogy Review 2016*. Accessed March 2018 www.tscouncil.org.uk/wp-content/uploads/2016/12/MFL-Pedagogy-Review-Report-2.pdf.

Tinsley, T. and Board, K., 2017. *Language Trends 2016/17. Language Teaching in Primary and Secondary Schools in England*. British Council. Accessed February 2018 www.britishcouncil.org/sites/default/files/language_trends_survey_ 2017_0.pdf.

Turner, K., 1999. Working with literature. In: N. Pachler, ed. *Teaching Modern Foreign Languages at Advanced Level*. London: Routledge, pp.209–229.

UNESCO, 2013. *Intercultural Competences: Conceptual and Operational Framework*. Paris: UNESCO.

University of Oxford Delegacy of Local Examinations, 1996. *Approved Specifications Advanced GCE French*. Oxford: University of Oxford Delegacy of Local Examinations.

Vidal Rodeiro, C., 2017. The study of foreign languages in England: uptake in secondary school and progression to higher education. *Language, Culture and Curriculum*, 30(3), pp.231–249.

# 3 | **Choosing the text**

## Introduction

Once a clear idea of the goals of teaching literature has been established, the first key decision to be made is which text(s) will best support these aims. Whilst it is difficult to label any text 'right' or 'wrong' *per se*, some works of literature will be more appropriate than others for the specific circumstances of a particular class and teacher. These circumstances are known best to the individual teacher and consideration of the factors outlined in this chapter may help to illuminate the choice.

## Prescribed texts

As this book is principally written with the Modern Foreign Languages A level syllabus in mind, teacher choice is limited by decisions made by the examination boards in relation to the texts which are approved for study, and by the examination boards adopted by the School or Department. Table 3.1 shows the syllabus choice across the examination boards for 2017/18, categorised by genre and date written for French, German and Spanish A level. Although certain texts (*e.g.* Molière's *Le Tartuffe*; Voltaire's *Candide*; Kafka's *Die Verwandlung*; Brecht's *Mutter Courage und ihre Kinder*; Lorca's *La casa de Bernarda Alba*) are old favourites from previous syllabi, many new texts have been included and Table 3.1 shows a predominance of prose writing of the late 20th and 21st centuries. This may not be surprising as teenage reading in the students' mother tongue is most likely to be prose, and of a more contemporary nature. Teachers are also likely to choose texts which are familiar to them.

Table 3.1 Examination Board A level set text choices by language, genre and date.

| | French | | | German | | | Spanish | | | Total |
|---|---|---|---|---|---|---|---|---|---|---|
| Exam board | AQA | Edexcel | WJEC Eduqas | AQA | Edexcel | WJEC Eduqas | AQA | Edexcel | WJEC Eduqas | |
| **Genre** *there is some discrepancy in classification of novel/novella of the same works between Boards | | | | | | | | | | |
| Novel | 8 | 10 | 4 | 4 | 5 | 3 | 4 | 6 | 2 | 46 |
| Short Story/Novella* | 1 | 1 | 1 | 2 | 5 | 1 | 3 | 5 | 2 | 21 |
| Poetry | 0 | 0 | 0 | 1 | 0 | 0 | 1 | 0 | 0 | 2 |
| Drama | 1 | 2 | 1 | 3 | 3 | 2 | 2 | 2 | 2 | 18 |
| **Total** | 10 | 13 | 6 | 10 | 13 | 6 | 10 | 13 | 6 | **87** |
| **Date written** | | | | | | | | | | |
| 17th century | 1 | 1 | 0 | 0 | 0 | 0 | 0 | 0 | 0 | 2 |
| 18th century | 1 | 0 | 0 | 0 | 0 | 0 | 0 | 0 | 0 | 1 |
| 19th century | 1 | 1 | 1 | 1 | 0 | 0 | 1 | 0 | 0 | 5 |
| Pre-1950 | 1 | 4 | 3 | 2 | 3 | 2 | 1 | 5 | 1 | 22 |
| Post 1950 | 3 | 5 | 0 | 4 | 10 | 4 | 7 | 8 | 5 | 46 |
| 21st century | 3 | 2 | 2 | 3 | 0 | 0 | 1 | 0 | 0 | 11 |

Total texts used by all 3 Boards:

| French | German | Spanish |
|---|---|---|
| 3 | 3 | 4 |

Total texts used by 2 Boards:

| French | German | Spanish |
|---|---|---|
| 2 | 3 | 4 |

Total texts used by only 1 Board:

| French | German | Spanish |
|---|---|---|
| 16 | 14 | 9 |

Total number of different texts offered for A level: French = 21   German = 20   Spanish = 17

Total number of different texts offered for AS level**: French = 15   German = 15   Spanish = 13

** (2 out of the 3 Boards reduce the number of texts available for AS level examination. AS texts are all part of the A level syllabus.)

Within the options available, teachers should seek texts through which students can develop their linguistic ability, cultural knowledge and personal engagement, whilst bearing in mind the final examination. The following factors (some of which intersect and overlap) may play a role here:

a)  Language;

b)  Student interest;

c)  Thematic content;

d)  Teacher preference;

e)  Genre;

f)  Resources;

g)  Examination requirements.

## Language

Ideally, an earlier programme of graded reading will have developed students' linguistic proficiency to the point where they can tackle the chosen examination text with confidence. The reality however, is that the A level text often represents a leap into new territory. **Linguistic difficulty** is therefore a significant consideration here. However, it is also useful to consider the opportunities for **linguistic development** and look beyond the potential difficulties. This decision will be influenced by **student ability** within the class. If the group is linguistically confident, a more difficult text could provide a welcome challenge and the opportunity to develop understanding of more literary registers, perhaps in preparation for University level study. For a different class, a more simply written modern text such as König's *Ich fühl mich so fifty-fifty* or de Vigan's *No et moi* may be more linguistically accessible and offer opportunities to develop students' everyday language and fluency. This choice will also depend upon how much time the teacher is willing or able to dedicate to helping students under-stand the text. A note of caution is sounded by Graham (1997), who suggests that teachers may underestimate the difficulty of a text for students (rather than for themselves), which risks demotivating them as they struggle with comprehension.

Elements which determine the linguistic difficulty of a text include **vocabulary** and **structure**. Vocabulary difficulties may be caused by not only archaic and dated language, but also by use of modern slang and idiom, dialect, specialised or technical language (*e.g.* flora and fauna in Pagnol's *Le château de ma mère*). Graham (1997 p.142) recommends works with everyday vocabulary and short, simple sentences. She also suggests that elements such as direct speech and exclamations can enliven the text for students.

The structure of a text is also important especially whether or not it follows the usual formal **schemata** or conventions of writing expected by readers. Research on reading (Barnett 1989) tells us that texts which do not follow a conventional chronological sequence of events (*i.e.* the use flashbacks as in Ruiz Zafón's *La sombra del viento* or where the narration jumps forward such as in Esquivel's *Como agua para chocolate*) make comprehension more difficult for second language readers. The **physical readability** of the text on the page can also be influential in comprehension. If the text is divided into short chapters, that can make it appear more accessible for both teaching and reading (*e.g.* Guène's *Kiffe kiffe demain)*. If the text is dense with long words and sentences with many clauses (a good indicator of readability in general) it is worth finding an edition with as much space as possible around the text to allow the eye some room to focus.

Ultimately, the more complicated the language and the structure of the text, the more difficult it will be for students to understand and analyse it independently and they will therefore need additional guidance and potentially teaching time. Given these factors, and the available lesson time, the **length** of the text may also become a consideration, especially if students' lack of fluency results in **low reading speeds** (Hill 1986) and a demoralising pace through a weighty tome. None of these difficulties are necessarily reasons to reject a text outright, but they are useful indicators of the support one might need to put in place for students when preparing the study programme.

## Student interest

Consideration of the students' experience and perspective on the text should be carefully borne in mind (Carroli 2008). The level of linguistic difficulty should be also weighed in relation to the **thematic content** of the work and its potential match with the interests and prior knowledge of the students. Indeed Benati (2013 p.96) indicates the desirability of choosing texts on subjects with which learners are **familiar** in order to aid comprehension as 'learners would find it difficult to process complex language *and* unfamiliar topics' (our emphasis) and Barnett (1989) also reports that **interest** influences what is understood. The dimension of student interest is important, impacting upon student motivation and perseverance (Parkinson and Reid Thomas 2000) and it is for this reason that it can be desirable to involve students in the choice of text. Paran and Robinson (2016) advocate this strongly and offer useful ideas about how to approach such involvement, such as writing synopses of a range of texts for students to examine. Chambers (1991) reports designing a programme of taster texts for students during the early stages of the A level course in order to prepare them for making a choice about examination texts. It may or may not be possible to seek students' views in a mainstream school context, but perhaps some degree of choice may be possible if a second text is studied. After all, reading in one's first language is often for pleasure and the dimension of potential **enjoyment** in second language reading should not be dismissed. If it is not possible to give students a choice, then at least the teacher can explain **why** the particular text has been selected for them.

It may be possible to consider how students' MFL studies fit in with their other **subjects of study**, for example linking literature concerning life in the former East Germany and the A level History course. Students taking A level Drama and Theatre Studies may be particularly equipped to study a play. Other links can be forged with the rest of the A level syllabus, such as through the pairing of a literature text with a film on a similar topic (*e.g.* in AQA, Hensel's *Zonenkinder* with Becker's *Good Bye, Lenin!* which both concern the fall of the Berlin Wall, or Joffo's *Un sac de billes* alongside Malle's film *Au revoir les enfants!* examining the treatment of Jews during World War II in France). The literary text may also be chosen to reinforce work on the **language content themes** of the A level syllabus. For example, there is a natural synergy between de Vigan's *No et moi* and the AQA sub-theme of 'life for the marginalised' and between García Márquez's *El coronel no tiene quien le escriba* and 'monarchies and dictatorships'. In Edexcel German, König's *Ich fühl mich so fifty-fifty* draws upon the background historical knowledge studied in the theme '*Die Wiedervereinigung Deutschlands*' (German reunification).

## Thematic content

The **thematic content** of a text is also significant in other ways. Kramsch (1993 p.105) sums up the twin difficulties faced by students trying to make meaning from foreign language texts:

> when faced with written texts, [language learners] often have the feeling of being confronted with a ready-made world of meanings upon which they have no control. Not only are many of the words unknown to them, but even if they know the words, their use is often out of the ordinary, with socio-historical connotations that are unknown to the non-native reader. Literary texts, that require an additional familiarity with a particular author, genre, period, or style, may be intimidating.

Kramsch alerts us to the, perhaps hidden, challenge (and possible reward) of what Hill (1986 p.26) terms 'cultural displacement'. This view acknowledges that the lack of background knowledge of the reader may mean that certain aspects of the text regarding social hierarchy and customs, historical, religious and political background, geography *etc.* may pose difficulties for the second language reader. They can involve specialised vocabulary and an unfamiliar underpinning to the world of the novel or play. Here the reader cannot rely on familiar frames of reference (e.g. Kramsch 1993) to help to decode and understand the text. A high degree of **intertextuality** (the number of external references within a work which are necessary to understand it) adds to students' load. This is not a reason to reject a work, but the teacher should plan carefully how to bridge the **cultural knowledge gap** in order for students who may be from different religious, social or familial norms to understand fully the text, and how much time this may require. It is also worth remembering that cultural barriers and remoteness from the world of the text can also exist in first language reading. Discussions with colleagues from the English Department may prove useful here.

As explored in Chapter 2, a key element of literature study is the student's ability to respond to the text and see beyond the specific cultural context and connect with its underlying personal and **universal themes** (Brumfit 1985). The student's **emotional maturity** is important and if cultural and affective factors are not taken into account, students may have difficulty in understanding the wider relevance of texts with relatively simple language demands. Kramsch (1993 p.126) reminds us to pose the question 'what personal experience can the students draw on to respond to the text?' White (1995) in her small-scale investigation notes that the study of Sartre's *Les mains sales* was an unfulfilling experience for the students who did not possess what she regarded as the required level of political awareness and engagement to appreciate the play. In Camus' *L'étranger*, issues of alienation from society and political and judicial hypocrisy proved equally problematic. A text which exemplifies a specific **literary technique** or underlying philosophy such as Brechtian *Verfremdungseffekt* or Latin American magic realism may also place further demands on students. When determining the difficulty of a text, it is important to look beyond linguistic challenges alone and to consider difficulties which Duff and Maley (2007 pp.6–7) term *referential* (i.e. the number of additional frames of reference to be mastered by the reader) and *conceptual.*

The genre known as **Young Adult Fiction** (YAL) may be well suited linguistically and thematically to some classes (Chambers 1991; Lasagabaster 1999). Schumm Fauster (2010) reports a successful project to raise intercultural sensibility among second language learners of English by using YAL texts. Her reasons for using works written for teenagers included the more modern language which was used, the themes and subplots which are designed to appeal to young people and the fact that the world of the text is seen through the eyes of teenagers, offering easier access to motivations and feelings. This is seen as particularly strong in the case of novels written in the first person (such as Guène's *Kiffe kiffe demain* or Joffo's *Un sac de billes*), which offers a very personal or **'insider' perspective** into the emotional and cultural world of the protagonists. Schumm Fauster's experience (*ibid.* p.190) leads her to stress the effect of empathy with the teenage protagonists which 'makes reading YAL a more personal experience. It also compels readers to come to terms with the emergent issues in a way that is similar to confronting a new culture in real life'. If part of the rationale for studying literature is to encourage aesthetic reading (see Chapter 2) and a personal response from the reader, this could be a powerful argument for including fiction which does not form part of the traditional literary canon in teaching programmes beyond the examination syllabus. Grimbert's *Un secret* (an AQA French A level text) won the *Prix Goncourt des Lycéens*, voted for by a panel of high school students, and a look at the list of past recipients would offer further suggestions. In Germany, the *Deutscher Jugendliteraturpreis* is awarded annually for youth fiction.

As a note of caution it is also worth considering whether the subject matter may touch upon any particular **sensitivities** in individual students' personal circumstances.

## Teacher preference

Teachers should also examine their own reaction to the text, indeed Kramsch (1993 p.138) states that 'the teacher's initial reaction to the text will be his most valuable asset in teaching it' and argues that even a strong negative reaction is preferable to indifference. Experience would indicate that where a choice is possible, it is far preferable, for all parties, if the teacher can convey genuine enthusiasm for the study of a particular text. Students respond (as in other aspects of the curriculum) to teacher enthusiasm (or lack of it). White's research (1995 p.74) indicated how instrumental the teacher's 'contagious interest' for a book could be in generating positive reactions from students and this should be taken into account alongside the students' linguistic and developmental needs.

## Genre

Genre may be a factor in each of the preceding considerations. The form of the work can contribute to both linguistic accessibility and teacher and student interest. The principal genres found in the Modern Foreign Languages A level syllabi and their potential advantages and challenges are examined in Table 3.2.

## Resources

It would be unrealistic to assume that **financial and time constraints** will play no role in the choice of text for study and school Departments may be keen to use existing sets of texts from previous syllabi. As teacher time is also a scarce resource, the recycling of existing notes and expertise may be a powerful consideration. The

Table 3.2 Advantages and challenges associated with different literary genres.

| Genre | Potential advantages | Potential challenges |
|---|---|---|
| Novel | • Opportunity for *extensive* reading<br>• Written model – rich linguistic content<br>• Extended story<br>• Interesting content<br>• Rich thematic material<br>• Engage imagination<br>• Encourage empathy and character identification | • Length<br>• Requires high reading speed<br>• Complicated plotlines<br>• Volume of vocabulary<br>• Challenging register<br>• Past historic in French<br>• Complicated syntax/lexis<br>• Unfamiliar structure<br>• May require extended background knowledge |
| Short story | • Manageable length<br>• Written model<br>• Universal themes may be symbolic<br>• Focus on a particular message<br>• Can convey attitudes of target culture succinctly or in symbolic form | • Restricted content<br>• Sophisticated lexis and syntax<br>• Requires specific knowledge of culture<br>• Often focus on form and language |
| Drama | • Length<br>• Avoids long description<br>• Often fewer characters<br>• Performance dimension – imagination and empathy<br>• Visual and aural impact: staging<br>• Encourages oral self-expression<br>• Connection with characters through direct speech empathy | • Difficult speech registers<br>• Less opportunity for extended linguistic models<br>• Distilled into short period of time and symbolic action<br>• May require specific background knowledge |

suitability of the text for students' linguistic needs and wider development should however be more compelling.

If considering teaching a text for the first time, it is useful to do a resource audit of both free and commercial materials in order to support teaching the text. A lack of readily available resources may dissuade the teacher from choosing an unfamiliar text. Research the availability of different **editions of the text**, e.g. versions for **e-readers** (some of which may be out of copyright) or study editions with background information and vocabulary aids. Investigate whether the text may be obtained more cheaply in the country of publication (if planning ahead) or whether 'as new' copies from book resale marketplaces are readily available. Some works (e.g. Voltaire's *Candide* and Maupassant's *Boule de Suif*) are freely available as pdf. downloads from the internet (see Appendix 1). Some thought may also be given to which **edition** of a text to choose: this may be an original language version or one edited for second language students. Some editions are packed with vocabulary and background information, but teachers hold different views on how helpful this is for students – either because it is in English, or because the original language used is too difficult or because glossaries may dissuade students from improving their reading skills. The correct edition will be the one which best supports your students.

Consulting **colleagues** and foreign language assistants to find out their reaction to or experience of the text is also helpful. They may be willing to share resources. Other resources which can support the teaching of the text are set out in Appendix 1.

## Examination requirements

Before making a final choice of text, it is sensible to consider the end goal in terms of **examination requirements** and the types of question which are set about the text.

- Is there enough substance to the text (and resources to support this) to allow the most able candidates to answer questions in the depth and detail required to attain high marks?

- Does the text allow all students to have a sufficiently strong grasp of the main themes and characters to ensure that they can approach the majority of questions with confidence?

## Conclusions

Ultimately it is important to choose a text which will ideally offer interest and enjoyment for the readers, enrich their cultural awareness and linguistic development, stimulate their curiosity and offer them the possibility of a broader understanding of (universal) themes relevant to their own lives. Teachers should seek to find a text which is linguistically accessible for a particular class of students given the teaching and examination context.

# Further reading

Chambers (1991) and Paran and Robinson (2016) discuss **student involvement** in text selection.

Hill (1986) offers further suggestions for assessing the **linguistic difficulty** of texts.

# Implications for teaching

- Reflect on one's own aims for teaching and learning in this section of the course and bear these in mind regarding choice of text(s).
- Consult the prescribed list of set texts with an open mind and read new texts for pleasure.
- Take into account a range of factors when choosing the text for study, focussing upon
  - linguistic and cultural accessibility to learners,
  - student (and personal) interest and contemporary relevance,
  - resources *and*
  - examination requirements.
- Note potential areas of student difficulty with the text.
- Consult colleagues.

# References

Barnett, M., 1989. *More than Meets the Eye: Foreign Language Reading: Theory and Practice*. Englewood Cliffs, NJ: Prentice-Hall.

Benati, A., 2013. *Issues in Second Language Teaching*. Bristol: Equinox.

Brumfit, C., 1985. *Language and Literature Teaching: From Practice to Principle*. Oxford: Pergamon.

Carroli, P., 2008. *Literature in Second Language Education*. London: Continuum.

Chambers, G., 1991. A-level literature in the 90s: a fresh start. *Language Learning Journal*, 3, pp.34–40.

Duff, A. and Maley, A., 2007. *Literature*. 2nd ed. Oxford: Oxford University Press.

Graham, S., 1997. *Effective Language Learning*. London: Multilingual Matters.

Hill, J., 1986. *Using Literature in Language Teaching*. London: Macmillan.

Kramsch, C., 1993. *Context and Culture in Language Teaching*. Oxford: Oxford University Press.

Lasagabaster, D., 1999. Literary awareness in the foreign language classroom. *Cultura y Educación*, 14–15, pp.5–17.

Paran, A. and Robinson, P., 2016. *Literature*. Oxford: Oxford University Press.

Parkinson, B. and Reid Thomas, H., 2000. *Teaching Literature in a Second Language*. Edinburgh: Edinburgh University Press.

Schumm Fauster, J., 2010. Promoting intercultural sensitivity through young adult literature. In: J. Aden, T. Grimshaw and H. Penz, eds. *Teaching Language and Culture in an Era of Complexity*. Brussels: Peter Lang, pp.179–192.

White, L., 1995. Reading literary texts at 'A' level. In: M. Grenfell, ed. *Reflections on Reading from GCSE to 'A' Level*. London: CILT, pp.59–90.

# Preparing to teach the literature text

## Introduction

This chapter examines the preparatory stages before teaching begins and suggests a sequence of actions which teachers who are new to teaching literature may wish to follow. Considerations such as **familiarisation with the text, seeking resources** and the **examination requirements** should be addressed early on. Teachers are also encouraged to consider the **principles** (in the light of discussions in Chapter 2) which will guide their approach to teaching literature and influence certain key decisions, including **ways of working**, how to approach **differentiation**, use of the **target language, integrating** literature more widely into lessons and gaining **student feedback**. How to establish a **'literature-friendly classroom'** environment and writing **a timeline** for the programme also merit consideration at this point.

## Understanding and analysis of the text

The process of choosing the text for study will have involved getting to know the book by reading for **pleasure** and in order to gain an overview of the language, plot and thematic content of the work. Now, a closer, **active** reading of the text has several purposes:

a) to analyse one's **own reaction** to the text (for in Kramsch's words (1993 p.137) 'in order to teach literature as dialogue between a text and a reader, teachers must first get in touch with themselves as readers');

b) to identify the **difficulties of the text** and how to **lessen** them (some difficulties may be associated with the **genre** (see Table 3.2 in Chapter 3), some may be

**linguistic**, some may stem from the cultural gap between text and reader (*i.e.* **socio-historical background**) and some may be **conceptual**);

c) to identify aspects of the text which will be key to answering the types of question found in sample and past **examination papers** or which are suggested by initial **reading around** the text. These should include **plot, characterisation, themes, socio-historical context**, and opportunities for **personal response** by the students;

d) to identify passages which could be exploited for **linguistic development**;

e) to highlight these **key extracts** (in c and d) and consider ways of teaching them;

f) to start to think about the text in **teaching units** (in preparation for planning a timeline).

With a short story or play, it is likely that several readings are possible, looking at different aspects each time, but with a novel, or if time is limited, then it is probably more realistic to work on a chapter by chapter basis and consider all areas at once. Individual teachers will have preferences of how they wish to record their notes, but a chronological reading journal (see Figure 4.1) is a possible tool for jotting whilst reading, using a grid which can be adapted as required.

Another approach is to analyse key aspects of the text in **categories**.

- What are the main events of the **plot**?
- What are the key **themes** and their **relevance** to the author and to today's readers?

| Chapter/Scene: | Summary: | | |
|---|---|---|---|
| Key passage: (page no. or photocopy) | Plot: | Characterisation: | Theme: |
| | Cultural background: | Style/structure: | Relevance to learners: |
| Language difficulties or opportunities | | | |
| Ideas for exploitation | | | |

*Figure 4.1* A chronological reading journal for teachers.

- How are the **characters** portrayed and how do they develop?

- What **stylistic features** are employed and what is their purpose and effect?

- What is the **socio-historical background** and its relevance?

  The following steps can help to do this.

- Write these questions down in separate documents and add notes (with page numbers) as reading progresses.

- Note down **queries to research** on one page and good ideas about **teaching the text** on another. This will save time later.

- Keep a **glossary** of unfamiliar vocabulary or cultural references.

- Reading the forthcoming chapters in this book on characterisation, plot and structure will offer **signposts** to look for.

- Looking at sample and past **exam questions** and other **critiques** of the work will provide ideas for categories.

- When **key passages** are identified, photocopy them and staple them together (or scan them into a document) under relevant headings, so that they can be easily referred to. These extracts will form the basis of teaching the text.

- Highlight different features in **different colours**: characters, themes, background context *etc*.

- Once key themes have been identified, **discuss** these with other teachers (or readers!) and listen to their interpretation of the text (Kramsch 1993). This will broaden and perhaps challenge one's own initial understanding of the work.

## Researching reference materials including media support

It is important to be able to contextualise the book for students. This requires knowledge of the author, the relevant socio-historical context to the work and the background information necessary to help students bridge the 'cultural gap'. Appendix 1 lists possible sources of information.

A good way to collect and collate online background material is through various **Pinterest** boards. This social media platform is probably familiar to students and has the benefit of being sharable within a group. It allows good use of visual material and the convenience of pinning websites together along thematic lines. Suggestions of new material also appear on the feed!

In addition to specific materials about the novel or play, there may be other short extracts or texts by the author which could illuminate the text to be studied.

Many of the websites discussed in Appendix 1 (*e.g.* Bibliothèque Nationale de France, TV5Monde) provide a good source of research material as they offer overviews of authors and literary periods with visual support.

## Understanding the examination

It is worthwhile spending some time at the outset gathering all the available information from the examination board via their website. The teacher should be familiar with

- the **requirements** of the examination (duration, word count, rubrics, question number and choice);
- the **types of question** asked, not just for the text to be studied, but for other relevant texts to give further ideas;
- the **assessment criteria** and mark scheme;
- **exemplar essays** and marking;
- previous **examiner reports** (commonly available via the school's examination portal);
- dates of **training events** (lectures, conferences, webinars) delivered by the examination board.

Highlighting key areas of importance will help when drawing up the programme of lessons and in preparing students for the examination. Attempting to write essays for sample titles offers a challenge and is a good way to focus the mind on what the students are working towards. Writing the essay is discussed in Chapter 10.

## Planning a timeline

It is helpful in advance to consider how best to allocate available teaching time to ensure thorough student preparation for the examination.

- On a calendar of the academic year, mark term dates, examination and study periods, mock exams and other relevant timetable events to ascertain how many teaching lessons are available for the literature study.
- Search for any additional external support (*e.g.* theatre visits; literature study days) which could be booked.
- Work backwards from the final examination to pencil in lessons for revision and examination practice.
- Divide the remaining teaching time into blocks to outline the time available for reading the text (by sections, chapters, acts) and working on the key areas of analysis (*e.g.* character, themes *etc.*).

- Consider how much time can be allocated to pre-reading activities and background research projects and whether there is scope for creative exploitation around the text.
- Divide the blocks into specific lessons or groups of lessons and include space for homework tasks.
- On the timeline, start to pencil in ideas for individual lessons.

This timeline should give an **overview** of the teaching programme in terms of learning activities, specific suggestions for which can be found in forthcoming chapters. Ideally, the plan will offer a **variety** of approaches.

- A balance of group and individual work and of skills practice (listening, speaking, reading and writing) will maintain student interest and support their general linguistic development;
- Opportunities for discussion, performance, creative output and even competitive games will keep lessons fresh and cater for different learning preferences whilst also developing transferable skills and student confidence;
- Examination practice is important and should not be left exclusively until the end of the course. Various challenges can be set, either guided in class or under test conditions, encompassing planning essays and writing opening and closing topic sentences;
- Regular opportunities for testing, feedback and reflection are crucial.

This timeline will need to be flexible of course, but it gives a structure around which to work and a roadmap of how to cover what is required. It also gives an early opportunity to review the programme by asking key questions *e.g.*

- Do the lessons offer opportunities for students to develop the full range of assessment aims and criteria?
- Are the overall aims of the literature course being addressed equally? *i.e.* Are there opportunities for linguistic, cultural and personal development?

# Ways of working

As in most lesson preparation, it is useful to think about:

- the balance of activities;
- what suits the particular class;
- what suits the teacher's chosen approach to literature;

- what is feasible in the classroom space (*e.g.* depending on student numbers, collaborative practices may suggest cluster seating or a discussion ring).

Students will feel also more secure in their learning if it is clear from the outset the expectations in terms of

- how much independent study is required;
- how they will take notes on their reading;
- how to record and learn new vocabulary;
- how their work will be monitored and assessed.

Both independent and collaborative working methods are important, as is the creation of a supportive physical and affective space in which to operate and it is worth giving some preliminary thought to this.

## *Promoting independent learning*

A level students need to develop autonomous working habits, including in their study of literature. Not only should this ideally promote an **independent**, personal response in each student (see Chapter 2), but if studying a lengthy novel, it is impossible (and undesirable) for this to happen entirely in lesson time (Turner 1999). However, due to the perceived difficulty or unfamiliarity of literature study, this is often an area where students and teachers may feel less confident and seek greater structure and control through a more didactic teaching approach.

It is important therefore to put systems in place to support students whilst still allowing **learner-centred activities**. Pachler and Field (1999) argue that literature both *requires* independent skills *and* also offers a vehicle through which to teach them. They see a continuum of '*guided* learner independence from the teacher' (our emphasis, *ibid.* p.63) from the learning tasks undertaken in the classroom to those required of students in external study time. Future chapters will suggest activities which may be conducted in both settings, and importantly, the development of independent skills should be evident either with or without the teacher's presence.

Specific skills required for effective learning in relation to literature study include:

- to read in the foreign language, deploying appropriate reading strategies and using dictionaries when necessary;
- to develop confidence and sensitivity to respond to the content of the text on a personal level;
- to express knowledge and opinions about the text effectively in the target language.

The development of these skills will help students to approach unfamiliar texts independently in the future and should inform the types of exercises they are given, both in and outside the classroom.

## *Differentiation*

Planning for independent learning also helps **differentiation** as students can move at their own pace (with guidance) through a range of tasks which support their individual learning needs. Students may also have different preferred **learning styles** and be used to different ways of working. A good place to start is to explore students' preferences and experiences and to plan to use a variety of tasks and materials. A helpful strategy could be to take different suggestions for activities contained in the following chapters and use them for different scenes or chapters at various stages of study. Alternating the focus of independent and group activities, oral and written, linguistic and cultural, factual and affective tasks should ensure that students find areas where they are comfortable, whilst expanding their capabilities in other ways. Offering students a degree of choice of activity related to their learning needs and interests (e.g. the type of summaries or characterisation tasks and the use of different media) can also be beneficial in boosting confidence and independence. Gifted and bilingual students can be encouraged to read more widely around and beyond the text and can be given additional research tasks to be shared with the group. The **personal library sheets** discussed in Chapter 11 may be useful to record additional reading (Appendix 3). During oral group work, it is often helpful to have a **confident linguist** to start discussions and supply vocabulary to maintain the group's momentum in the target language.

Many of the activities suggested in forthcoming chapters can be adapted to provide a lesser or greater degree of **linguistic support**. Gap-fill exercises, walking dictations, jumbled sentences, true or false statements, matching activities are just some of the ways of supporting less confident students as at the end of the exercise, they have full, correct sentences about the plot or characters which they can then reuse in their own writing. Open-ended questions, sentence starters or some more imaginative role plays require greater linguistic input from the students themselves. It is important not to overwhelm students at the start, but as the teaching progresses and students become more familiar with the text and the vocabulary, the level of support can be reduced. Whatever the task, student outcomes are always improved if the teacher provides a **clear model** and framework for the completion of the task, so that all students have the basic structure to follow. More confident students can extend the model. Giving students **preparation time** before writing and speaking tasks can build confidence and preceding these tasks with **partner discussion** can be beneficial. Importantly, if this is the first time that students have embarked on in-depth literary study, a **gradual progression** in activities from factual to description to analysis is sensible.

## The collaborative classroom

Leland *et al.* (2013 p.195) remind us in their book about teaching literature to young children in their first language that 'reading is a social process of meaning construction'. This principle holds good for older learners exploring literature in a second language. Modern Languages classrooms are, by necessity, spaces where discussion, interaction and idea-sharing are promoted and students regularly engage in pair work, group work and collaborative learning. They are used to giving their opinions and justifying these with (often well-worn) reasons. Teachers are skilled at fostering a collaborative environment and this assumes even greater importance in the literature classroom. Genuine learner engagement with the set text requires students to respond to the themes and form of the narrative, at least in part, on a personal level. The expression of these **personal thoughts** may seem risky to the students who are also exposing themselves **linguistically** as they struggle to express **conceptually** difficult thoughts. This situation may be heightened in regional tertiary colleges where students are unfamiliar with the teacher and each other at the beginning of the course.

Consideration of how to achieve a safe space for literary study and discussion is important as students benefit from oral, interactive tasks which help them to clarify their ideas and express them in the target language. Chambers (1991 p.6) reminds us however that the use of the target language 'takes time, patience, co-operation and understanding'. It is helpful therefore to start in a less threatening way, adopting 'think, pair, share' approaches such as championed within **assessment for learning** (Jones and Wiliam 2008 p.10). Depending upon the class size, these pairs can then join to form fours or sixes, each time negotiating and forming a new collective view and taking joint responsibility for the ideas subsequently shared with the wider group. Swapping pairings around maintains freshness and challenge and results in students taking different roles in the interactions. Many of the activities suggested in later chapters, including role play, hotseating, jigsaw discussions, filming, all require collaboration and can often be a gateway to developing both linguistic and other transferable skills.

Whilst pair work allows a degree of anonymity vis-à-vis the whole class, it is important also to develop the **confidence** that students can hold and share an **individual view**. A particularly helpful aspect of literature study is fostering the knowledge that no opinion will be 'wrong'. Three points may be borne in mind here.

- Firstly, a **plurality of views** is encouraged.
- Secondly, the teacher's approach to **error correction** is important and should be handled sensitively especially in the early stages when students are grappling with linguistic or conceptual complexity or are expressing personal beliefs. Simply noting a couple of significant errors to refer to later in class is preferable to inhibiting students' oral composition.

- Thirdly, students may need help in order to be comfortable **critiquing** a text. They may either be reluctant to criticise a text for fear of revealing their own lack of understanding or may be determinedly negative and unwilling to see positive aspects. It may help for the teacher to model a negative (reasoned) critique of perhaps another text which he or she did not enjoy, to show that it is acceptable to hold critical views.

### Structured controversy

A modified approach to what Hill and O'Loughlin (1995 p.56) call **structured controversy** provides another way for students to practise a critique or seeing an argument from both sides with the linguistic support of other students.

- Pair A decides on three positive features of the text (or arguments in support of a particular proposition or opinion or character's action) and Pair B works out three negative features (or arguments against it).
- A and B present their ideas to one another.
- A and B switch positions in order to add three more features in support of their new pro or contra stance.
- With some arguments laid out before them, students are then, as individuals, more likely to feel empowered to select those which best reflect their personal views – which may be nuanced with both positive and negative facets.
- They then combine their arguments again to form a balanced perspective which can be written up. (Hill and O'Loughlin *ibid*. require participants to come to a final verdict on the proposition.)

Collaboration can also be with **external groups** such as classes in other schools and also via links abroad. The use of email, Skype, social media and other online platforms as well as e-learning facilitates collaboration with other students to share views and research on the text. At this preparation stage, it is worth investigating how contacts through twinning, exchanges, the foreign language assistant, colleagues or personal links can be used. This may be particularly useful if the A level class itself is very small.

## The literature classroom

As well as ensuring a positive affective climate for literary study, the teacher can create a positive physical space. Reading (literature) is a core feature of language learning. A visit to an English primary school or secondary English classroom reveals many ways of promoting a reading culture in students' mother tongue. Students and teachers are, for example, encouraged to share reviews of what they are reading and illustrations of book jackets, newly published books, booksellers' sales charts and classic old favourites are celebrated in often colourful displays. A possible model for such reviews may be found in Chapter 5, but they can be easily differentiated. (Appendix 3 contains a fuller example of a personal reading record in French, Spanish and German.) Teachers may consider creating a **'literature corner'** in the classroom, library or other shared space. This could include enlisting the help of other colleagues (from within and beyond the languages faculty) to create a changing display of the type often seen in bookstores. The format can be more or less complicated (and demonstrate different grammatical structures!) A simple outline can be found in Figure 4.2.

Drama can also be included and teachers and students could record which plays have been seen at the theatre. Favourite short poems could be displayed. **Films** (e.g. adaptations of Pagnol's novels), TV or radio productions of foreign stories could also be included. Students could be encouraged to add their own film reviews. An 'Infos' or **bulletin board** could show updates on e-reader releases or new DVDs or foreign books picked up cheaply in charity shops or from online sellers. Some platforms allow readers to download or borrow **digital books** free of charge and these can be highlighted, as well as sites which offer excellent **visual material** on authors and books. An eye-catching description of the book is a good way to attract students' interest. Winners of annual foreign prizes for literature could also be featured – or researched by the students (see for example French lists on *Culturethèque* in Appendix 1). Highlighting links to podcasts of **book clubs** (e.g. BBC World Service Book Club) where foreign authors are discussing their works (in English if necessary) may get students reading more widely beyond the actual syllabus, or at least broaden their awareness. This sort of discussion is good preparation for thinking about the themes in novels and how writers go about writing *etc*. This is particularly useful if some students are interested in pursuing literary studies at university.

If space allows, another project (perhaps a task for Year 12 Induction) could be to display a **cultural timeline** by century for the target language country. Major

| Frau Jones liest … | *Emil und die Detektive* von Erich Kästner |
| --- | --- |
| Monsieur Brabant vient de lire … | *Sous les vents de Neptune* de Fred Vargas et *La gloire de mon père* de Marcel Pagnol |
| Señora Cuevas recomendaría … | *El amor en los tiempos del cólera* de Gabriel García Márquez |

*Figure 4.2* Prompts for reading displays.

events and authors are placed on the timeline and new ones added through the course of literary and non-literary lessons. Students could be initially prompted to name key events or figures associated with the country – e.g. World Wars I and II in France and Germany, *le 14 juillet*, building *la Tour Eiffel*, Napoléon Bonaparte, Hitler, Franco and the Spanish Civil War – and challenged to assign them to the right century on the timeline. Where do literary texts and their authors sit e.g. Hugo's *Les misérables* or Grimms' *Kinder- und Hausmärchen*? Students may be able to suggest other events or personalities from their Art, History or Science courses. This is a good way of helping the students to see how literature connects to their wider knowledge.

## Integrating literature

Seeing literature as an integral part of the A level programme will support students' engagement with the text. As studying literature contributes to all the aims of the A level syllabus (linguistic, cultural and personal), it sits comfortably within the whole. The activities suggested in later chapters include speaking, listening, reading and writing and provide ample opportunities for individual and group work. The language of discussion and argumentation transfers easily between literary and non-literary topics and building the confidence to present information and offer personal opinions is important for the oral examination. Skills learnt by analysing intentions and meanings in the set book can also be applied to other sources of written and spoken information. Teachers can integrate excerpts from literary texts when teaching themes e.g. poverty or history and can use literature as a spark for grammatical exercises and showing a new construction in action. Chapter 11 approaches literature as a stimulus for students' own creative written and spoken language use.

Importantly, if the A level course is taught by two members of staff, it is beneficial if links to the literature are exploited in both classes to avoid the literature being seen as a separate unit.

## Using the target language

To ensure that the literature lessons are part of an integrated A level programme, it is important that they should be conducted in the target language as far as is possible. As the students will write their examination essay in the target language, it is of course essential that they have plenty of practice in expressing their views in French, German or Spanish. It is the teacher who will set the expectations here.

Students will inevitably find discussion in the target language challenging due to the complexity of what they may wish to say. They can be supported throughout the course in giving and justifying opinions and the specific vocabulary for talking about literature can be learnt in the same way as that of other topic areas and regularly tested and reinforced. Appendix 2 contains vocabulary in French, German and Spanish and **wordmats** with key phrases *etc.* can be produced and students challenged to include the words as often as possible.

Importantly, students will need clear oral and written **models**, writing and speaking frames in order to help them to stay in the target language and giving students the opportunity to **prepare work in advance** (e.g. at home) for discussions will help them to gather their questions, facts and arguments before going 'live' in the lesson. Students can be given different degrees of support materials according to their needs and encouraged to use them more sparingly as their confidence grows.

As discussed, allowing students to use '**think, pair, share**' techniques, helps to support less confident students and prepare their points for speaking. Games-type activities in groups also allow students to receive support from other team members and to build their collective linguistic capability.

Wherever possible, it is helpful for students to hear people talking about literature (e.g. the author talking, podcast discussions, film or stage production trailers) and to read written reviews in order to feed into their own vocabulary.

Reading aloud can be difficult at first for students and is discussed in Chapters 6 and 7 but practice with pronunciation can help to build their confidence.

Overall, it is useful initially to encourage students to put forward their views in the target language rather than to focus on error correction. Recurrent mistakes can be noted and dealt with separately. Where students stray into English, it is also helpful to have a **strategy**. This may be a protocol of asking for the word in the target language, using a dictionary or trying to paraphrase the sentence. If necessary, this can then be a teaching point later or the teacher (or appointed student) can keep a note of all the language required in a particular lesson. This can then be shared with the class to learn and use next time.

## Evaluating the programme

Carroli (2008) insists that listening to students' voices and their expectations of what they will learn from their study of literature is vital. They should also have the opportunity to evaluate their progress and the effectiveness of the approach taken. For the teacher, this feedback will help shape the teaching and identify any difficulties experienced by the students. Gathering views can be done informally, but it is also helpful to allow individual responses through a more formal questionnaire. These can be paper-based, but online survey tools offer templates for writing questions and can be quite efficient in collating responses. (Many online tools have restricted free access e.g. Survey Monkey, but schools may also have in-house tools or subscriptions.) This can also be a better way of offering students anonymity in their responses.

Nguyen (2016) gives examples of before and after questionnaires to investigate student perspectives on their learning experience compared to their expectations and previous courses. In this study, the questions were open-ended and qualitative data was then gathered and analysed. This type of question allows teachers to decide what they want to find out from students and then to give them the freedom to respond however they wish. This is appropriate for small groups and allows the teacher to gain deeper insights into what students think and the underlying reasons for their views.

Alternatively, a quantitative approach is quicker for students to complete and produces numerical data. Questions can be built using a Likert scale (e.g. 1–4) for students to strongly agree, agree, disagree or strongly disagree to various statements, or to rate various elements on a numerical scale. As well as exploring what students find generally useful, enjoyable or challenging, it is helpful to focus on specific aspects such as particular types of exercises (discussions, pair work, role plays, *etc.*) or activities. When using this approach, it is also wise to leave an opportunity for further explanation of the answer given in a 'free text' box. If an online tool is used, then answers can either be obligatory or optional.

## Conclusion

This preparatory phase gives the teacher the opportunity to think about his or her aims for this aspect of the A level syllabus and to plan how to achieve them. However, although literature has some novel features which require additional thought, many considerations simply reflect normal classroom practice and literature teaching does not need to be seen in a fundamentally different way from the rest of the syllabus. It does perhaps offer a fresh opportunity for teachers to review their overall principles and enrich their lessons with this new dimension.

## Further reading

Pachler and Field (1999) discuss **learner independence** at A level.

Hill and O'Loughlin (1995) suggest a range of practical activities for promoting **collaborative working** with literature.

Bell and Waters (2018) provide a useful guide for writing questionnaires and researching classroom practice more widely.

## Implications for teaching

* Think broadly about how the linguistic, cultural and personal benefits of literature study can be incorporated within the course.

- Read the text for pleasure and then analytically. Take notes on plot, characterisation, themes, structure, style and relevance to learners.

- Note potential areas of difficulty for students and plan strategies to help them.

- Understand the examination requirements and digest all the support offered by Examination Board materials.

- Research materials available to support teaching the text and talk to colleagues.

- Research the thematic and socio-historical background to the text and the author. Read around the text where time permits.

- Consider how to promote independent learning in class and at home.

- Plan opportunities for discussion and collaborative learning.

- Create a timeline to guide teaching across the time available.

- Plan opportunities for gaining student feedback.

# References

Bell, J. and Waters, S., 2018. *Doing Your Research Project. A Guide for First-Time Researchers*. 7th ed. Buckingham: Open University Press.

Carroli, P., 2008. *Literature in Second Language Education*. London: Continuum.

Chambers, G., 1991. Suggested approaches to A-level literature. *Language Learning Journal*, 4, pp.5–9.

Hill, S. and O'Loughlin, J., 1995. *Book Talk. Collaborative Responses to Literature*. Victoria Australia: Eleanor Curtain Publishing.

Jones, J. and Wiliam, D., 2008. *Modern Foreign Languages inside the Black Box: Assessment for Learning in the Modern Foreign Languages Classroom*. London: GL Assessment.

Kramsch, C., 1993. *Context and Culture in Language Teaching*. Oxford: Oxford University Press.

Leland, C., Lewison, M. and Harste, J., 2013. *Teaching Children's Literature. It's Critical!* New York: Routledge.

Nguyen, H.T.T., 2016. How does an interactive approach to literary texts work in an English as a foreign language context? Learners' perspectives in close-up. *Innovation in Language Learning and Teaching*, 10(3), pp.171–189.

Pachler, N. and Field, K., 1999. Learner independence. In: N. Pachler, ed. *Teaching Modern Foreign Languages at Advanced Level*. London: Routledge, pp.60–75.

Turner, K., 1999. Working with literature. In: N. Pachler, ed. *Teaching Modern Foreign Languages at Advanced Level*. London: Routledge, pp.209–229.

# 5 | Introducing the text

## Introduction

Due to the new challenge which studying literature in a foreign language can present, students and teachers may approach their first text with some trepidation. The lessons in which students first encounter the text therefore assume considerable significance and the key purpose of this chapter is to suggest ways in which teachers may **engage student interest** in the task and text ahead. We will examine ways of engaging students initially with the **cultural world** of the text through pre-reading, research and presentation tasks in order to prepare the way for deeper study. An important principle underpinning these activities is that of **initial group discussions and activities**. From the outset students are encouraged to share ideas (where opinions and interpretations are sought rather than 'correct' answers expected) in preparation for their personal responses to the text. This initial phase is particularly important for students who do not have a strong existing group identity. It will allow the teacher to establish a 'baseline' understanding of students' starting points in terms of motivation, literary taste and knowledge, and of their discursive language skills both individually and as a whole.

Additionally, we suggest that students should be supported by a clear explanation of the **examination requirements** they will face and an overview of how the study programme is structured to meet these goals. A **framework of expectations** can also be reassuring for students.

## Pre-reading

The study of a foreign language text is potentially complex and the process is often broken down into stages. Lazar (1993) espouses a widely accepted three-part structure of pre-reading; while-reading and post-reading. Pre-reading also corresponds to the first phase of Parkinson and Reid Thomas's (2000 pp.108–109) proposed framework for reading novels, which they characterise as 'transformation'. This is essentially a combination of a teacher-led introduction to explain the context of the text and highlight key ideas, and the initial personal engagement of students with the context and the author, before any detailed reading of the text itself.

It is perhaps helpful to think of this stage as **pre**-paration for reading which encompasses the discussions, activities and tools given to students which prepare them to read the foreign language text itself. Pre-reading exercises and principles may be applied to any genre and specific activities for novels and drama will follow in Chapters 6 and 7.

The aims of the pre-reading stage may include:

- to generate interest in the text;
- to initiate reader engagement around the text;
- to engender confidence in the students that they are able to meet the goals ahead;
- to reassure the student that s/he will be supported to meet these goals;
- to offer preliminary support with linguistic and conceptual content as a gateway into the text;
- to 'bridge the gap between the reader and the text' (Benati 2013 p.97) or supply 'the missing link between books and students' everyday lives' (Bredella 2000 p.391).

## A note of caution

In Chapter 2 we discussed the reader-response dimension to literature study. These texts were initially written to be enjoyed directly on the page or on stage, not through classroom scrutiny before the book has been opened or the curtain raised. It is reasonable therefore to remember the limits of pre-reading, which should not detract from the reading experience itself. A work of literature is powerful when interpreted personally and this individual response could be inhibited by imposing (albeit inadvertently) a particular interpretation on students in this pre-reading stage. Teachers are seeking a balance between providing students with the knowledge to access the text successfully whilst not hampering their ability to discover it as the author intended. The ability of the class may also influence these decisions.

A guide in finding this balance may be the 'native speaker' or **'cultural' gap**. Does the pre-reading material cover information with which the author would have reasonably expected his or her audience to be familiar? Examples of this may be a contemporary German speaker's knowledge of the reunification of East and West Germany (König's *Ich fühl mich so fifty-fifty* or Hensel's *Zonenkinder*) or a Spaniard's awareness of Franco's rule (Ruiz Zafón's *La sombra del viento*), knowledge which provides the background setting for the story. A specialised lexicon of (technical or regional) vocabulary may also fall into this category. The teacher is aiming to provide the students with a frame of reference for their reading, which can increase their confidence and understanding (Turner 1999).

## Preparing the ground

As discussed in Chapter 3, the teacher will have already considered the strengths of the chosen text but will also be aware of any potential challenges to be overcome. Asking how easy it will be for the students to engage with the text linguistically, conceptually or personally and judging their level of motivation towards literature study (along with the teacher's learning goals), will guide this initial stage of introducing the text with each particular class.

It is worth noting that

- the sequencing and use of these activities will depend upon how involved the students have already been in choosing the text;
- the timing of these initial encounters may vary depending upon the overall study programme and examination (AS or A level) to be targeted. Some activities could be undertaken early in Year 12 or at the end of Year 12 with tasks to complete over the summer holiday before Year 13. Another option for some schools may be to incorporate this as part of a pre-Year 12 induction programme after the completion of GCSEs and as a precursor to a holiday project. The timing and choice of activity will depend upon the ability and motivation of the students.

## Reading in one's first language

A starting point is to involve students in a discussion about reading or going to the theatre as a leisure activity in their own language. Depending upon the class, their linguistic level and their prior experience, some or all of the following areas may be considered, to build on or reactivate existing language in the area:

- Why do students read in their own language?
- What types of material do they read and why?
- What makes a 'good read'?

If a play has been chosen, then questions about reading and viewing drama in the theatre would be appropriate.

- For homework, students may be asked to write a brief synopsis of a favourite book or play (read in any language they choose). Some students may benefit here from a framework (Figure 5.1 which can be translated into the appropriate language) to guide them, and it is always useful if the teacher shares a synopsis as a model. This is an ideal activity for a foreign language assistant (FLA) to get involved with. He or she can also offer a synopsis and possibly take charge of the feedback of students' synopses outside main class time.

Whilst this activity is probably best completed at home, it could be used as the basis for a short oral presentation to the class or small groups in the next lesson (or with the FLA) where other students are encouraged to pose questions and give their own opinions about whether they would like to read the book or see the play. The written versions could be displayed as part of the 'literature classroom' suggested in Chapter 4.

| Title | |
| --- | --- |
| Author and nationality | Sentence starters may be added if necessary to support students *e.g. L'écrivain s'appelle … … .* |
| Date of publication | |
| Genre | |
| Setting: historical | |
| Setting: geographical | |
| Main characters | 2 sentences to describe each one |
| Plot | Summarise in a maximum of 5 sentences |
| Why you liked it | |
| For whom would you recommend it? | |
| 3 adjectives to sum up the text | |

*Figure 5.1* Possible framework for student book synopsis (translated into French, German or Spanish). The framework can be adapted according to the ability of the students.

# Reading in a foreign language

Discussions of first language reading are a preamble to considering foreign language literature. The following activities ask students to consider the following questions:

- What is their experience of foreign literature to date? (which may have been in English or on television or film e.g. Hugo's *Les misérables*)
- Why read in a foreign language?
- Why do they think it forms part of the syllabus?
- What do they hope to get from reading in French, German or Spanish?
- What challenges do they envisage?

This can provide the teacher with a valuable baseline of students' prior experience. The teacher may use some visual prompts (e.g. a still from *Les misérables*) to get the ball rolling. Students share experiences in pairs before leading to whole-class discussion.

Depending upon students' experience of literature in previous years (and this may have increased in line with more recent Key Stage 3 guidelines or simply due to a diverse bi- or multilingual heritage group), it may also be interesting to see if they can name any works from the target language canon as a quick starter. This could take the form of a multiple choice *Who Wants to Be a Millionaire?* format, a Quizlet.com or Memrise.com matching exercise. It could be a group challenge and draw upon clues from the titles to supplement any actual prior knowledge.

Different ways to approach this could include:

- Filling in blanks for either author or title or both e.g. Les F_ B _ _ S de L_ F _ N T _ _ _ E (*Les fables* de La Fontaine; the difficulty can be easily adapted to the group). Extra points could be offered for guessing the century correctly. Some titles with amusing possibilities to guess are shown in Figure 5.2. Guessing what the story may be about can also be fun!

| | |
|---|---|
| *Le rouge et le _ _ _ _* | *Stendhal* |
| *Les mains _ _ _ _ _* | Sartre |
| *Die verlorene _ _ _ _ der Katharina Blum* | Böll |
| *Der _ _ _ _ _ _ der alten Dame* | Dürrenmatt |
| *Como agua para _ _ _ _ _ _ _ _ _* | Esquivel |
| *La _ _ _ _ de Bernarda Alba* | Lorca |

*Figure 5.2* Literature titles for students to guess.

- Matching and grouping exercises could be done on the interactive whiteboard or using cards
  - matching author and title; author and century;
  - grouping titles by category as plays, novels, short stories, poetry;
  - grouping authors into dramatists, novelists, short story writers and poets (with perhaps some overlap e.g. Camus as novelist and dramatist!).

## The benefits of studying literature in a foreign language

Asking students why they might read in a second language can help teachers to assess the starting points of their class. A discussion of the benefits could be done informally as a guided discussion, perhaps with pair and share techniques, or given a more structured exercise to support their own target language use for discussing the topic e.g. with a diamond 5 or **diamond 9 ranking exercise** (in Figure 5.3). Here the potential benefits of literature study are put on pieces of card in the target language and students, after discussion, rank them in terms of what they feel to be the most important. With such ranking activities it is often helpful to leave one or two cards blank to encourage students to contribute their own reasons. The cards should be structured in a way that will assist students to put forward their points of view e.g. starting with an infinitive which can easily be used with a construction such as, 'Reading French literature can help me to … '. The question of what the students hope to gain from studying literature is important and will support both motivation and personal engagement. The teacher will wish to outline the reasons why literature is on the syllabus and explain his or her own rationale and learning goals for the unit of study.

| to learn about Spanish culture | to improve my reading | to improve my own writing |
|---|---|---|
| to learn new vocabulary | to enjoy an interesting story | to make me think about issues |
| to think analytically | to learn about the world | to feel proud of my achievement |
| to understand myself | to … … … … … … … . | to … … … … … … … … … . |

Figure 5.3 Possible benefits of studying literature for use in diamond ranking activity (to be translated into French, German or Spanish).

## *A plan for success*

However, it is also important to acknowledge that students may have concerns and to listen to what they feel the **challenges** may be for them. This can be handled positively and students reassured when they understand how the course will be structured to support them to move confidently towards examination success – and a real sense of achievement. The exact **framework** will depend on the text, the class, local circumstances such as time and resource allocations and the possible availability of a FLA. The teacher is essentially communicating to students the plans decided in Chapter 4. (Depending on group and stage of study, this may not all be delivered at once, the trick being to reassure but not overwhelm!)

The areas to cover may include:

- An explanation of the rationale for their study of literature, highlighting how they will benefit;
- An overview of the structure of the literature teaching unit, explaining how much class time will be devoted to it and the further requirements for private study;
- A summary of the examination requirements to demystify the end goal. They **will** be able to talk about characters, plot, the author's intentions and (as appropriate) understand about an important historical, social or cultural aspect linked to the target-language-speaking world;
- An expectation that they will work both individually and collaboratively in order to develop their understanding, critical arguments and oral and written fluency. By working together, they will share aspects of the workload and have a sounding board for their ideas;
- The expectation that they will keep glossaries to support their vocabulary learning;
- An illustration of the thematic note-taking and chapter summaries they will be completing (see Chapter 6);
- An overview of useful sites and sources of information to assist with their research skills.

Many of these topics will be revisited in more detail throughout the course.

## Meeting the text

First impressions count. If this is the first time the students have been shown the text, a simple **familiarisation and prediction** exercise can be quite effective in sparking discussion. Book jackets and theatre posters are designed to attract attention and their artwork can be used to elicit aesthetic opinions in advance of more focused literary ones. It is easy to find pictures of books from online book sellers and publishers' websites, a Google image search and often on the homepages of contemporary authors. The websites of theatres such as the *Comédie-Française*, the *Weimar Theater* and indeed the National Theatre or Cervantes Theatre in the UK often display posters from previous productions. Pinterest is a useful collection point for images and students can compare different graphical representations.

If there are different translations of the title into English (e.g. Camus's '*L'étranger*' as The Outsider, The Stranger or The Foreigner; Colette's *Le blé en herbe* as The Ripening Seed or The Green Wheat), this may also be worth noting. Book jackets also often contain an indication of the plot and brief reviews, which can be collated and given to students. If the book jackets are not particularly stimulating, bringing in any picture related to the text could prompt discussion (Chambers 1991).

Asking 'opinion' questions ensures that students are offering personal opinions and interpretations from the outset. For some texts and covers, it may be possible to challenge the students to identify the passage from the text which inspired the cover once they start reading the text.

- Which cover / poster attracts you most and why?
- What emotions does the cover evoke in you?
- What does the cover tell you about the story / play? e.g. its genre, tone, plot
- Why might these images have been chosen?
- Does the jacket 'blurb' make you want to read on?
- Can you predict what the story is about?
- Why do you think I chose this text for study?

It is helpful if students keep a **record of their first impressions** which can be revisited once they have completed the text. After reading the book, their opinions on the most appropriate cover may have changed! They may also be able to offer better reasons why one translation of the title is better than another or why that text was chosen by their teacher. (If time allows, Chapter 11 suggests how this pre-reading phase could be used for some creative writing based on clues about the text.)

## Preliminary projects

Preparation for reading the text may focus on aspects of its linguistic or conceptual content. This background knowledge offers opportunities for either independent research or group projects about the author and the socio-historical, geographical or lexical content of the work. For all these projects the use of visual materials should be encouraged.

## *The author*

- One approach is a straightforward lecture on the **author's life** by the teacher to include key biographical details and explaining milieu and events which may be relevant to the work in question, *e.g.* Camus's upbringing in Algeria (*L'étranger*) or Molière's position at the court of Louis XIV (*Le Tartuffe*). This is principally didactic but if used as a listening exercise, students could be challenged to complete a factsheet. This may then act as a springboard for further research by the students and include YouTube clips and TV clips from the excellent, searchable resource www.ina.fr which has interviews with modern authors such as de Vigan and Guène and documentaries on other literary and historical topics.

- A more student-led approach could involve simply offering a loose framework for students to research in groups or individually. A '**puzzle**' approach could be adopted. A number of key objects or dates or words or images (of the author, quotations, names of other works) are given to students who must research their significance to the author's life and put them together as a biography to be presented in writing and/or as a class presentation. In this case one slide for each 'hook' would provide a tight structure. This type of approach combines the benefit of partial guidance for students whilst encouraging them to read and discover about the author independently and offering scope for their own interpretation of the importance of the 'hooks' or clues. Students could divide the clues between them and then combine for a coherent presentation, thus developing a collaborative and discursive approach from the outset. Students could also be asked to include three other 'hooks' which they feel are important to the author's story.

- The use of a **webquest** could be another, complementary approach and is a useful initial guide to both the author and their work and where to find and how to use information. Teachers give students, in pairs or groups, a series of questions to answer about the author and a list of foreign websites where this information can be found. Online sites make it very easy to access information about most authors and their books in the target language. However, students may be tempted to devour wholesale or 'copy and paste' indiscriminately the author biographies, plot summaries and character studies which they find. Pedagogically therefore it is important to prepare tasks which, at least initially, guide students to the use of reputable sites for the collation and extraction of information. It can also stop students becoming too immersed at this stage in, for example, Camus's philosophical writings. Appendix 1 gives some useful information sources.

Students must also be supported to develop confidence in their own ability to understand and interpret the text and online commentaries about it. Online content is only one interpretation of the work, which may inform but not replace their own personal response.

## *The geographical and/or socio-historical setting*

- Where a text is strongly rooted in a particular setting, students can become familiar with this before reading the text itself. In Pagnol's *Le château de ma mère*, the landscape of Provence is integral to the story and a key feature of the vocabulary used. It is also reasonable to imagine that Pagnol's French audience would be familiar with this area. Students could be asked to put together a presentation on the region with guidelines to include particular information *e.g.*

  - its location in France;
  - key towns;
  - images of the landscape (could include links to artists);
  - images of village life, contemporary to the setting of the novel (before World War I);
  - flora and fauna (which is important in the novel).

A similar approach could be taken with East and West Germany in Hensel and König's works and a map of Barcelona is an essential tool to get to grips with Ruiz Zafón's *La sombra del viento*.

- For texts which are situated against a backdrop of actual **historical events**, understanding this context may be necessary before students approach the text. For König's *Ich fühl mich so fifty-fifty* or Hensel's *Zonenkinder*, students could put together a **timeline** of historical events. This could be a simple matching and ordering exercise of key dates and events followed by an explanation of the political events. Again, images of events and social indications (advertisements, propaganda posters *etc.*) can enrich the account and stimulate student questions and opinions significantly. Online reports and film clips of historical events could provide listening comprehension exercises.

- Students could be given **tasks** such as researching what Jews could and could not do in Occupied France during World War II or the restrictions on life in East Germany, or the dangers faced by opponents of General Franco in Spain. Giving students some key texts as sources will make it easier for them and if different students are given different extracts initially, they can summarise these orally and present their findings to pool their new knowledge.

- Individual students can be given **specific** areas to research which they then explain to the class as they are met when reading the text.

- If students use **technology** to present their findings, the research work of the group is reduced and students can have ready access to everyone's files. In addition to Pinterest boards and blogs, **QR (quick response)** codes could be used. Before students begin the research, the teacher needs to check that they have downloaded a QR code reader app to their mobiles and gives them a website link for creating a QR code (www.qr-code-generator.com). After doing the research task, students incorporate a QR code in their displayed work; other students can then click on this, using the QR code reader app. This takes them to a further linked document, website or podcast on the author or text.

- Using **film** to gain a sense of time or place can be powerful. This is not the stage at which to watch a film adaptation of the text for the reason that it necessarily imposes another person's interpretation on the text and may be heavily abridged or altered. However, a film such as *Molière* (Ariane Mnouchkine 1978) can transport the students into 17th century France quite effectively. Similarly, contemporary films treating a similar historical period *e.g. Good Bye, Lenin!* (directed by Wolfgang Becker 2003) or *Das Leben der Anderen* (Florian Henckel von Donnersmarck 2006) can throw light on the period in question and be viewed at home.

- Other **visual** media such as paintings and photos can help to evoke a sense of place and history (*e.g.* the Spanish Civil War, or Algeria in the interwar years).

## *Lexical and thematic content*

- Once the students know the subject of the text, then a useful preliminary exercise might be for them to predict words which could be useful and produce a **glossary**. In Esquivel's *Como agua para chocolate* the framework of recipes would prompt a collection of relevant culinary terms.

- Similarly, where the text's themes overlap with other non-literary topics, *e.g.* immigration or homelessness, these topics could be taught in advance of the literature text.

- Giving students **conflicting viewpoints** on a central theme (*e.g.* the role of women within the family or what drives someone to murder) to discuss in groups can help to generate interest and opinions before tackling the issue within the text itself. Carter and Long (1991) stress the benefits of helping students to relate such themes and discussions to their **own personal experience** where possible, in order to help them to get to grips with the issues at this initial stage.

## Conclusion

Teachers themselves are in the best position to judge how to introduce the literature component of the course and the text itself to their class. From the start, students should understand how their literature lessons will help them to develop as linguists and how they will be supported to achieve this new challenge. Their interest and engagement can be sparked by thinking and talking about the text and relevant themes before starting to read it in detail. Students can also be given research tasks which will help them to understand the text and be able to relate their reading to its cultural context in the examination.

## Further reading

Paran and Robinson (2016 from p.29) give further examples of how to explore learners' prior **experiences of reading**.

## Implications for teaching

- Encourage students to think about their own reading in advance of meeting foreign literature.
- Discuss the purpose of studying the text and their perceptions of the benefits.
- Generate interest in the chosen text through visual clues and asking for students' first impressions.
- Think about where the difficulties with the chosen text lie and help students to enter the world of the novel or play in order to develop a frame of reference ahead of reading the text itself.
- Encourage guided research projects where possible in order to encourage student-led collaborative learning rather than a strongly didactic approach.
- Explain how to meet the examination requirements and what will be expected in lessons and at home.

## References

Benati, A., 2013. *Issues in Second Language Teaching*. Bristol: Equinox.

Bredella, L., 2000. Literary theory and literature teaching. In: M. Byram, ed. *Routledge Encyclopaedia of Language Teaching and Learning*. London: Routledge, pp.387–391.

Carter, R. and Long, M., 1991. *Teaching Literature*. Harlow: Longman.

Chambers, G., 1991. Suggested approaches to A-level literature. *The Language Learning Journal*, 4, pp.5–9.

Lazar, G., 1993. *Literature and Language Teaching: A Guide for Teachers and Trainers*. Cambridge: Cambridge University Press.

Paran, A. and Robinson, P., 2016. *Literature*. Oxford: Oxford University Press.

Parkinson, B. and Reid Thomas, H., 2000. *Teaching Literature in a Second Language*. Edinburgh: Edinburgh University Press.

Turner, K., 1999. Working with literature. In: N. Pachler, ed. *Teaching Modern Foreign Languages at Advanced Level*. London: Routledge, pp.209–229.

# 6 Teaching the novel and short story

## Introduction

Novels are well represented in the set text lists and remain a popular choice for teachers and students. They are a rich source of language and allow students to explore characters, situations, cultures and beliefs which may be very different from their own experiences to date. This chapter offers suggestions about how to study a novel in order to exploit these opportunities and to address the challenges posed by the genre.

Before appreciating the novel, students need to be guided through the complexities of **length, language** and **plot** in order to read and understand it. It is useful therefore to start by reviewing **strategies** to facilitate independent reading and considering how techniques can aid **vocabulary** retention and retrieval, improve **dictionary** usage and speed up **reading rate**. These strategies can also benefit students' linguistic development more generally.

Deciding how to use **class** and **independent study** time when first reading the text is another important consideration. This requires identifying key episodes to review together in class and constructing meaningful tasks to support students' individual reading at home. The use of **audio recordings and film productions** is also considered. During this initial reading phase students should build a firm knowledge of the **plot** of the novel and start to gather the information required for future analysis of **characterisation, structure, style and underlying thematic content**, all of which will be explored in Chapters 8 and 9.

Whilst many of these topics apply equally to the study of the **short story**, some particular features of this genre are considered separately at the end of the chapter.

# Reading the novel

The first difficulty with a novel is ensuring that, whatever the **length** of the work, students have read the text and understand it sufficiently to be able to think and write knowledgeably and critically about its content.

Teachers often face the dilemma of wanting to ensure comprehension of both language and content through close reading in class, but do not have sufficient lesson time to devote to this. Such line by line reading of lengthy works would, in all likelihood, prove unwieldy for both students and teacher. This may also be counter-productive in terms of student motivation and of achieving the key aims of literary study (Turner 1999). 'Spoon-feeding' texts (or reading in translation!) will not encourage students to develop their own reading strategies and may inhibit their ability to form their *own* relationship with the text. The practical solution to this dilemma is to design a programme where some close reading is done **in class** and the rest undertaken **at home** by students themselves.

This challenge of extensive independent reading is made easier for students if they are helped to develop their second language **reading skills**. As outlined in Chapter 3, readers rely on **schemata** – their expectations of both content and form – in order to decode texts in both their first and second languages. Texts which do not conform to these schemata are harder to understand and novels, where both content *and* language are likely to be unfamiliar, significantly increase the demands placed upon the reader (Schramm 2008). This 'cultural' or thematic gap can be bridged by the type of **pre-reading exercises** suggested in Chapter 5 where students are encouraged to predict content on the basis of various markers and acquire an awareness of the broad context of the novel and its author. This is why 'pre-reading' is the first stage in most frameworks for teaching literature (e.g. Lazar 1993; Benati 2013). This chapter assumes that such activities have already taken place for the text as a whole. However, they may still have a part to play in preparing for smaller sections of the novel, especially where these will be read independently by students. In this second stage, readers become familiar with the plot and characters of the novel before moving to a deeper and more personal third stage of analysis.

## Learning strategies

For several decades there has been interest in the use of explicit **learning/learner strategies** in order to support second language learners. In the English Language context, O'Malley and Chamot (*e.g.*1990) and Oxford (*e.g.*1990) led the discussion, exploring strategies employed by effective learners to support their progress. Strategies are often characterised as cognitive, metacognitive, social or affective and some may be largely subconscious, whereas others are more likely to be explicitly taught

(Macaro 2001 pp.24–26). Most importantly, teaching students to use these tools effectively helps them to become more **active participants** in their learning and more independent as a result.

In England, strategy use is embedded in the National Curriculum Programme of Study for Key Stages 3 and 4 (DfEE/QCA 1999), the Framework for languages at Key Stage 3 (DfES 2003) and Key Stage 2 (DfES 2005). Teachers are therefore familiar with teaching strategies for learning vocabulary and tackling reading and listening texts in the early years of language study (e.g. Harris 1997) and may imagine that A level students are proficient in helpful reading strategies. Studies have shown, however, that this is not always the case (Graham 1997) and that usage can be very patchy. Additionally, different strategies correspond to individual learners' preferences (Grenfell 2007) and so using and teaching a wide range of strategies is most likely to be beneficial to a class.

Whatever students' prior experience, it is worth investing some time in **explicit instruction** in using strategies before students are faced with reading a literary text. As reinforcement and repeated practice are known to be necessary for strategy use to become embedded (Wright and Brown 2006), teachers can use the new task of literary reading as an ideal opportunity to review, reinforce and potentially extend students' current practice. Students can learn from **discussion** of their own existing strategy use and from hearing that of their peers. **Modelling** some strategies during class reading is very helpful at the start. 'Thinking aloud' during the process helps to ensure that students understand both how to go about deploying strategies and what their purpose is. Specific reading activities can be given to support strategy use during home reading (see next section). Weaker students may need **intervention** to help them to use strategies effectively. Barnes (2000 pp.28–29) enumerates some of the problems experienced by readers at A level and **diagnosis** of where the particular problems lie may be extremely helpful.

## *Reading strategies – how do we read?*

In order to understand a text, in either one's first or second language, it is generally recognised that two categories of reading process are employed (e.g. Benati 2013). These are commonly defined as a **top-down** approach where the reader uses his or her wider knowledge beyond the individual text (*i.e.* information about the topic in question, cultural background or conventions of text structure) to make sense of what is being read in conjunction with selected key words and text markers. A competent reader will also check the validity of these predictions based on information which emerges later in the text. In a **bottom-up** approach, by contrast, the reader focuses on small units of language and uses vocabulary, grammar and syntactic knowledge to work out meaning in a more atomistic manner.

Successful second language readers use a combination of these strategies (see the **interactive model** of reading, Macaro 2003), mimicking the approach they have already mastered when reading in their first language. However, research indicates that in second language reading, learners tend to focus disproportionately on bottom-up, linguistic knowledge, which slows the reading process down significantly (Benati 2013). This problem is compounded because strategies which might support this approach are also less frequently discussed by teachers (Graham 1997). This second language reader bias towards bottom-up approaches is in part due to the difficulty of employing top-down strategies to unfamiliar material such as literary prose. Even familiar lexical items are not recalled automatically in the second language, making it more difficult to quickly gain a broad (global) understanding of the text (Schramm 2008). (This argument supports the use of pre-reading familiarisation activities to provide an initial frame of reference for reading the novel.) So, teaching students how to transfer their existing first language reading strategies to their second language study, and how to make judge-ments about which kind of strategy works best (Macaro 2001), can benefit literature study *and* also contribute to other areas of the course. As reading becomes more difficult at advanced level, students can also benefit from learning **affective strategies** which may help them to maintain their motivation when the going gets tough.

## *Strategies for successful reading*

In order for students to navigate the challenge of reading a novel successfully, they should be equipped with a bank of effective strategies for coping with the combined challenge of the **length of text**, the **amount of new vocabulary** and the **complexity of structure**. The following strategies and suggestions taken from observations of the reading habits of effective language learners may benefit *all* A level readers.

1. **Define a clear reading goal** (Schramm 2008; Benati 2013). Guided reading with shorter tasks and activities offer an immediate goal, *i.e.* the desired **focus** for a particular passage or chapter may be

   - to understand the next episode in the story;
   - to analyse character or character development;
   - to identify aspects of the author's style or use of language;
   - to examine thematic content;
   - to prompt students' responses to a particular situation in the novel *etc.*

Understanding this main purpose is important as it allows students to focus their efforts and avoid being distracted or becoming bogged down in irrelevant details (Schramm 2008).

2. **Activate background knowledge of the topic.** This is an important **top-down** strategy which allows other strategies to be used. It gives a reference point against which other suppositions can be developed and evaluated. In a novel this may most usefully refer to what is known of the plot, characters and setting up to this point.

3. **Activate existing lexical and syntactical** knowledge. Students can be alert to the stylistic habits and vocabulary of the author. These may be past historic forms, repeated turns of phrase or a specific set of vocabulary (e.g. technical, regional or colloquial terms). Keeping a **glossary** of recurring words can save time and help to provide 'anchors' within dense unfamiliar text.

4. **Infer from context**. Using context to guess unknown vocabulary will speed up reading considerably, as long as **checking mechanisms** (e.g. does this still make sense in the light of any new information?) are also used.

5. **Skim** the surface of the text to grasp the gist of a passage. The beginnings and ends of sections may be particularly useful, as are any captions or subtitles (although rarer in literary works) which can give the reader clues about the general content of the passage.

6. **Scan** for specific details such as key words or ideas. As both skimming and scanning techniques are designed to encourage rapid reading of the text, giving a time limit for such exercises in class is useful. This will help students to try to get the message quickly and to learn to determine which words are crucial to understanding (and may be looked up) and which are less important and can be ignored.

7. **Use temporal markers** (time expressions) to understand the chronology of a narrative. Words and phrases which indicate the opposition of ideas (e.g. however; in contrast etc.) are also helpful in determining the structure of a passage. Lists of these could be studied in advance.

8. **Use grammatical markers** (e.g. capitalised nouns in German, typical suffixes e.g. for adverbs (-ment); forms of past participles) to orientate oneself in a complex sentence.

9. **Dissect** compound words into **constituent parts**. This is particularly useful in German but it can also be helpful to identify other known words with a similar root or etymology.

10. **Use punctuation** to identify separate clauses, main verbs or where dialogue starts and ends or the speaker changes.

11. **Reading aloud** often helps to jog the memory about words and to untangle difficult syntax as it may be possible to recognise familiar oral patterns.

12. **Know** when to use a **dictionary** and when not to. It has been reported that less successful readers tend to focus on the meaning of nouns and to overlook verbs, so this may be an area to discuss with students (Macaro 2001).

13. **Use cognates** (known as **transfer**). It is important however that readers are also aware of *'faux amis'* (it may be useful to supply students with an initial language-specific list). Interestingly, Macaro (2001) reports finding that less successful readers focussed *too* heavily on cognates, leading to errors.

14. **Focus** when reading, keep going and do not panic!

15. **Combine** strategies to assist comprehension.

16. Constantly **monitor** understanding, using new information to confirm or re-evaluate earlier decisions and to notice any inconsistencies. Keep asking 'does this make sense?'

17. **Put oneself in the text**. Considering how one may act in this situation can also be an effective top-down strategy.

18. **Reflect** on the reading process and **evaluate** one's own strategy use. By asking what worked for them, students can refine and develop their strategies (Schramm 2008).

## Embedding reading strategies

Teachers can assist students in using these strategies by:

- allowing students to discuss and share their own use of strategies in English and the foreign language;
- explaining that good readers make use of a range of effective strategies to improve their reading;
- helping students to see that they do not need to look up every word in order to understand;
- showing learners a range of different strategies;
- modelling strategy use with learners when reading an unfamiliar passage;
- encouraging learners to monitor the effectiveness of their strategy use over time.

Reading tasks given at home can also encourage these types of reading. For example, questions that just ask for a broad understanding of key events (e.g. the sequencing of sentences or word limited summaries) will help students to read for gist (skimming). Questions which focus on specific details (e.g. gap filling or completing grids) require students to scan the text for the required information.

## Tasks to support active reading

In order for teachers to support students to tackle the extensive reading required by a novel, both independently and in lesson time, it is important to bear in mind the principles that students should have a clear (short-term) **reading goal** and be required to be **active** in the reading process (Grellet 1981). The most tangible way to do this is to provide students with **tasks** to be completed based on their reading of a passage or chapter.

Many teachers will be familiar with the concept of **DARTs** (Directed Activities Related to Texts), which has formed part of the literacy toolkit within schools for many years (DfES 2004). Indeed, many of the successful ways of exploiting non-literary second language texts from the early stages of language learning would fall naturally into the categories of supporting students to understand texts. The purpose is to make texts which are challenging to read and understand more accessible to students.

DARTs activities are often categorised as either **reconstitution** or **analysis.** Reconstitution exercises usually involve distilling information and reproducing it in a condensed form. The principle is to allow students to become familiar with and manipulate key aspects of the text and language in readiness for the more challenging analytical tasks. Techniques of skimming and scanning are often used (and can help to speed up the reading process with a lengthy and complex text). Such reconstitution activities may include representing the **key facts or events** in a **visual format** such as completing tables or grids, flowcharts or diagrams. **Gap fill exercises, true or false questions** or **reordering jumbled sentences** can all ensure that students have a grasp of the basic sequence of the plot and some sentences in the target language to support their spoken and written discussion. It is also helpful here, where appropriate, to use the types of exercises which may be found in the reading papers at AS and A level.

With most A level classes it is wise to allow students the chance to do some recognition and manipulation work before moving on to interpretation activities (Barnes 2000). However, at this level, exercises will most usefully fall into the **'analysis'** category. Students work, often collaboratively, not to find the 'right' answer, but to look deeper into the text to uncover possible meanings and deduce reasons for what happens. Questions should be open rather than closed and invite students to prioritise, speculate, rank, categorise and offer their own opinion. Students should be prepared to support their views with evidence from the text. (These principles underpin many of the activities suggested throughout Chapters 6–9 in this book and can be adapted to many different texts and situations.)

It is timely here to mention the difference described in Chapter 2 between **efferent** and **aesthetic** reading. Whilst students and teachers will be primarily concerned with understanding the plot of the novel as they start to read, the tasks to accompany the reading should also recognise the 'aesthetic' element of reading. Teachers can model this aspect of reading by a 'thinking aloud' technique where they explore the questions, thoughts, feelings and interpretations which arise whilst they read a particular passage (Kramsch 1993). In this way students are encouraged to look beyond the mechanics of the story, to consider the meaning of the story for themselves as the reader.

The starting point for approaching any reading passage is to decide what the students should learn from it.

- Why is this excerpt important?
- How will it help the students to understand the text, in terms of language or content?
- Is efferent (for information) or aesthetic (for a more personal response) reading most appropriate?
- What type of activity will best serve this goal? (N.B. activities which check factual understanding are different from those which will encourage reflections on the bigger picture.)

Teachers may wish to focus on passages which highlight:

- plot;
- narrative technique;
- characterisation;
- socio-historical context;
- style and structure;
- thematic content;
- learner response to situations.

## Working with key passages

Exercise types could include **highlighting or underlining** key words, phrases or ideas in the passage. This could be to focus upon *content* or *language* and could have varying degrees of difficulty. Students could for example be asked to read and underline

- an aspect of the argument, marking statements for and against in different colours;
- opinions of a particular character using different colours to indicate the different holders of these opinions;
- aspects of a character's motivation;
- a description of an event as seen from different perspectives;
- factors which explain an event;
- every reference to a particular colour or to nature (where these are symbolically significant);
- adjectives or adverbs (to highlight a particular stylistic device);
- subordinate clauses (to focus on sentence structure *etc.*).

The list here is potentially endless and can be adapted to help students focus on particular aspects of the text and then to start to make judgements based on the information they have extracted. Highlighting also enables quicker participation in subsequent discussions as students can find examples more easily to support their views.

This works best if students have their own text (perhaps on a tablet to highlight electronically) or an enlarged copy of the specific passage with colours to categorise further what they are highlighting. Highlighting may be a prelude to extracting information to represent in a **tabular form**, for example:

- contrasting views of characters;
- the positives and negatives of a situation;
- similarities and differences between characters, events or stylistic passages;
- the cause and effect of events and actions.

These tables can then serve as a springboard to add further detail from later in the text. At this stage, such visual representations are really a framework for focussing and supporting student reading and for alerting them to areas for further analysis. Other ideas may be found elsewhere in the book to help students to focus on particular aspects of the text, e.g. using a **flow chart** or **timeline** to represent events. Another DARTs approach is to transform the text into a **different format** such as an advice leaflet, a diary entry, a police report, a newspaper article or a poster and activities to stimulate students' creativity and language production in this way may be found in Chapter 11.

Students should also be guided in the most time-efficient and useful way of **note-taking** and recording their reading. Where should they keep their notes? Will they be required for monitoring by the teacher? Should they focus on particular areas? Should they be in full sentences? Teachers and students will have their own preferences but will both benefit if important ideas from reading the novel are recorded in a format which does not overburden the students and which allows information to be easily retrieved when required. Collating ongoing thoughts in key categories can be done in a similar form to that suggested for the teacher in Chapter 4, for example as seen in Figure 6.1.

In addition, grids for recording character traits are suggested in Chapter 8 and specific plot summary tasks are detailed later in this chapter. A good policy is to ensure that the tasks given throughout the reading and analysis phases (as suggested in Chapters 6–9) will together constitute a record of all the key areas for the examination. This will help all students to develop a firm basis of knowledge and language about the text in a structured, manageable way.

A key principle of the DARTs approach is that **discussion** underpins the construction of meaning amongst students. So, although students may complete such exercises as part of independent reading at home, they will still benefit from discussion of their findings in class, where they can be challenged to support their views. This may be teacher-led or between pairs and groups.

| Chapter/Scene: | Summary: | | |
|---|---|---|---|
| Key passage: (page no.) | Plot: | Characterisation: | Theme: |
| | Cultural background: | Style/structure: | My response: |

Figure 6.1 A chronological reading journal for students (to be translated into French, German or Spanish).

## Improving reading speed

As it is unlikely that the whole novel can be read together in class, learning techniques which can help students to speed up their independent reading at home may be beneficial. The reading strategies discussed previously are designed to help students to 'keep going' when reading rather than interrupting their flow over every unfamiliar word, but Hill (1986) looks specifically at increasing reading speed. She suggests techniques such as:

- covering what has been read to prevent students from rereading it;
- masking a line so that students guess what is hidden beneath;
- giving decreasing time limits for comprehension texts over the year;
- using graded readers which students complete as quickly as they can.

An updated approach could be to use the timed entry function on PowerPoint in order to gradually speed up the entrance and exit of sentences onto the screen. Some students may not respond well to trying to read under the pressure of time, and the novel in question may demand slow and deliberate decoding by students at this level. However, over a period of practice, this focus may help some students to get used to making quicker judgements about meaning and give them the confidence that, as long as the text is not too far beyond their linguistic level, they do not need to read and reread sentences several times.

## Vocabulary

Exposure to vocabulary is an important component of reading ability because learners use the words they recognise as the basis for reconstructing meaning

(Benati 2013). Research points to the fact that one of the key difficulties of the transition to Year 12 for students is the volume of new vocabulary, which can seem both frustrating and overwhelming (Graham 1997; Gallagher-Brett 2006). It leads them to underestimate their progress during this first year of A level study and can be demoralising. Reading literature can appear particularly problematic as students are faced with a vast amount of unfamiliar vocabulary at once.

However, the acquisition of less common vocabulary in Year 12 has been found to be a key indicator in differences in students' overall progress and attainment (Richards *et al.* 2008). It is perhaps not surprising that students with a wider, more sophisticated vocabulary forge ahead, and the goal for teachers should be to ensure that all students work on developing their knowledge of low-frequency vocabulary. The authors of this longitudinal study (*ibid.*) recommend graded readers as an incremental way of developing learners' vocabulary. Literature also offers a rich supply of vocabulary, but the author's words have not been chosen with the needs of the second language learner in mind and students will need more support to assimilate them.

It is helpful to review how students learn vocabulary. Snow (1998) includes a range of strategies to use with younger learners, but as language learning is an iterative process, revision and reinforcement of techniques can be invaluable for learners who struggle in particular areas. Indeed, in a smaller A level class, there is also perhaps a greater opportunity to address individual learner difficulties in this area than in larger lower school groupings. Able students with reasonable memories may have coped well with the linguistic load of GCSE but at A level they need to become increasingly self-reliant in order to absorb large amounts of vocabulary and may benefit from some strategy instruction.

In order to help students to assimilate new vocabulary, Richards *et al.* (2008 p.210) recommend the 'systematic revisiting and recycling of lexis in order to maximise exposure, attention and use'. So, when teaching literature, creating opportunities to revise the vocabulary encountered during reading, is important. Learners could be encouraged to try the following activities.

- Keep a dynamic glossary of useful and recurring words in the novel;
- Choose words or phrases to learn explicitly and use in their own work. Putting words in context helps to fix them in the memory. Teachers can help by signalling words useful for writing about the texts;
- Regularly test one another in pairs;
- Build topic webs, such as culinary terms if reading Esquivel's *Como agua para chocolate* or flora and fauna in Pagnol's *Le château de ma mère*. In such cases, students are unlikely to reuse the specific terms themselves and simple recognition is more appropriate;

- Students can predict words they might need about a certain topic to focus on particular areas of vocabulary;

- Exercises on synonyms are also useful in building vocabulary. For example, novels with significant direct and indirect speech are likely to use many different synonyms for 'to say'. Students could be challenged to note down a list of these as they read the novel and then tick off the synonyms as they use them orally or in their own writing. New synonyms can be added to the list as the reading continues;

- Other categories for similar treatment could include conjunctions, adjectives, abstract nouns, or adverbs *etc.*

### Written literary forms

This is a specialist type of vocabulary or grammatical construction which students will only encounter in literary prose. The *passé simple* (past historic), for example, is a tense which students of French are unlikely to meet in other circumstances. Teaching the basic forms of the tense, especially those of the high-frequency irregular verbs such as *faire, être* and *avoir* (with a handy crib sheet) will speed up reading for students until they recognise the forms automatically.

## *Use of the dictionary*

Developing the reading strategies discussed will hopefully help students to become less reliant on looking every word up in a dictionary. Students should aim to decide if the word is really necessary at all or to work out the meaning from context or from cognates, or from related known words or grammatical knowledge.

- Berwick and Horsfall (1996) suggest an activity where students take a photocopy of a passage, score out all the words they do not understand and see how much of the text they can grasp.

- Lazar (1993) suggests that students eliminate all the unnecessary words from a paragraph until only those essential to the overall meaning remain. Alternatively, students could underline only those words that are required (different colours of highlighter pen could indicate 'essential', 'helpful' and 'unnecessary' vocabulary). Students then compare their versions and work out which words are important and why.

- Students can then annotate a paragraph with the strategies they used to work out various words: unnecessary; cognate; grammatical marker; context *etc.*

New technology such as **e-readers** with built in dictionaries and **online dictionaries** also may make life easier for students.

Advanced learners will already have received instruction on using a full-size **bilingual dictionary**, but this does not always guarantee effective use in practice (Graham 1997). Teachers could share the following tips with students, perhaps by modelling them aloud with a difficult passage in the novel:

- Use reading strategies to check whether it is really necessary to use the dictionary;
- Look beyond the first meaning in the dictionary;
- Question whether the meaning actually fits the context, and if not, look for another meaning;
- Understand the terminology e.g. *lit / fam / fig*;
- Look at the syntax of the sentence and work out whether the word required is a noun or adjective or verb;
- Be aware that the unknown word may be an inflected (irregular) verb or past participle e.g. *fit* in French or *gewesen* in German;
- Think about what the headword in the dictionary might be. This is especially significant for separable verbs in German.

Teachers may wish to introduce a **monolingual dictionary** to advanced learners. These contain a wider set of words and access to synonyms which can help to develop students' writing. They can also be used to cross-check a meaning from a bilingual dictionary in order to verify that they have chosen the correct meaning in context.

## The spoken word: reading, listening and speaking

The use of spoken versions of the novel can be very beneficial for students and develop their listening skills alongside supporting their understanding of the text. It is possible to purchase **audiobooks** of many foreign classic and popular novels in original or abridged forms (and with www.audible.co.uk a free month's trial is often offered as a promotion). Students are then able to hear a native speaker give a professional reading of the novel. Online sites (see Maupassant in Appendix 1) also give free access to audio versions of some stories and it is possible on YouTube to find clips of readings of extracts of novels (sometimes by the author such as Camus' reading of the opening to *L'étranger*).

Playing audio versions of excerpts from the novel can help to bring some variety to lessons and has the benefit of **supporting students' understanding** by the expression, emphasis and tone in the reader's voice and any accompanying sound effects. It can convey the novelist's style by reproducing and highlighting stylistic devices such as alliteration, repetition, rhyme and onomatopoeia. The rhythm of the prose or its changes in pace and intensity can also become apparent to second language readers through the spoken text. By bringing the words alive, the reading can help students to create mental images and fix the episode (or the characters) in their mind.

- In class, choose key episodes which will help students with characterisation, evocation of place or mood and thematic content. The recordings can reinforce dramatic or climactic moments around confrontations, grief, pathos or joy *etc.*

- When students have read some of the novel at home, they can be asked to nominate which episodes from the text they would choose to hear read aloud.

- After listening they can present why they chose the passage and what they have learnt from it. They can also critique the reading itself.

As they read along with the written and spoken text in parallel, students can also hear the correct pronunciation of unfamiliar words and if different clips are available, students may also benefit from hearing a variety of voices. Using different recordings also helps to illustrate another benefit, or pitfall, of using an audio or video version. Students should be aware that whenever a novel (or play) is 'performed' in some way, the actor, reader and director all add an additional layer of interpretation to the author's original text. The way the novel is read is a product of how the reader and director have interpreted its meaning and how to convey that most convincingly. Where more than one version is available, these can be compared by students to note differences between them, but also between how the students may themselves have imagined the text (the type of voice, the emotional undertones *etc.*).

The use of a spoken excerpt is also a way of reinforcing grammar and spelling.

- A cloze exercise can be used where students have to fill in key words (with correct spelling, conjugation, agreements) after listening to the reading and then check with the written version.

- Alternatively, they can be given sentences from a passage they have not read and try to order them into a paragraph or dialogue. As they then listen to the passage, they can confirm or change their order. This helps students to really concentrate on the text and is useful if the teacher wishes to focus on how a description, a dialogue or an event is structured by the author. They can then discuss why the structure was chosen and the effect on the reader.

- Playing an unread passage can also act as a springboard for a discussion about a particular issue or theme, or speculation about what is happening (and will happen) before tackling the written text. The success of this approach will depend upon the competence of the students and difficulty of the text, as listening without the text for support is often very challenging, especially when read at native-speaker speed.

Similar techniques can also be used with a DVD or radio production of a drama. However, a film of a novel requires different treatment as it will differ greatly from the written text.

## Reading aloud

If a professional recording is not available, it is worth remembering that, for students, reading aloud can often be awkward and counterproductive. It is a challenge for many students to read out loud, even in their mother tongue, especially from an unfamiliar text in front of an audience. They must pronounce words intelligibly and also understand their meaning in order to use intonation and stress appropriately across the sentence. If reading aloud is considered to be appropriate for a particular class, students can be given short passages to prepare in advance or bilingual students asked to highlight particular episodes.

## The place of film

Another means of 'hearing' the characters of a novel speak and helping students to enter the world of the novel is by using a film version of the text. Many of the novels on the syllabus have been made into films, some in English versions as well as in the original language. Using recorded productions of plays is discussed in Chapter 7, but the issues are more problematic with novels and the teacher should be aware of several pitfalls.

- A novel is written to be read on the page and many of its integral features are lost in translation to a visual medium.

- The language used in a film is very different, often relying on dialogue rather than description. Students need to work with the original language to see how the novel is constructed.

- Most films diverge greatly from the original novel, usually through omitting events or characters, or sometimes by changing the sequence of events, plots and even endings. The setting may be brought vividly to life or may be significantly altered. Students can find it difficult to remember what is in the novel once they have seen the more visually powerful screen version.

- There is the danger that students may refer to the film rather than the novel in the examination (this has happened!), creating a poor impression and using inaccurate evidence to support their views.

Teachers should always watch a film version carefully in advance and decide whether there are any scenes which can be used to illustrate episodes accurately when the class are first meeting the text. Teachers can then design activities which are relevant to specific parts of the novel using clips from the DVD or perhaps online (*e.g.* YouTube). As a rule, it may be prudent to wait until the students have a good grasp of the original novel, before seeing the full-length film version.

Using a film version can have several benefits when the reasons behind seeing it (usually in sections) are clearly explained.

- Seeing the film illustrates how the novel's meaning can be interpreted and re-interpreted differently according to the reader's (or director's) perspective.
- Clips can be used intermittently to help students examine the text from a different standpoint.
- Early exposure to clips of the film may engage students more fully in the subsequent study of the text.
- Students can watch the film as private study in order to save valuable lesson time and then prepare for the discussions in class.
- The film version may often highlight the key characters and themes of the novel.
- A good film version may help students to appreciate the novel more fully and to see it as a whole.
- As a footnote, if students are also studying film for the examination it gives them another opportunity to discuss film techniques and recycle their technical vocabulary.

## Activities whilst watching film clips

- If students have the task of identifying where the film and novel diverge, this can prompt useful conversations (or as a written task) about **why** this might be and focus student attention on the construction of the novel.
- Students can also be asked about where and how they feel the film differed from their own expectations. This can be organised in categories *e.g.* particular key episodes or plot strands, or characterisation, setting or themes. These reflections can then prompt discussion about whether the students have now changed their interpretation and why. It also offers an opportunity to compare, evaluate and make judgements in the target language.
- Attention can also be focused on these categories more generally as a basis for discussion.
  - Is the **action** the same in the film as in the novel?
  - Where are the differences and why might these be?
  - How are particular **characters** portrayed on screen?

- ○ Would you have chosen these actors to play them? Why is this?
- ○ What details reflect the social and historical **setting** of the novel?
- ○ What mood does the director create?
- ○ How is a particular **theme** portrayed and what impression does this create?
- ○ **Why** is this scene important in relation to the novel as a whole?
- ○ Describe how the clip makes you feel.
- ○ What is your reaction to the director's portrayal of this part of the novel?

*Activities prompted by film*

- A trailer for a film can provide a very good 'spark' for discussion or a creative exercise such as students directing their own trailer. Deciding what the key 'hooks' are in the story can be a good collaborative exercise as students are really being asked to distil the essence of the film into a few short frames.

- Students can watch a clip without the sound and then create the dialogue or voice-over themselves. They can imagine what sort of music could be used for effect.

- They can also hear the sound without the images and imagine the actors and staging, before viewing the clip itself.

- Students can also recreate the clips themselves, perhaps with the brief to adapt them to more closely portray the novel. They can film them and justify their choice and the finished result to the class.

- If reviews of the film are available, students can decide which best reflects their view of the whole film and why. They can then act as a model for students' own reviews.

# Reading the novel in class

These aspects will all help to structure how teachers support students in reading the novel, at home and in class. Time in class will largely focus on ensuring that students understand key episodes of the plot and the main features of the novel's characterisation, themes, style and structure. This will emphasise discussion and sharing, developing and valuing individual views and responses. Explicit practice of reading strategies can also be useful and some passages may be useful for linguistic exploitation.

Teachers should first identify the passages of the novel to **read together**: Hill (1986) suggests that episodes which show the development of the story, characterisation, the social setting and stylistic devices should give the overall framework for the story. It is likely that the opening paragraphs of the novel will also be important.

Barbour (1995) gives a detailed description of how to approach this with Mauriac's *Thérèse Desqueyroux*, with a focus on students asking questions and uncovering clues about the whole novel. All the questions which the opening paragraphs or chapter raise for students can be listed in a grid and as the story unfolds, the table can be completed. In a different approach, Turner (1999) suggests that reading does not need to start at the beginning, especially if the start of the novel contains a difficult 'stream of consciousness' or problems with 'flashback'. In this case, other relevant passages may offer an easier 'way in' to the novel. The conclusion of the novel will also merit significant discussion in class.

Students often benefit from preparation at home for passages which will be read in class. A simple skimming or scanning task at home could give students what Turner (1999 p.219) calls a 'surface level' understanding of the text to enable class discussion at a deeper level. Asking students to come to the lesson with questions can highlight any comprehension difficulties.

Where a long novel is concerned, the passages looked at in class may not necessarily follow on from where students have read to at home (Collie and Slater 1987). Indeed, Carter and Long (1991) suggest that if the whole of a long novel is read in great detail, there is the danger that students will focus on small details rather than having time for the bigger picture. **Summaries** (as described later in this chapter) may be given to students to fill in less important sections of the novel when time is tight.

# Reading the novel at home

Not only is reading the novel at home a practical necessity, Collie and Slater (1987 p.12) argue that it 'allows them [the learners] to form a personal relationship with the text and to feel, at the end, that they have coped satisfactorily with the challenge of a complete book'. The process should foster student independence and confidence but does need guidance from the teacher.

The aims of this guidance may include the following:

- to give students a focus and a (time) framework for their reading;
- to make the reading manageable by dividing it into sections;
- to help students to understand the plot, often condensing complex language into simpler highlights;
- to alert students to wider issues of the novel's style, characterisation and themes;
- to give them the language which they can use to talk and write about the novel;
- to encourage them to value their own opinions and interpretations;
- to make reading a more collaborative and interactive process.

The DARTs-type activities discussed earlier in this chapter have a role to play in ensuring that students read '**actively**' in order to extract key information in various written, tabular or diagrammatic form. In fact, most exercises used with non-literary texts are valuable here.

Thought should be given to **sequencing** of DARTs-type activities as students will need more guidance at the start and less as they become more confident readers. One fairly simple activity is to give students a list of key events in the chapter. They tick off when they have read them (perhaps giving the page number). To make this more difficult students could be asked to write an additional sentence about each of the events, providing more information or giving an opinion. This can also be made more difficult by adding an incorrect event to the list or missing out something vital (Collie and Slater 1987).

As **translation** into English is now part of the AS level examination, students can practise by translating short extracts from the novel. Passages could be chosen where close scrutiny both of meaning and how the author uses language would be beneficial.

It is important that these tasks do not become too **repetitive**. They should allow students to practise different skills and read both efferently and aesthetically, encouraging analysis and interpretation as well as gathering factual information.

## Collaborative reading

Group interaction remains important in order to help students to generate and test ideas and to practise expressing themselves in oral discussion. Not only can many of the DARTs-type activities be done in pairs and groups in class, but students can also collaborate to share the 'out of class' reading load.

For example, students can take it in turns to lead other students through parts of the novel by preparing at home:

- a glossary of vocabulary for a particular passage;
- a summary of the main points of the passage;
- ten questions for others to answer about the chapter (perhaps incorporating true or false or matching type exercises or simple gap fills).

In class, they can then lead on the six most important events in the chapter, or the three most important things they learnt about a particular character (the focus being agreed with the teacher in advance).

Students could all read the chapter but be given different areas of focus for the ensuing class discussion, along the lines of a **book club** (Hill and O'Loughlin 1995).

(This could also be used at the end of the novel as a summary and review activity). Possible roles could include:

- the chairperson who will lead the discussion by asking the group what they thought of the chapter and asking them to introduce their areas of expertise;
- the summariser who gives a brief outline of what happens in the chapter and why it is important to the novel;
- the highlighter who picks one or two key passages to read aloud and explain why he or she thinks they are important;
- the observer who describes the main protagonists, how they develop and what we learn about them in the chapter;
- the sociologist who describes what we learn about the geographical, historical or social setting of the novel;
- the wordsmith who picks out notable stylistic features of the chapter;
- the interpreter who describes how the themes of the novel develop and the possible relevance to the contemporary audience (of the novel).

Of course, the exercise does not need to be as elaborate as this, with roles combined and two or three students simply preparing to report back on plot, theme or character development in the chapter. Alternatively, if the class is large enough to have several students covering the same focus, then these students can meet to discuss their findings and then reconstitute in groups with one representative from each of the other areas. This type of **jigsaw** reading activity can be adapted in many ways. This encourages discussion, pooling and developing individual students' ideas and supporting students who find reading the literature particularly challenging.

Alternatively, to encourage students to discuss their reading in pairs, Collie and Slater (1987) suggest giving one half of the class one set of questions, (which may be about the chronological events of the chapter or be more thematic or character based) and a similar, but different, set of questions to the other group. Each group completes their questions at home, and then the students pair up with someone from the other half to share their answers orally with the result that eventually both students have answers to both sets of questions.

## Plot summaries

Students must have a firm grasp of the plot of the novel and the sequence of its events in order to see it as a whole. This knowledge also allows them to draw on specific evidence from the text to support their arguments and therefore score highly in the examination. With a lengthy novel, summaries of the action teach learners to identify the key points from the narrative and are essential revision aids. There are several ways of doing this, and using a range of approaches helps to vary the process with a long novel. Some summaries will be simply for students' individual revision, whereas others may be shared with the class or assessed by the teacher. Ideally summaries should also offer some catalyst for analysis or evaluation.

Brief summaries could be aimed at distilling the nub of each chapter (or section) for revision:

- Decide upon **titles** for each chapter;
- Create a **wall display** with visual representations for each chapter (Collie and Slater 1987);
- Groups create a PowerPoint **slide** per chapter. Share with the class and then compare what each group has considered to be the key points;
- Write a synopsis of each chapter within a strict **word limit** or number of sentences;
- Write the chapter as a **tweet**;
- Write the plot in five lines on the back of a **postcard**.

More **extended summaries** can be designed by the teacher to offer students varying degrees of support.

- As a revision exercise after reading the whole novel with the class, write **key facts** per chapter on index cards but without numbering them. Groups then have to order the **index cards** in the correct sequence and use the facts as a basis for their own synopsis. If the facts on the cards are bullet points this will be harder for them than if full sentences are used.
- Prepare **questions** on each chapter for the students to answer. The responses will make a full synopsis of events. Ensure that questions also ask students for their interpretations and feelings about the characters, events and style.
- Alternatively, students are given statements about the chapter which they have to decide are **true or false** (and then correct) to complete a summary. It is made more difficult if some of the sentences are neither true nor false but elicit some doubt or ambiguity. (These could be about motivation or feelings *etc.*) These sentences support weaker learners by providing a bank of phrases to summarise the action. Multiple choice questions can also be used here with students choosing the option which corresponds most accurately to the text.
- Provide short summaries of each chapter for students to extend to a specific length. Where students need more support, more writing can be given with less material to add. Summaries with gaps to fill also ensure that all students have a basic synopsis in correct French, German or Spanish. As an added linguistic

challenge, these gaps could also test particular grammatical knowledge. This technique could be used for character analysis, discussion of themes *etc.*

- Give students summaries containing a specific number of factual errors which they have to (compete to) correct as quickly as possible.

- Give students several summaries (these can be taken from the group anonymously). They have to amalgamate points from the different summaries to produce their own, better summary and be prepared to justify what they have included or omitted (Turner 1999). Alternatively, students decide which summary they feel is best and explain why.

- Collie and Slater (1987 p.52) suggest 'snowball summaries' which are added to over time as more of the novel is read.

- For a greater challenge, as students become more familiar with analysing the action and the characters, they could write a summary of the chapter from the perspective of one of the characters. Students in the class could choose different protagonists and their summaries could reveal interesting differences in perspective.

## *Analysis*

At the end of reading each chapter or section, the teacher will want to review not just what has happened but also what has been learnt in relation to the novel's characters, themes, setting, structure and style. How does this chapter link to other chapters in the novel? What is each student's personal response to the chapter?

Suggestions for the analysis of these aspects are detailed in Chapters 8 and 9.

## Short stories

In comparison to the demands of reading a novel, the choice of the short story may seem less daunting for students who are not used to extensive second language reading, and for teachers faced with limited curriculum time. For this reason, studying a short story is often a good introduction to literature in a second language. Many of the principles and strategies already discussed can also be applied and because of its length, there may be time to focus more intensively on a greater proportion of the text. Some *specific* features of short stories are also relevant to classroom study.

Firstly, there is usually a requirement to study a **collection** of short stories. For Maupassant, the *Contes de guerre* encompass four stories, the longest of which is *Boule de Suif*. This introduces a new dimension, namely how different narratives fit together. Examination questions will often ask students to consider characterisation, style or themes in relation to at least two of the stories studied. Students must be able to analyse points of similarity and difference between stories and consider the author's stylistic features and thematic concerns at this overall level. This can require students to look more closely at these features and promote a greater degree of analysis.

## *Pre-reading*

When reading a short story, it is possible to offer students more support in the pre-reading phase. As the text is shorter, the pre-reading activities can also be more comprehensive and this can be helpful for less confident students. Ideas for pre-reading can be found in Chapter 5, but to summarise, preparation in the following areas can help to prepare students for reading the whole story. (Barbour (2000) provides some useful suggestions of activities based on Maupassant's *Boule de Suif*.)

* **Language:** tasks which focus on pre-teaching key **vocabulary** or exploring a particular area of vocabulary such as military terms in Maupassant's *Boule de Suif*. For some students, work on a particular unfamiliar grammatical feature (e.g. the past historic in French) may be helpful. As short story writers have to convey their story with a limited number of words, the language is often particularly condensed and may be allegorical or draw on significant symbolism and imagery. This can be difficult for second language learners and could also provide a focus for pre-reading.

* **Content:** exercises which encourage students to **predict** aspects of the story. This may arise from the title of the story, or around an opening line (or paragraph) or a brief exchange of dialogue, from which students can imagine what happened before and what will happen after the encounter. Making a **wordcloud** of a summary of the story (where the most frequent words appear in the largest font) is also a way of setting students' imagination running. (There are many videos online which show how this can be done for free using Microsoft Word or web tools.)

* **Context:** activities which focus on the socio-historical background of the story, such as the Franco-Prussian war in Maupassant's *Contes de guerre*. Students can research this themselves, access the period through pictures or be given audio or written texts to practise their comprehension skills in class. Knowledge of the particular cultural milieu (attitudes and tensions) can be important in understanding a short story as the author does not have the luxury of extended explanations, and so giving students some initial insight into this world can substantially support their appreciation of the story.

* **Personal response**: tasks which invite students to explore the **theme** or central dilemma of the story from a personal perspective. The themes dealt with in short stories often have a relevance beyond the parochial situation of the story itself

and it is important that students can see how they might apply more universally to the human condition. Questions generated by the short story's particular theme, could include:

○   What makes people act in the way they do?

○   How would you react if ...?

○   Have you ever been in a situation where ...?

○   Is it ever right (or wrong) to ...?

○   Could this situation occur today?

## Structure and style

Structure in a short story is particularly important: Parkinson and Reid Thomas talk of 'postcard fiction' (2000 p.101) and suggest asking students to write a story on the back of a postcard as a way of identifying the particular characteristics of a short story. This device of using a postcard reinforces the idea that for a successful short story there are fewer characters and one main plot line, with a situation that can be resolved or exposed in a relatively compact physical space and timescale.

A useful way of extracting key elements in a short story is to ask the following questions (Paran and Robinson 2016):

•   What? (the main event)

•   Who? (the main characters)

•   When?

•   Where?

•   Why? (the reason behind the events and characters' actions)

•   (How? – the details of how the event came about are sometimes important)

Students can answer these questions in a grid to focus on the **core** of the story and then consider the stylistic and structural features employed by the author. A clear representation of the plot (and characters) of each story in a collection helps students to avoid mixing up characters and events between the stories. The suggestions for **plot summaries** of the novel can also be adapted to use with the short story in order to fix the different narratives clearly in the students' minds. One approach could be to substitute paragraph or groups of paragraphs for 'chapter' when summarising. Reducing a paragraph (or page) to a single sentence or within a number of words, is a useful linguistic exercise which also ensures that students really analyse the nub of the narrative.

This focus also draws attention to the **style** of the prose, the use of language for **description** and scene-setting. In short stories, characters and situations are often established with minimal description. The use of striking imagery can convey atmosphere and meaning more economically than words and students can extract examples and explain what they convey in plainer prose. This lends itself to synonym hunting and matching exercises.

Short stories often make use of a surprising plot twist, and suspense is created to build tension about what might happen. This is another area for students to focus on, working out the techniques used to heighten the **dramatic tension**.

When considering the **structure** of a short story, it can be helpful to distinguish between what Parkinson and Reid Thomas (2000 pp.103–104) call scene and summary. The former is where we see the action played out through dialogue, where the characters' voices are heard, whereas the latter is simply a summary of what happened, told by the narrator. The contrast of scenes and summaries has an effect on the rhythm and the pace of the story, highlights certain episodes and adds interest for the reader.

## Post-reading

Exercises which explore characterisation, the style, structure and themes of the stories are described in Chapters 8 and 9. However, when working with a collection of short stories, students will need to make comparisons across the stories studied. Using grids to compare characters from the different stories, but also the settings and the recurring themes provides a good visual framework for students.

- Do the stories reveal a common preoccupation with a particular group (or class) of people?
- Do the characters display similar traits (strengths and frailties)
- Is the setting the same?
- Is a similar mood created?
- Is the story told in a similar manner?
- Do similar themes recur?
- Are the endings similar?

Chapter 11 lists creative ways of exploiting literature but activities that may be sparked by the short story in particular include:

- dramatising the story;
- writing a continuation of the story (or a prequel to the action);

- writing a new paragraph in the style of the author;
- retelling the story in the student's own contemporary context.

# Conclusion

This chapter has focused primarily on the challenges of reading an extensive, authentic narrative with second language learners. Helping students to become more confident and effective readers is a key benefit of literature study, and hopefully, with support, they will experience a sense of genuine achievement after having completed their (first) novel. It is not always easy to balance the demands of preparing students for the examination and preserving the pleasurable aspects of reading fiction, especially in a second language. However, offering support and a varied diet of individual and collaborative activities should help students to feel confident in their knowledge of the novel and also in forming and expressing their own opinions about it. They have a firm basis for investigating other features of the novel such as characterisation, themes, style and structure, for which complementary activities are discussed in Chapters 8 and 9.

# Further reading

Naiman *et al.* (1996) and Grenfell (2007) provide an overview of the development of **learning strategy research**.

Graham (1997) researches the difficulties which modern languages A level students experience during the transition to advanced study and explores how they can be supported through the use of **learning strategies** to become more effective learners.

Macaro (2001) provides a readable exploration and explanation of strategy use, written with the purpose of guiding the classroom teacher through an **action research project** to investigate this in the classroom.

Wright and Brown (2006) also discuss reading strategies in a practical modern languages classroom setting. The authors set out strategies and how to teach them and then how to **investigate their usage** by GCSE students. In the limitations section of the paper they highlight how difficult it is to assert causation, due to the many unknown variables, in this type of **classroom research**.

For teachers working with younger students, the Classic Pathfinders give examples of how to develop basic **reading skills** with basic texts, *e.g.* (Turner *et al.* 2005).

Barnes and Powell (1996) provide an easily accessible and practical introduction to helping to develop reading skills with A level students.

Collie and Slater (1987) provide many examples of working with **novels** for students with English as a second language. Barbour provides specific examples of working with Mauriac's *Thérèse Desqueyroux* (1995) and Maupassant's *Boule de Suif* (2000). Turner (1999) also provides helpful examples of work with Ernaux's *La place*.

Some interesting ideas for using **film** to explore literature may be found in Faber (1998).

## Implications for teaching

- Ensure that learners can apply a range of strategies to support their reading of the novel. Teach these explicitly and monitor effective implementation.
- Divide the novel into sections for close reading in class and independent reading at home.
- Provide structured activities to guide and support independent reading. Inform students of the purpose and focus for each section and use a range of exercises which help them to achieve these goals.
- Ensure that students have clear summaries of the novel in accurate language for reuse in their discussions and essays.
- Include questions which ask for students' interpretation and personal response to the novel and build their confidence in expressing their views.
- Focus time in class on discussion of key passages and use audio and video materials where appropriate.
- Use collaborative exercises to help learners to develop their ideas and the ability to express them in the target language.
- Build students' knowledge of the novel so that they can begin to analyse its literary features.

## References

Barbour, S., 1995. Teaching a level literature in the target language: some suggested approaches. *The Language Learning Journal*, 11, pp.36–38.

Barbour, S., 2000. Discovering literature through the target language. In: G. Shaw, ed. *Aiming High 2: Straight As*. London: CILT, pp.37–49.

Barnes, A., 2000. Developing advanced reading skills. In: G. Shaw, ed. *Aiming High 2: Straight As*. London: CILT, pp.26–36.

Barnes, A. and Powell, B., 1996. *Developing Advanced Reading Skills in Modern Foreign Languages Handbooks for Language Teachers: Concepts 8*. Cheltenham: Mary Glasgow Publications.

Benati, A., 2013. *Issues in Second Language Teaching*. Sheffield: Equinox.

Berwick, G. and Horsfall, P., 1996. *Making Effective Use of the Dictionary*. London: CILT.

Carter, R. and Long, M., 1991. *Teaching Literature*. Harlow: Longman.

Collie, J. and Slater, S., 1987. *Literature in the Language Classroom: A Resource Book of Ideas and Activities*. Cambridge: Cambridge University Press.

Department for Education and Employment and Qualifications and Curriculum Authority (DfEE/QCA), 1999. *Modern Foreign Languages. The National Curriculum for England*. London: QCA and HMSO.

Department for Education and Skills (DfES), 2003. *Key Stage 3 National Strategy. Framework for Teaching Modern Foreign Languages: Years 7, 8 and 9*. London: DfES publications.

Department for Education and Skills (DfES), 2004. *Pedagogy and Practice: Teaching and Learning in Secondary Schools. Unit 13: Developing Reading*. HMSO.

Department for Education and Skills (DfES), 2005. *The Key Stage 2 Framework for Teaching Languages*. Accessed January 2019 https://webarchive.nationalarchives .gov.uk/20110512174848/https://nationalstrategies.standards.dcsf.gov.uk/node/ 85274.

Faber, P., 1998. Through the camera's lens: an innovative approach to analysing literature. In: W. Gewehr, ed. *Aspects of Modern Language Teaching in Europe*. London: Routledge, pp.83–92.

Gallagher-Brett, A., 2006. *Hard Going but Worth It: A Snapshot of Attitudes to Reading among Language Undergraduates*. Southampton, UK: Subject Centre for Languages, Linguistics and Area Studies, University of Southampton.

Graham, S., 1997. *Effective Language Learning*. London: Multilingual Matters.

Grellet, F., 1981. *Developing Reading Skills: A Practical Guide to Reading Comprehension Exercises*. Cambridge: Cambridge University Press.

Grenfell, M., 2007. Language learner strategy research and modern foreign language teaching and learning. *Language Learning Journal*, 35(1), pp.9–22.

Harris, V., 1997. *Teaching Learners How to Learn. Strategy Training in the Modern Languages Classroom*. London: CILT.

Hill, J., 1986. *Using Literature in Language Teaching*. London: Macmillan.

Hill, S. and O'Loughlin, J., 1995. *Book Talk. Collaborative Responses to Literature*. Victoria, Australia: Eleanor Curtain Publishing.

Kramsch, C., 1993. *Context and Culture in Language Teaching*. Oxford: Oxford University Press.

Lazar, G., 1993. *Literature and Language Teaching: A Guide for Teachers and Trainers*. Cambridge: Cambridge University Press.

Macaro, E., 2001. *Learning Strategies in Foreign and Second Language Classrooms*. London: Continuum.

Macaro, E., 2003. *Teaching and Learning A Second Language: A Guide to Recent Research and Its Applications*. London: Continuum.

Naiman, N., Fröhlich, M., Stern, H. and Todesco, A., 1996. *The Good Language Learner*. Clevedon: Multilingual Matters.

O'Malley, J. and Chamot, A., 1990. *Learning Strategies in Second Language Acquisition*. Cambridge: Cambridge University Press.

Oxford, R., 1990. *Language Learning Strategies: What Every Teacher Should Know*. Boston, MA: Heinle and Heinle.

Paran, A. and Robinson, P., 2016. *Literature*. Oxford: Oxford University Press.

Parkinson, B. and Reid Thomas, H., 2000. *Teaching Literature in a Second Language*. Edinburgh: Edinburgh University Press.

Richards, B., Malvern, D. and Graham, S., 2008. Word frequency and trends in the development of French vocabulary in lower-intermediate students during year 12 in English schools. *The Language Learning Journal*, 36(2), pp.199–213.

Schramm, K., 2008. Reading and good language learners. In: C. Griffiths, ed. *Lessons from Good Language Learners*. Cambridge: Cambridge University Press, pp.231–243.

Snow, D., 1998. *Words. Teaching and Learning Vocabulary*. London: CILT.

Turner, K., 1999. Working with literature. In: N. Pachler, ed. *Teaching Modern Foreign Languages at Advanced Level*. London: Routledge, pp.209–229.

Turner, K., Mitchell, I. and Swarbrick, A., 2005. *Learning by Ear and by Eye. Classic Pathfinder No.5*. London: CILT.

Wright, M. and Brown, P., 2006. Reading in a modern foreign language: exploring the potential benefits of reading strategy instruction. *The Language Learning Journal*, 33 (1), pp.22–33.

# 7 | Teaching the play

## Introduction

Many of the areas discussed about studying the novel will apply in similar ways when teaching a play. However, the two genres do differ significantly and these differences have implications for how to approach drama in the classroom. This chapter will examine the **particular characteristics** of drama and explore the opportunities which it offers to students. The collective performance aspect of drama encourages the development of both oral and listening skills and, especially when a play is seen in production, the students can become transported powerfully into the world of the characters. This 'front row' seat invites students to empathise with the characters' dilemmas and actions and to reflect upon how they themselves might act in similar situations and on the wider message which the playwright may be trying to convey.

Indeed, students of drama should not simply be 'passive recipients', but 'active meaning makers' (Nicholson 2000 p.164). It is important that students *experience* a play as a work of drama rather than simply words on a page in order to be able to engage with it fully and forge their own meanings from its substance. Drama should stimulate students' imagination as they contemplate bringing a play, its characters and message to life.

## Setting the context

As with the novel, deciding how much contextual information to give students about a play in the pre-reading phase will depend on how integral this context is to understanding the action and the time available. Ideally, students will discover the play for themselves and bring their own interpretation to it, backfilling any relevant context after this initial encounter. This may not always be possible however, as the references within a play may require knowledge that could not be expected of a modern audience. If students are studying Brecht, then some initial discussion of this style of Epic Theatre and *Verfremdungseffekt* may help to prepare them for the plays themselves (see Further reading).

Additionally, some students find it reassuring to have a clear framework about author and genre, period and thematic underpinning before trying to understand the play itself. Again, as discussed in Chapter 5, different approaches to acquiring this context are available, which require differing degrees of student participation and research. As a rule, students benefit from actively researching, presenting and sharing this background knowledge. If time is tight however, and if students have already undertaken such familiarisation activities for another text, then brief summaries of key information or listening and reading comprehension exercises of the historical background, for example, may be an efficient starting point.

If a decision is made to set the scene and explain the context from the outset, it is still worth starting with an excerpt from the play itself.

- Choose a scene or an exchange which is easily accessible to the students and, if possible, show this in performance (on YouTube or a DVD). This could be the scene in Molière's *Le Tartuffe* where Orgon is hiding under the table or from the Prologue in Anouilh's *Antigone* where the Chorus explains the heroine's impending fate or in Dürrenmatt's *Der Besuch der alten Dame*, where Claire announces that Ill must be killed.
  - The excerpt can be chosen to highlight a particular key feature of the play: comedy, tragedy, predestination, alienation from the audience, historical setting *etc.* or
  - Choose a protagonist's key scene which acts as a 'spark' for students to speculate about his or her character, situation or relationship, or what happened just before the scene and what will happen next.
  - Questioning can be quite open, letting students form their own opinions of what the scene might mean and what they might expect from the rest of the play
    - What is the tone of the play?
    - Is it modern or historical?
    - Who are the main characters?
    - What might it be about?
    - What questions would they put to the characters?

Starting in this way should put the play at the heart of the contextual information to follow and spark student interest in what is to come.

## Engaging students

A somewhat more light-hearted way of introducing the background setting of the play (and setting students' imaginations running) is to bring in some of the props (or pictures of them) that would be required in the play. For Sartre's *Les mains sales*:

- Props: a wartime radio; 12 childhood photos; a typewriter; a revolver; a coffee pot; a bomb and some lipstick.
- Set dressing: a calendar marked 'mars 1943'; some Communist party posters
- Names: Hugo; Hoederer; Jessica; Olga
- Lines of dialogue: *e.g.* Hoederer 5e Tableau, Scène III (*'les main sales'*); Hugo 7e Tableau; Scène unique.

Students discuss what they think the play will be about and how the objects and other pieces of information will figure in it. Speculation will encourage the language of debate as students offer their suggestions and reject those of others. Students may then be motivated to discover if their guesses were accurate.

# Experiencing the play

Critics have talked of a duality in the text of a play: one aspect which is literature and one which is for performance (Parkinson and Reid Thomas 2000). It is important that students demonstrate through their answers in the examination that they have studied a **play** rather than simply a written script (or indeed a novel). Drama is not designed for individual silent reading, but collective spoken performance. However, this can pose additional challenges for classroom study.

## Seeing a live production

To experience the full power of a play as the dramatist intended, students should have the opportunity to see a theatre production. The physical dimension of the shared audience experience (of laughter, shock or tragedy *etc.*) is an important element in understanding how the play functions. Many theatre companies stage productions of A level texts but if not, original or English language versions of plays by the same author (*e.g.* particularly Brecht or Molière) will also help students to enter the theatrical world of the dramatist being studied. Productions on DVD or the internet can also show the play in performance and breathe life into the words on the page. Radio productions may also be available.

## *Reading in class*

The nature of drama presents the teacher with the question of how best to go about 'reading' the play with the class. On one hand a play lends itself to being spoken aloud and offers students a legitimate opportunity to practise oral and aural skills. However, to do this well requires not only the ability to pronounce possibly unfamiliar and foreign words intelligibly, but also to use the correct phrasing and intonation to give the words meaning. Listening to one another read in a dull monotone will probably do nothing to enhance students' enjoyment (or understanding) of the play.

As lack of confidence may also be a factor here, allowing students to work on lines of text together can act as a useful prelude to students performing parts of the play. Students work on key exchanges, building up meaning and the confidence to speak the words aloud. Their goal is to make the dialogue sound *believable*. Parkinson and Reid Thomas (2000) suggest that reading the play aloud should be likened to delivering a **radio broadcast** so that the tone, pauses, intonation and even sound effects allow the readers and audience to enter more fully into the spirit of the drama. The playwright may also have included instructions in the script which will help students with the following activity.

- Students first annotate the scene deciding
  - where to pause;
  - what gestures to use;
  - what the tempo of the lines would be (spoken more quickly or slowly);
  - which words would be spoken more loudly or more quietly;
  - what emotion would be in their voices (lines spoken ironically, comically, desperately *etc.*)

  This could be a good trigger for work on adverbs.

- Different pairs of students could work on different parts of the scene or on different exchanges before coming together to share their interpretations in larger groups or as a whole class. This is a good way of helping students to fix scenes in their minds and to learn key quotations for use in their essays.
- Alternatively, pairs could swap their script with another pair and try to follow their instructions.
- In order to vary the exercise, on a separate occasion the class could divide into the number of characters in the scene. One group all work on Character A's lines together, deciding on their delivery, and groups B and C do the same. Then the students regroup into jigsaw groups of A, B, C *etc.* to perform the whole scene.

- Scenes such as in Dürrenmatt's *Der Besuch der alten Dame* where the citizens often chant lines in unison or the Chorus in Anouilh's *Antigone* offer additional scope for group reading.

Hearing the lines spoken on an audio or video performance first provides a model for the students' own reading and working with the foreign language assistant where possible or using other native speaker expertise within the class or from the teacher can also build confidence.

Practice like this also legitimises the concept of **rehearsal** and recognises the fact that not all speaking is spontaneous (Parkinson and Reid Thomas 2000).

## *Using a recorded production*

In addition to reading aloud in class, using a DVD of a performance is a good way of familiarising students with the play and simultaneous watching and reading (in small sections) can support students' own reading. Showing sections of the production at key points when reading the text can also help students to understand the action, and the subtext which lies beneath the words. Listening to the rhythm of a monologue or the cut and thrust of the dialogue helps the students to 'feel' the language used by the playwright.

It is also important that students appreciate the play in its entirety, and therefore watch the full production at some point. Teachers may prefer to do this before or after reading the play in sections and there are benefits to both approaches. If students watch the production before reading, they may have a better understanding of the action (supported by the performance) and be motivated to read the play. However, depending on the students and the play, significant pre-reading and contextual work may need to be carried out to ensure that students do not feel overwhelmed by action which they do not understand.

Students will usually benefit from some preparation *prior* to a theatre visit to allow them to follow the action and identify the characters. If using a DVD production however, there is greater flexibility to show the play, or part of it, at a time of the teacher's choosing. A third option of seeing the play 'in performance' may be a film adaptation. This is generally less desirable but could be shown once students have a good grasp of the text and exploration of the inevitable differences between stage and screen could prompt interesting discussion. For example, Dürrenmatt's *Der Besuch der alten Dame* was filmed, with a different ending, as *The Visit* (directed by Bernhard Wicki) in 1964 with Ingrid Bergmann and Anthony Quinn. The official trailer for the film, which is available on YouTube, provides a great stimulus for discussion along the lines described in Chapter 6.

## *Different interpretations: using stage productions and film*

The one caveat which teachers may bear in mind is that watching a production can impose a particular interpretation of the play on students, which may then colour their own reading of the play. For this reason, it is worthwhile trying to find more than one production, and then discuss the different interpretations with the class.

- Students can be asked about
  - the differences in the staging of the productions (e.g. set; costumes; era);
  - which characterisation was more convincing and why;
  - any difference in the emotions raised by the two performances;
  - which production was closer to how they had imagined the characters and the intention of the play.

- If a recorded production (or a film version) is shown **after** studying the text, the teacher could pose questions for group discussion.
  - Are there **differences** or omissions between the production (film) and the text?
  - Where are the differences and why might these be?
  - What details reflect the social and historical setting?
  - Does the version bring out specific aspects of the **action**?
  - What **mood** does the director create?
  - How are particular **characters** portrayed?
  - Would you have chosen these actors to play them? Why is this?
  - Which character would you like to play?
  - How would you divide the play for a 3/4/5-part TV production?
  - How is a particular **theme** portrayed and what impression does this create?
  - Has it changed your **opinion** of the play, action or characters?
  - What is your **reaction** to the director's portrayal of (this part of) the play?

Different groups of students could be asked to note and report back on different aspects of the staging e.g. costumes, set, lighting, how the characters were played, ways of speaking *etc.*

# The play in class

It is possible to take a global approach to studying drama by taking the whole play and working thematically with characterisation, themes, language and staging after viewing a performance. However, it is likely that teachers and students will feel most secure in taking a **scene by scene** approach to the play.

A first task is to consider the length of the play and the time available and decide how many scenes can be worked on together in class, and how much reading will be done at home. Because of the collective nature of drama, and especially with a short play, it may be possible to read the whole play in class. Homework activities however, can help to prepare students and encourage independent exploration of the text. Ideas for exploiting reading at home and in class are discussed in Chapter 6 and are applicable to drama, although it is important to bear in mind the performance dimension. Areas of focus include **plot, characterisation, use of language, structure, themes and dramatic effect**.

Active tasks help to focus students' attention on a particular reading goal for each section. As the text is less dense than that of a novel, this task may be questions which pick out the key points of the action or characterisation during the scene. There should also be some opportunity for students to evaluate what they are reading or place themselves critically at the centre of the dilemmas portrayed.

- What would they do when asked to kill Ill in return for Claire's money?
- Or, what lines might they cross if overwhelmed by debt? (Dürrenmatt's *Der Besuch der alten Dame*);
- Would they bury their brother whatever the consequences to themselves?
- Or, where would they draw the line between loyalty to family and breaking state laws? (Anouilh's *Antigone*);
- How difficult is it to defy peer pressure and stand up for the outsider?
- Can they understand the reasons behind der Lehrer's initial lie about Andri? (Frisch's *Andorra*).

If YouTube clips or an audio version of a production are available, encourage students to listen as well as to read as this supports understanding through actors' intonation and sound effects.

Language in drama can be more difficult for second language learners as it may be poetically condensed or archaic or colloquial. Some editions of texts have **glossaries**, which can be very helpful for independent reading Otherwise, giving students some key vocabulary for each scene can enhance the reading process. Alternatively, students can be given responsibility for providing key words on a particular scene for the rest of the group, thus **sharing the load**.

## *Summaries*

The act and scene structure of plays assists in chunking the text and it is helpful for students to build a **scene by scene summary** of the play. This helps students to fix in their minds the sequence and rhythm of the action and allows them to locate evidence for their essays. Where plays do not follow a conventional structure, *e.g.* Anouilh's *Antigone*, it is helpful to impose artificial breaks such as whenever a character enters or exits. The scene structure in Sartre's *Les mains sales* follows this French tradition of scenes being simply markers for characters' entrances and exits.

Questions answered during independent reading form a good basis for a scene by scene summary and students can also be encouraged to fill in a response grid as with a novel (Figure 6.1). Chapter 6 offers a range of suggestions for summarising the action which can be used. In addition, it is worth considering the following, as they emphasise the dramatic aspects of the play.

- Students invent a title which captures the dramatic focus of each scene or act;
- For selected scenes, students stage a tableau of a key moment and take a photo for use in a pictorial summary of the action;
- Depending on the complexity of the play, students write the setting and key items of props on separate cards for each scene (or group of scenes) and jumble them up. Characters' names or a key line of dialogue can also be added if necessary. These can then be placed in the correct order as a challenge to remember the sequence of the play. Students can also use the cards in pairs to sum up the action of each scene in turns as they turn over each card.

## *Focus on key scenes*

Time in class is likely to focus on key scenes in the play. These may include:
- when we first meet the main protagonists;
- when main characters meet;
- when the background to the current situation is explained;
- when (internal or external) conflict occurs;
- turning points;
- when key decisions are made;
- examples of physical drama on stage;
- examples of comedy;
- where the language or action is particularly difficult to follow;
- the dénouement.

The following techniques may help where scenes are problematic:

- If the scene is very complicated, students rearrange sentences describing the action into the correct order. This will support students' understanding of the scene and also provide a correct summary of the action.

- If particular lines are difficult to understand, students can be given modern or simpler equivalents in the target language. Students find the matching phrases in the scene to help them to work out the meaning for very poetic, metaphorical, archaic or colloquial language (Collie and Slater 1987).

To increase student familiarity with an important scene, the following activities are helpful:

- Students are given the lines of (part of) a scene which they reconstitute by ascribing the lines to the right characters and then placing them in the correct order.
  - Unless the extract is very short, it is better to allow students some time to reread the relevant exchanges first.
  - If the lines are in rhyme, this is an excellent way of drawing attention to the language and pronunciation e.g. Molière's *Le Tartuffe Acte V, scène 5*.
  - This activity can be made easier by giving the students the whole scene in the correct order and only removing the lines of one character. In this way they can use the context and conventions of dialogue to support them in reinserting the jumbled-up lines.
  - In order to be more creative, students could be given just one half of the dialogue and asked to make up the responses for the other character (in keeping with the sense of the scene). Half the class could be doing one half of the conversation whilst the other half takes the other role (Lazar 1993). This is a useful language practice activity if students try to express the meaning of the scene in contemporary dialogue.

## Stage directions

Stage directions are often a valuable aspect of key scenes. The use of clear stage directions enables the playwright to convey an authorial voice and, in framing the dialogue, stage directions help the reader watch the play 'imaginatively' (Margetts 2000 p.43). They also give the printed text more clarity and authenticity for theatrical production. Occasionally stage directions replace the dialogue, while some are implicit through actions in the text (Wallis and Shepherd 2002).

Among the current set texts for French, use of stage directions varies greatly; in Molière's *Le Tartuffe* they are sparsely used, but clarify who is being addressed or indicate relative positions of the actors; in Sartre's *Les mains sales* however they are much more detailed and refer to décor, objects, positioning of the characters, sounds offstage, the way characters speak and the speed with which they communicate. Lorca in *La casa de Bernarda Alba* and *Bodas de sangre* uses stage directions particularly to convey movement, clothing and colours. In Dürrenmatt's *Der Besuch der alten Dame*, the scene is set in some detail at the start of each Act, where sound and movement are carefully specified.

In order to focus students' attention on the stage directions, various activities could be used.

- Firstly, students could answer the following questions in pairs:
  - What is the purpose of the stage directions in the play?
  - Who are the stage directions for? The director? The audience?
  - Why does the dramatist give detailed (or very few) stage directions?
  - What effect does this have on the play and the audience?
- In a second activity, students could be presented with a page of text from the play with the stage directions removed:
  - Each pair of students devises stage directions for the blanks, subsequently giving the page to another pair, who act out the scene following the new stage directions.
  - The two new versions are then compared to see what effects the stage directions have on the action.
  - Finally, the students compare what they have written with the original stage directions for that page and discuss the effectiveness of each.
  - The class could then run through the original version and reflect on their new understanding of the stage directions in the play.
- Alternatively, if the students are taken to see the play in a theatre, they could then devise and implement different stage directions to see how the action is altered by this.

# The staging

The setting for the play also provides a rich backdrop for study and students should be encouraged to think about the visual impact of the play. Discussion can be around the set itself, furniture and props, costumes, sounds on and offstage, video projections and lighting. If students have seen the play in a theatre, an interesting discussion can ensue around lighting effects and how subtle changes in lighting can enhance or alter mood.

As in the last activity for stage directions, students working individually or in pairs could examine details of the setting act by act. Students with a drama background should be divided up amongst the groups to share their expertise.

- Students work in groups
  - to list the number of different set changes required during the play (and work out how many sets in total);
  - to write a list of props that would be required for each scene/act of the play;
  - to draw the set layout in the different acts (and imagine how the transitions may be achieved);
  - to sketch out costumes;
  - to consider the lighting (level of lighting; use of spotlights; use of darkness);
  - to think about the music in the play (e.g. the jukebox in Frisch's *Andorra* and the songs in Brecht's *Mutter Courage und ihre Kinder*). What is required and what is its effect?

For a play such as Frisch's *Andorra*, where the stage is effectively split between the action and the 'witness accounts' in the foreground, the staging is integral to the message and structure of the play.

- Using an image search, students can mock up a **mood board** for the staging of their production (e.g. set, costumes). This might be influenced by YouTube clips or productions of the play.
  - The theatre posters designed by theatre companies for previous productions often give a flavour of the production (contemporary or period, with minimalist or complex staging). Students could take inspiration from these and design their own.

## Performance activities

The logical way for students to get a sense of staging and stage directions and the importance of the play in performance is to try their hand at acting out scenes. However, whilst performing gives the opportunity for students to practise oral skills and to engage with the form and meaning of the language, not all students will enjoy this. It is important not to make students feel anxious and scene reading aloud (with careful preparation) is a good place to start before moving on to scene practice in pairs and small groups. On the other hand, any drama students in the group may be more willing to be adventurous.

- One approach is to encourage students to **walk through key scenes**. Scenes may be acted out but just with gestures to accompany the audio of a video or radio production (or confident readers within the group). One student can act as director, instructing 'actors' according to the stage directions. Students focus on the non-verbal dynamics of scene.

  - How close are the characters to one another and to the audience?
  - Are they seated?
  - Are they moving or stationary or doing something else?
  - What body language are they displaying?

As an alternative to performance here, it may also be worth mentioning Carter and Long's (1992 p.125) concept of 'reader's theatre'. This essentially is a discussion of all the questions surrounding staging, how lines are delivered, lighting, actors' movements, costumes, props *etc.*, but in groups without the performance element.

Acting out key scenes or exchanges can also really help students to understand characterisation, how tension builds within the scene or the thematic core of the drama.

- It is often more efficient to have students work in pairs to practise (or groups of three if the scene requires it). Each pair or group practises their role, perfecting pronunciation, intonation, gestures and movement and interaction. Students then change pairs or groups and perform again, aiming to share and refine their performances through working with others. Eventually they may be able to perform without the script.

  - A 'director' could be nominated for each group to give notes and supervise the rehearsal. He or she could lead discussions about the interpretation of various lines and staging.

With a confident class, it may be possible to encourage greater spontaneity in language and deeper conceptual engagement with the play.

- Firstly, students may be asked to improvise the scene which precedes the start of the play, or happens after its conclusion, taking their inspiration from the characterisa-tion and clues in the play. In Lorca's *La casa de Bernarda Alba*, students could recreate Bernarda's husband's final conversations with his wife and daughters. Action which we do not see on stage could also be imagined, such as Hugo receiving the poisoned chocolates in prison in Sartre's *Les mains sales*. First meetings of key characters such as Jessica and Hugo (*Les mains sales*) or earlier partings *e.g.* Claire and Ill (Dürrenmatt's *Der Besuch der alten Dame*) or der Lehrer and die Señora (Frisch's *Andorra*) could require students to understand these characters and in the latter cases, the origins of the play's action.

- Students could also take the nub of the characters' situation or a key two- or three-line exchange and use their imagination to script the scene which they then perform. This could either be in character or as themselves in a modern setting *e.g.* How might der Lehrer and die Señora in Frisch's Andorra explain to Andri the truth of his parentage?

### Legislative theatre

An alternative approach for confident students who enjoy performance could be borrowed from the work of Brazilian writer, political activist and theatre practitioner, Augusto Boal (1998) who created Legislative Theatre in the 1990s. A short play involving a set of issues is performed and the audience is encouraged to interject, sometimes with an audience member replacing one of the actors on stage. The actors react to their suggestions and alter the dialogue. Another member of the audience can then request they return to the original script or suggest another twist. In this way, the audience and the actors respond and collaborate. The path of a play could be changed in this way. Sartre's *Les mains sales* might lend itself to this form of intervention since different scenarios are possible as Hugo struggles to make key decisions. Audience participation may also have an interesting effect on Lorca's *La casa de Bernarda Alba*.

# Dramatic devices

When studying a play, students should be aware of the devices a playwright uses to bring his or her story to life on stage and hold the attention of the audience. It is less easy in a play than a novel to convey the characters' inner thoughts, so the playwright makes use of devices such as soliloquy and asides to the audience in order to externalise inner conflict. Dramatic irony, comic relief, satire, foreshadowing and flashbacks are all techniques which can be employed to engage the audience in the action.

Students should be encouraged to use the appropriate technical terms in their essays and these are supplied as part of the French, German and Spanish vocabulary lists in Appendix 2.

- Pairs of students could study the play act by act in terms of dramatic devices. Figure 7.1 can be consulted for meanings of the terms and Figure 7.2 (translated using the vocabulary in the Appendix 2 lists) completed with examples from the play being studied. Pairs of students can then compare their findings. Students should try to explain, simply, the purpose and effect of the use of the device.

# Style and structure

General questions of style and structure are considered in Chapter 9, but it is worth flagging up features to be aware of specifically while reading a play at this point.

## Language and dialect

The way in which the protagonists speak contributes to the impact of the play in performance. Different registers and accents (regional, metropolitan) play a part in characterisation and vary the rhythm and tone of the scenes. These differences are not necessarily easy for second language learners to detect however and seeing a performance of the play should help to highlight them. In *Les mains sales* the young intellectuals speak in modern French whereas the uneducated Party bodyguards Slick and Georges use coarser working-class idioms and the aristocratic Prince Paul uses more elevated language. In Anouilh's *Antigone* different speech registers differentiate the characters (poetic Antigone as she dreams of secret solitude; the informal style of her nurse; the coarse language of the guards and the brutal realism of Créon).

## Comedy

Language can also be a tool in creating comedy, and in bringing interludes of comic relief in tragedies. Identifying these episodes, how they are created and what purpose they serve in the overall arc of the play will help students to understand the construction of the play. Students can most easily recognise elements of physical comedy (farce or slapstick e.g. in Molière's *Le Tartuffe* or Dürrenmatt's *Der Besuch der alten Dame*) and these can be a focus for exercises to explore stage directions as discussed above. Smutty and vulgar language or innuendo may also need to be highlighted for students.

Understanding satire in a play like Molière's *Le Tartuffe* can be closely linked to the thematic content of the work. It is helpful for students to be aware of how the comedy was received in its own time in order to understand the potency of such satire. Poking fun at religious hypocrites was viewed as extremely subversive in 17th century France, and King Louis XIV was pressurised by religious groups to ban the play. In more recent times, dramatists such as Brecht use humour to mock aspects of human nature and society.

| Dramatic devices in plays | |
|---|---|
| antagonist/foil | an opponent for the main character (protagonist) |
| aside | a brief comment for the audience to hear |
| catharsis | a purging of emotions, especially pity or fear, leading to renewal |
| climax | the turning point or decisive moment |
| chorus | their function is to describe and comment on the action of the play |
| comic relief | witty or humorous scene in a serious play |
| conflict | psychological conflict between two or more characters |
| dénouement | the final part of a play, where strands of the plot are drawn together and resolved |
| Deus ex machina | an unexpected person or event resolving a situation |
| dramatic irony | the audience is aware of full significance of a character's words or situation |
| dynamic characters | characters who undergo a change in attitude or personality during the play |
| flashbacks | memories or scenes from the past |
| flat/static characters | characters who do not undergo any change during the course of the action |
| foreshadowing | a literary device which prepares the audience for a future event |
| hubris | excessive pride or self-confidence (in classical theatre, towards the gods) |
| monologue | a long speech by one character |
| props | objects used on stage – these can take on great significance |
| rising action | character flaws, decisions and circumstances leading to the climax |
| satire | the use of irony or ridicule to expose people's stupidity or vices |
| secondary characters | characters who shed a new perspective on the situation or on other characters |
| soliloquy | a character speaks his/her thoughts aloud |
| tragedy | a play dealing with tragic events, and which has an unhappy ending |
| tragic flaw | a character trait which leads to a character's downfall |
| Unities of time/ place/action | In classical plays, the action of one main plot takes place within 24 hours in one place |

*Figure 7.1* Dramatic devices in plays.

| Dramatic device | Example in text | Purpose and effect of device |
|---|---|---|
| antagonist/foil | | |
| aside | | |
| catharsis | | |
| chorus | | |
| comic relief | | |
| conflict | | |
| dénouement | | |
| Deus ex machina | | |
| dramatic irony | | |
| dynamic characters | | |
| flashbacks | | |
| flat/static characters | | |
| foreshadowing | | |
| hubris | | |
| monologue | | |
| props | | |
| rising action | | |
| satire | | |
| secondary characters | | |
| soliloquy | | |
| tragedy | | |
| tragic flaw | | |
| unities of time/ place/action | | |

*Figure 7.2* Dramatic devices activity (translations of the devices into French, German and Spanish may be found in Appendix 2).

## Dramatic structure

Some plays will follow a typical three or five act structure e.g. Lorca's *La casa de Bernarda Alba* where the three acts introduce, develop and then (tragically) resolve the action. In Sartre's *Les mains sales*, the action is told in flashback in Tableaux 2–6.

As with Anouilh's *Antigone*, the fate of Hoederer is therefore known from the start (but not how his murder would occur), but that of Hugo is not decided until the final line. As well as writing summaries of the action (as described above), students should think about the full arc of the story.

- **Timeline** exercises are useful in sorting out the sequence of events and also for mapping the dramatic arc of the action. (Different colours could be used for the following activities so that they can be compared on the same chart.)
  - ○ Students mark the scenes on a horizontal axis and indicate the length of scenes to see where the pace of the play is speeded up or slowed down. Pace can be increased by using short scenes, rapid exchanges, a succession of events and lots of changes of characters on stage. In contrast, long scenes with lengthy monologues or little action can slow down the action.
  - ○ The number of characters, or the presence of the main protagonists, could also be marked on each scene.
  - ○ The scene-line could also be used to mark the turning points in the action.
  - ○ The same activity could be used to mark the rising or declining tension of each scene to give a visual outline of the dramatic rhythm of the play. Tension may be the result of plot twists, misunderstandings, dramatic action on stage, suspense, or conflict between characters.

## Themes

The thematic content of the plays is very important, especially as the plays on the syllabus address significant human issues. Activities for exploring the central concerns of the plays are discussed in Chapter 9 but students could use the particular feature of this genre in a number of ways.

- Students identify and act out exchanges which best illustrate the themes of the play to fix them in their minds;
- Students are given lines which pertain to the core themes and sort them by character and identify the circumstances in which they were said.
- Students could script mini-scenarios to illustrate similar concerns in a contemporary way.
- Given the tragic outcomes of most of the set plays, students could also be asked to imagine how a happier ending could have been secured. How would the protagonists have to behave differently in order to change their fate?

# Conclusions

Studying a play has much to offer A level learners. The plays on the syllabus often centre clearly around a meaningful dilemma, a difficult choice which the protagonists have to make in situations which can be related to modern life. The dramatic power with which the play can communicate the essence of human behaviour and motivation offers exciting opportunities to discuss relevant themes with students.

Students should not lose sight of the fact that they are studying a play and be able to discuss the particular features of the genre. This leads to exploration of staging and opportunities for student performance. More creative opportunities using drama can be found in Chapter 11 and activities to develop understanding of characterisation, themes, style and structure are discussed in Chapters 8 and 9.

# Implications for teaching

- Where possible, organise a visit to see the play, or an associated play, at the theatre.
- If relevant, ensure that students understand the playwright's views of drama and the socio-historical context of the play.
- Divide the play into sections for close reading in class and independent reading at home.
- Identify audio and video resources which can support reading the play in class and at home.
- Provide structured activities to guide and support independent reading. Inform students of the purpose and focus for each section and use a range of exercises which help them to achieve these goals.
- Ensure that students have clear act and scene summaries of the play in accurate language for reuse in their discussions and essays.
- Help students to become more confident in reading and acting parts of the dialogue and remind them of the performance dimension of the play when discussing it.
- Help students to think about staging and the visual and auditory impact of the play on the audience.
- Build students' knowledge of the play so that they can begin to analyse the dramatic devices and language used to affect the audience.
- Help students to understand the characterisation, themes, structure and style of the play.
- Include questions which ask for students' interpretation and personal response to the play and build their confidence to express their views.
- Promote collaborative learning and interactive exercises to help learners to develop their ideas and the ability to express them in the target language.

# Further reading

The National Theatre has a video on YouTube entitled *An Introduction to Brechtian Theatre* produced in conjunction with their production of *Mutter Courage*. The British Library has interesting articles on Brecht's theatre (in English) in its Discovering Literature: 20th Century strand (along with other European influences).

Theatres will often produce notes for their productions and a good place to start is Das Berliner Ensemble. The National Arts Centre, Ottawa, has extensive study notes on *Mutter Courage* http://artsalive.ca/pdf/eth/activities/MotherCourage.pdf.

The Théâtre National in Belgium produces teaching dossiers including for Anouilh's *Antigone*. The Association Bourguignonne Culturelle has an extensive dossier on Molière's *Tartuffe* (saison 2011/12). La Comédie Française has a range of online resources on its productions, including Molière's *Le Misanthrope* and even Lorca's *La casa de Bernarda Alba*, which could be interesting for students studying Spanish and French. These performance notes also help the students to see the creative process behind staging from the director's perspective. The Cervantes Theatre in London often stages works by Lorca.

Lazar (1993) has ideas for exploiting a play in a second language and Collie and Slater (1987) describe exercises used with drama in English.

# References

Boal, A., 1998. *Legislative Theatre: Using Performance to Make Politics*. Abingdon: Routledge.

Carter, R. and Long, M., 1992. *Teaching Literature*. Longman Handbooks for Language Teachers, 3rd impression. Harlow: Longman.

Collie, J. and Slater, S., 1987. *Literature in the Language Classroom: A Resource Book of Ideas and Activities*. Cambridge: Cambridge University Press.

Lazar, G., 1993. *Literature and Language Teaching: A Guide for Teachers and Trainers*. Cambridge: Cambridge University Press.

Margetts, D., 2000. Reading and writing plays in an electronic classroom. In: H. Nicholson, ed. *Teaching Drama 11–18*. London: Continuum, pp.37–50.

Nicholson, H., 2000. Conclusion: changing cultural landscapes. In: H. Nicholson, ed. *Teaching Drama 11–18*. London: Continuum, pp.160–166.

Parkinson, B. and Reid Thomas, H., 2000. *Teaching Literature in a Second Language*. Edinburgh: Edinburgh University Press.

Wallis, M. and Shepherd, S., 2002. *Studying Plays*. 2nd ed. London: Hodder Education.

# 8 | Understanding the characters

## Introduction

Characters play a major part in most literary fiction. It is likely that they drive the action and the reader's first emotional engagement with a novel or a play, positive or negative, often results from early encounters with the main protagonists.

- Has the author succeeded in bringing the characters and their motivations credibly to life?
- Do we care about what happens to them?
- How do they interact?
- How do they develop over the course of the story?

Analysing the characters created by the author is a key aspect of appreciating a literary text and unsurprisingly this is the focus of many A level questions. The ability to understand characterisation is also required when studying films and here these two areas of the Advanced level syllabus usefully overlap.

The exploration of characterisation meets the aims of teaching literature as discussed in Chapter 2 in a variety of ways and can bring many benefits, which it is helpful to bear in mind as a guide.

### Linguistically

- It is often relatively easy to garner basic evidence for discussion of character as the relevant information may be identified through clear textual markers (*i.e.* names) and simpler syntactic structures.

- Vocabulary used for the description of characters may be more familiar for A level students from their earlier language learning.

- Character study can be a way to promote close examination of the text (*i.e.* with close reading of paragraphs and gap fills *etc.*)

- Character study can also broaden students' basic vocabulary and lead to a greater degree of sophistication in their own writing.

- For the most able candidates it also encourages the possibility of high level analysis to demonstrate linguistic subtlety and analytical depth.

## *Culturally*

- Exploring a character's situation and seeing through his or her eyes can assist students in understanding the historical, political or geographical context of the work.

- Character study can provide a bridge to understanding more difficult concepts within the work.

## *Reader response*

- The discussion of characters and their motivations is a good way to engage readers and can encourage opinions from less confident students about how the novel or play may relate to their own experience.

Students will, of course, need support in their progression from simply identifying character traits to being able to analyse and discuss the characters fluently in the target language. Opportunities for structured practice will allow students to build confidence in both their opinions and linguistic ability to express them. This chapter will look at what the examination requires and suggest activities to help students achieve this.

# Examination focus

One of the two essay choices offered to candidates in the A level examination will usually focus on characterisation. Even where this is not the case, characters may provide a vehicle through which other thematic aspects of the work can be examined.

Character-based questions fall broadly within the following areas:

- The study of an **individual character or group**;
  (this includes minor characters and groups of characters – e.g. portrayal of gender or the Prussians in Maupassant's *Boule de Suif* which are used as archetypes)

- A character's **relationship with other characters**;
  (including the relative importance of characters; the influence of characters upon one another; how characters are seen by others)

- A character's **relationship with events**;
  (including the effects of events and external pressures on characters *and* the effects of the character on events e.g. the consequences of a character's actions)

- A character's **relationship with the author**;
  (including how characters are used to portray the author's message or theme and how close the identification between author and character is seen to be)

- **Time** is also an important dimension: how does the character **develop** as a result of interaction with other characters and events?

If students have a good knowledge of these areas, then they will have a firm grasp of the characters and the wider text. Additionally, a thorough understanding of character can be used and adapted to answer (seemingly) more complex questions and practice for this should be part of pre-examination revision. Students should be wary however that repeated practice of 'character study' essays does not lead to their wholesale regurgitation in exams. Adapting knowledge to the specific question is essential for a good mark.

The ideas for activities which follow are intended to help teachers and students consider these key areas for character study. Activities may be used at different stages in the course as a general introduction before the text is read in full, some as each individual chapter is discussed, and others after reading has been completed. Teachers may choose to use different activities when approaching different characters and activities can be varied by the use of group or individual work, undertaken in class or at home. Different activities will also be more or less applicable to the particular text under study.

## Critical distance

As students work to understand the characters, it is important to remember that they are creations of the novelist or dramatist. Students' views are an *interpretation* of how the characters, their meanings and motivations are *presented* to us by their creator. It is helpful if students acknowledge this dimension within their discussion and the language they use (e.g. by using verbs such as dépeindre, darstellen or representar.)

# Introducing character analysis

Although students may be able to draw on ideas about character study from their English literature study, using these skills in the target language adds additional challenge. Preliminary exercises will help students to understand how to approach the subject and to build the necessary vocabulary for discussion of character traits.

## *Dramatis personae*

- After an initial familiarisation with a novel or short story, students write a list of *dramatis personae* as they would find in a play (it may be helpful to have some examples of such lists to look at first).
  - What information is given?
  - In what order are the characters presented? This could lead on to discussions of the importance of the individual characters.

- This exercise also allows students to focus on the **names** of the characters, and what this might mean in some texts. For example, most of the characters in Dürrenmatt's *Der Besuch der alten Dame* are simply called by their occupation (Der Arzt, Der Lehrer *etc.*) or are numbered as citizens. This could be seen as dehumanising, showing them merely as representations of their social institutions. The name of Mann's eponymous hero *Tonio Kröger* is also unusual and foreshadows his dual Italian/German heritage, which is an important part of his personality.

## *Role*

- Once they have read the text, students (in groups) divide characters into the **importance** of their respective **roles**. Suggested divisions could be **main, secondary** and **minor roles**:
  - Students are challenged to justify their results and find a consensus.
  - They discuss the function of the most minor characters and decide why they exist.

When considering the full list of characters in a novel or play, students should not overlook **absent friends**. These may be characters which do not appear on stage *e.g.* Pepe in Lorca's *La casa de Bernarda Alba*. The Colonel's dead son in García Márquez's *El coronel no tiene quien le escriba* is nevertheless a continual presence in the novel. Thaïs, Lou's baby sister who died, is also a character whose *absence* has huge ramifications for the characters and the story in de Vigan's *No et moi.*

When students are more familiar with the characters and plot, the activity *'Without me'* (discussed later in this chapter) will help students to assess the importance of a particular character or group of characters within the story.

## *Groupings*

Another way of approaching character function (and thematic content) is to look at **groups** of characters. Students may be asked, for instance, to consider how women are presented in a text. This may be in contrast to the male characters or may centre on their role in or treatment by society (e.g. Esquivel's *Como agua para chocolate* or Lorca's *La casa de Bernarda Alba*). A question like this can be answered with reference to individual key women. Another example may group together minor characters, such as the Prussians in Maupassant's *Boule de Suif* or the individuals whom Joseph and Maurice meet on their flight from Paris in Joffo's *Un sac de billes*. Students may be asked to consider their presentation and function in the narrative.

- Students suggest groupings of characters which strike them. (These will of course vary greatly depending on the text itself and be linked to its thematic content.) They can begin with simple pairs of **factual categories** such as men and women; adults and adolescents; family and non-family; married or unmarried; urban and rural; East and West Germans; Prussians and French; wealthy and poor *etc*.
    - They then decide which are the most significant groupings for the text and *why*.
- A second round of grouping can encourage students to think beyond surface characteristics and include **character viewpoints** or **internal traits** e.g. rational or emotional; kind or cruel; socially accepted or outcast; powerful or weak; honest or dishonest; traditionalist or rebel. Specific vocabulary can be given to support students and guide them.
    - More complicated Venn diagrams could then be drawn to map the main characters against these groupings *i.e.* Maupassant's *Boule de Suif* is a woman, French, working class, kind *etc*.
    - Groups discuss why these divisions exist and start to identify similarities and differences between the characters and the oppositions and tensions created within the narrative.

This type of exercise also helps build familiarity with characters in a long or complicated novel.

## *Character profile*

Students can think about the information needed to build up a picture of someone's character, and then use this to write more sophisticated analyses. In the following discussion, ideas should emerge from the students themselves, but it is useful to have key questions prepared to move each stage along as is appropriate for the group. Initially only the first categorisation takes place. Raising awareness of these areas will help the students to be alert to aspects of character as they read the text.

- Students suggest the information they need about a character and then group their ideas into categories. At this stage the discussion is not specific to the chosen text. Categories may broadly divide initially into:
  FACTUAL: e.g. physical description/family/background/education
  AFFECTIVE: e.g. dislikes/likes/temperament

- Students are encouraged to explore what else the author may tell us?

  What are his or her goals?

  What motivates him/her?

  Who are his or her friends or enemies?

  What or who influences him or her?

  Does he or she have any strong beliefs?

  What obstacles has he/she had to overcome?

  What difficulties still await?

  What don't we know?

  What might be hidden?

  What effects might he or she have on other characters and on the action?

- To develop the discussion to a higher level, the question of *'how do we know this?'* about a character is introduced.

  Is it through what the author tells us – either explicitly or through inference?

  Is it through what the character tells us about him/herself?

  Is it through how the character acts?

  Is it through what other characters tell us?

  How reliable are these voices – are they biased or deceived by the character?

  Do we make judgements and assumptions based on our own perspectives, values and experiences?

- It may be helpful for students to be challenged to think about themselves: *What categories should someone use to get to know 'you'?*

- Asking the question *'Do you change over time?'* could alert students to the idea of character development and change.

# Gathering the evidence

Students need tools to collect evidence as they read or reread the text, especially when tackling a novel, so that they have a bank of language and ideas at their fingertips for discussion.

## *Identity cards*

Students are asked to fill out a basic profile sheet which records an overview of key personal (factual) identification for characters. This task could be divided around the class for different characters and then the answers shared and perhaps revised or enhanced through collective discussion.

## *Character grids*

Completion of a character grid (or profile) can be an efficient aid for keeping track of ideas on individual characters. Figure 8.1 suggests a possible format (or the more general grid suggested in Chapter 6 may be preferred).

- Students fill in the grid as they read each scene/chapter/section (in note form). It is important to record clear factual information (key quotes and page numbers) for reference at a later date. Students will be able to write more convincing and well-reasoned essays if they get into the habit of supporting each characteristic by **evidence** from the text.
  - This **evidence** should be analysed however:
    - Is a particular characteristic explicit or implied?
    - Is it demonstrated (through the character's own words or actions)?
    - Is it reported by another character or the author?
    - How reliable is this evidence?
    - Is there evidence to contradict this character assessment elsewhere in the book?

| Name of character: | | | |
|---|---|---|---|
| **Page** | **Quality (Change in character)** | **Evidence from text** | **Type of evidence 1–6** |
| | | | |
| | | | |
| | | | |
| | | | |
| | | | |
| | | | |
| *How do we know?* | | | |

1. By the character's actions
2. By what he or she says
3. By what another character says
4. By what the narrator says
5. The evidence is reliable
6. The evidence is implied rather than explicit

*Figure 8.1* Character grid.

## *Sharing the load*

If the responsibility for gathering information about the characters (and perhaps the minor ones lend themselves to this activity) is distributed amongst students in a collaborative activity, some simple guidance makes the task more manageable and ensures that each student plays his or her part. Hayhoe and Parker (1984) suggest the following steps:

- Students write down the page numbers (or scenes) when the character is present, or when he or she is referred to by others.
- Students decide which are the character's most important appearances and whom he or she is associated with at these moments.
- This information can then be used to summarise the part the character plays in the text.

# Exploring individual characters and building language

Once students have gathered some textual evidence through their character grids, they can start to develop the language they need to express their conclusions about the characters. A useful starting point here is a focus on **adjectives**, which are more nuanced and abstract than those with which the students may already be familiar.

## First impressions

Hares (1984) suggests starting with a broad-brush approach where students are asked general questions such as whether their initial reactions to a particular character are positive or negative. They must justify their answer with evidence. Further probing can help the student to unpick why they feel that way. Is this a gut reaction or is it because of their lack of common ground with the character or their own prejudice? Other broad contrasts could be used such as tragic or comic.

Students can then be challenged to think in more detail about a character's personality by identifying individual characteristics which they regard as positive and those which are more negative.

## Light and shade ping-pong

Following on from first impressions, to encourage students to see **nuance** in the main protagonists' character, they can be challenged to a metaphorical game of ping-pong. One team has to find positive aspects of a character, whilst the other team finds the negative, citing examples from the text. Teams take it in turns until one side runs out of arguments and concedes the point. As actions can often be interpreted positively and negatively, it may open up lively debate in the target language and challenges to the referee! Complex or morally ambiguous characters are particularly good choices for this activity, e.g. Meursault in Camus' *L'étranger*.

## Favourite characters

To encourage students to look across the entire cast list they could be asked to decide (as appropriate to the text) which character:

* they would choose as a friend;
* they would prefer as a parent;
* they would trust with a secret;
* they would avoid at a party.

*Or* which character:

- is the most sympathetic / most inspiring / most vulnerable / most convincing;
- is the least important / least engaging / least humane *etc.*

Here key adjectives and descriptive phrases can be introduced for students' use. These prompts could be designed to practise a particular structure, *e.g.* conditional or superlative.

Students could then be given time to prepare a justification for their choice, citing evidence from the text and their own perspective. Other students can then challenge or vote for the most convincing argument. This dimension of **personal engagement** is an important element in the assessment criteria. The important dimension of **criticality** can also be introduced here as students consider how realistic they find the characters in their roles of friend, parent, teacher *etc.*

## Casting director

As students' familiarity with the characters grows, they may decide who they would cast in the roles in a film adaptation of the book or play. This will require them to think about how they envisage the character in their mind's eye, physically but also in terms of psychological portrayal. If a film version is available or a stage production can be seen, a subsequent area for discussion could be any disparity with the students' own mental picture of the characters.

## Using film

To make further use of films, Parkinson and Reid Thomas (2000) suggest that students pick scenes in the novel they are studying which illustrate certain character traits of the main protagonists. Once they have discussed the written text, students then watch the relevant episodes in the film and compare the portrayal of the characters. Again, the film version may differ from their interpretation of the text, and therefore lead to either new insights into the characters or negative student critique.

## Pick and mix

Grouping more sophisticated adjectives together helps students to build their vocabulary and also to think about character in a more detailed and precise way. Hares (1984) gives an example of a character profile format where four adjectives are given per line and students must select one (or no) characteristic(s) to describe the subject's personality. At the end of the grid, the student can add any other qualities, but has a solid basis of adjectives (and their feminine forms where necessary) to begin their own compositions. It is also useful to ask students to rank the adjectives from most to least apt for the character.

## Diamond ranking

A more interactive way of ranking characteristics is to use the familiar 'diamond 9s' activity. Traits associated with a character (perhaps from the previous grids) are written on cards and students rank them into a diamond shape (essentially 5 rows with 1, 2, 3, 2 and 1 cards respectively). Students can work individually or in pairs and then join with other groups to share their ranking and the reasoning behind it.

## The character continuum

Whereas Hares groups unrelated characteristics, another approach is to think about characteristics in terms of opposing pairs of adjectives. The adjectives are set out on a continuum, with an adjective on the left and its opposite on the right. Hayhoe and Parker (1984 p.29) suggest a grid where students use a five-point scale to show which of the poles best describes the character. This encourages the use of qualifying phrases such as:

- not at all; a little; rather (or quite or somewhat); very; extremely;
- never; rarely (or seldom); sometimes (or occasionally); usually (or generally); consistently (or fundamentally).

Where there are a small number of characters in the novel or play, students work to place each character on the continuum for a quality, marking the line with the character's name and possibly using colour. If there are a large number of characters, the chart could be redone in landscape format. Examples of contrasting adjectives in French, German and Spanish are shown in Figures 8.2, 8.3 and 8.4. These phrases can be adjusted to the characters and the adjectives can be used for describing and comparing characters.

## Un portrait chinois

This activity is well suited to introducing literature before A level since little language, but a lot of imagination, is required. However, it remains a fun way to analyse a character and, at this level, can throw up some interesting insights, which can then be justified using more complex language. Any internet search on 'Chinese

| gentil, aimable | cruel | kind ... cruel |
|---|---|---|
| content, heureux | mécontent, malheureux | happy ... miserable |
| sympathique | antipathique, déplaisant | nice ... unpleasant |
| patient | impatient | patient ... impatient |
| amusant, drôle | sérieux | funny ... serious |
| stable | instable | stable ... unstable |
| réfléchi | homme/femme d'action | thoughtful ... man/woman of action |
| calme | agité | calm ... agitated |
| loyal | déloyal | loyal ... disloyal |
| mûr, (attitude) adulte | immature, puéril | mature ... immature |
| sensible | franc | sensitive ... direct |
| flexible | rigide | flexible ... unyielding |
| généreux | radin (argent) / malveillant | generous ... mean |
| altruiste | égoïste | altruistic ... egoistic |
| honnête | malhonnête | honest ... dishonest |
| optimiste | pessimiste | optimist ... pessimist |
| aventureux | prudent | adventurous ... careful |
| confiant | craintif | confident ... scared |

*Figure 8.2* French character adjectives.

portrait' or 'portrait chinois' will result in pages of suggested prompts which can be used to construct a metaphorical description of an individual. These can be concrete items (e.g. an animal; a car; a sport; a fruit; a household item; a book; a film; a place; a landscape etc) or more abstract concepts (a mood; a colour; an emotion; a vice; a time of day etc). The portrait can be written in the first person (the character's self-perception) or the third person as judged by the student, the author or another character. In fact, in works where deception, duplicity or self-delusion feature prominently, then conflicting portraits of the same character can help to illustrate these differences. Molière's *Le Tartuffe* provides a good example of where the other characters' (Orgon and his wife) portrait of the central protagonist, Tartuffe, may be markedly different! If the novel or play centres around the contrast between two protagonists, (e.g. Hugo and Hoederer in Sartre's *Les mains sales*), then two contrasting portraits could be constructed.

In French the basic structure of the portrait uses the conditional 'si' clause:

| lieb, nett, freundlich | unfreundlich, grausam, hart | kind … unkind |
|---|---|---|
| fröhlich, zufrieden | traurig, unzufrieden | happy … unhappy |
| entscheidungsfreudig | zögerlich | decisive … hesitant |
| geduldig | ungeduldig | patient … impatient |
| witzig, humorvoll | ernst | funny … serious |
| stabil | beständig | stable … unstable |
| nachdenklich | Mann/Frau der Tat | thoughtful … man/woman of action |
| ruhig, gelassen | bewegt, aufgeregt | calm … agitated |
| loyal, treu | treulos | loyal … disloyal |
| erwachsen, vollentwickelt | kindisch | mature … immature |
| sensibel, empfindlich | unsensibel, unempfindlich | sensitive … direct, blunt |
| flexibel | unflexibel, unbeweglich | flexible … inflexible |
| freigebig, generös | geizig, durchschnittlich | generous … mean |
| selbstlos | egoistisch | unselfish … selfish |
| ehrlich | unehrlich | honest … dishonest |
| optimistisch | pessimistisch | optimistic … pessimistic |
| abenteuerlich | einfallslos, nicht abenteuerlich | adventurous … unadventurous |
| selbstbewusst, überzeugt | unsicher, nicht selbstbewusst | confident … lacking in confidence |
| rücksichtsvoll | rücksichtslos, unbedacht | considerate … inconsiderate |

*Figure 8.3* German character adjectives.

Si *Tartuffe* était *une saison*, il serait *l'hiver … …*.
The sentence can then be extended either by a simple *'parce que'* clause as justification for the student's choice:
Si *Tartuffe* était *une saison*, il serait *l'hiver* parce qu'il ne possède pas de chaleur humaine.
A relative clause could also complete the sentence:
Si *Tartuffe* était *un métal*, il serait *l'or* qui pour lui est tout ce qui compte.
Alternatively, students can be encouraged to use *'pour plus infinitive'* or *'pour que … plus subjunctive'* to imagine **why** the character would choose to be represented by that particular item:
Si *Tartuffe* était *un oiseau*, il serait *le coucou* pour s'installer chez les autres.

| simpático | antipático | kind, nice … unpleasant |
|---|---|---|
| feliz | infeliz | happy … unhappy |
| decidido | indeciso | decisive … hesitant |
| paciente | impaciente | patient … impatient |
| gracioso | serio | funny … serious |
| estable | inestable | stable … unstable |
| tranquilo | nervioso / inquieto | calm … restless |
| leal | desleal | loyal … disloyal |
| maduro | inmaduro | mature … immature |
| sensible | directo | sensitive … blunt |
| flexible | inflexible | flexible … inflexible |
| generoso | tacaño/mezquino | generous … mean person/mean with money |
| poco egoísta / altruista | egoísta | unselfish … selfish |
| honesto | deshonesto | honest … dishonest |
| optimista | pesimista | optimistic … pessimistic |
| aventurero | poco osado | adventurous … unadventurous |
| seguro de sí mismo | falta de confianza, inseguro | confident … lacking in confidence |
| cortés, educado | grosero | polite … rude |

*Figure 8.4* Spanish character adjectives.

In German, 'wenn' clauses with the subjunctive and conditional can be completed with 'weil' or 'um…zu' clauses, creating a complex sentence. In Spanish, 'Si' clauses with the imperfect subjective and conditional can be completed with *por qué* followed by a clause or *para* followed by the infinitive. It is best to give the class a couple of examples first in order to get the ball rolling and establish the pattern. It is also fun if these examples come from the teacher's own portrait!

## Key paragraphs

Close reading of a chosen paragraph or scene can help students to link their analysis to the text. The teacher chooses key sections (when a character is first introduced or during a key interaction or possibly an internal monologue). Students are asked to find as many details about a character as possible from a short passage of text. This can be done competitively in pairs for additional discussion and motivation (or even as a 'ping-pong' match as discussed earlier in this section). They scrutinise each sentence carefully for information and think about some of the questions posed earlier regarding how this information is presented and how reliable it may be. If students are given different excerpts for the same character, this could prompt interesting discussion and expose possible contradictions or developments in character (especially from different stages in the action). Students can be encouraged to choose their own passage and carry out a similar analysis at home, and then share this in class.

## Quotation challenge

As a revision exercise and to ensure that students are able to anchor their character analysis in the text itself, they can play various games with quotations. The simplest is a team game where a character's words are read out or displayed on the whiteboard and teams gain points for identifying the speaker, whom they were speaking to, when it took place during the narrative and what was the context. After guessing some set by the teacher, the students can find quotations themselves to try to outwit the opposing team.

## Character mood charts

Charting a character's moods helps students to see different facets of their personality and their development over time. Some texts lend themselves particularly well to this, as they also highlight the influence of events and other characters on the main protagonist. Voltaire's *Candide* is a particularly good example: most chapters in the book involve a high point, where Candide sees his love, Cunégonde, before the downward spiral towards the end of the chapter where he is confronted by the reality of a natural disaster, or similar tragedy. It is only after many adventures and disasters towards the end of the novel that Candide reaches an equilibrium. Similarly, the highs and lows of Joseph's escape from Paris in Joffo's *Un sac de billes* could be charted, where, for example, having escaped the camp, the brothers immediately run into the interpreter from the hotel.

* Students draw a **timeline** of the novel or play, perhaps divided into chapters or scenes, marking on significant episodes in the action which relate to a particular character.

* A vertical axis is drawn on the left with a scale indicating a particular emotion. Happiness provides a simple place to start. The horizontal timeline itself is a neutral baseline with degrees of happiness (and euphoria) above and degrees of sadness below. At each point in the timeline, students decide on the

character's 'happiness quotient' and plot the graph accordingly. This visual representation can help students to see patterns and the shape of the character's passage through the narrative. Other emotions could be substituted according to the character and text.

# Character development over time

This dimension of character study is particularly relevant to much of the adolescent or coming of age literature featured on post-16 syllabi. It also demonstrates a deeper analysis of the protagonist. Character development is often seen in relation to growing up, for example sexual maturation (Vinca and Phil in Colette's *Le blé en herbe* or Michael in Schlink's *Der Vorleser*). Different factors contribute to the wider picture of growing up through exposure to events and other people. Young characters move from naivety to a deeper understanding of self, others and the world. Examples include Josyane in Rochefort's *Les petits enfants du siècle*, Daniel in Ruiz Zafón's *La sombra del viento* and Marcel Pagnol in his memoir *Le château de ma mère*.

Adult characters also change through the influence of other characters or events, or a combination of both. This development often lies at the heart of the narrative and may exemplify the central **theme**. In Kafka's *Die Verwandlung*, Gregor undergoes the ultimate physical transformation into a giant insect which necessitates both physical and psychological change. In Sagan's *Bonjour tristesse* Cécile, on the threshold of womanhood, is presented with two contrasting models in Anne and Elsa to follow as she contemplates her own path. Tita's development leads to the point where she is able to defy convention and consummate her love for Pedro after many years of denial in Esquivel's *Como agua para chocolate*.

Sometimes, a protagonist's character may only be revealed over time. In Schlink's *Der Vorleser*, Hanna's true identity is kept secret until her trial. This missing information illuminates many aspects of her behaviour during her early relationship with Michael. Not only does the trial reveal important aspects about Hanna to Michael, but the trial and her time in prison seems to reveal a new understanding of her own past to Hanna herself.

- A timeline can also be used to plot a character's development against key episodes and events in the text. A range of adjectives can be added to describe the protagonist's character at different stages of the narrative.
  - ○ Different colours can be used to indicate which of these adjectives are regarded by the students as positive and which as negative.
    - *Is the character becoming more or less sympathetic over time?*
    - *What other trends are discernible?*
    - *What causes these changes?*

○ New information could also be added about the character at the relevant stage, such as when Hanna's past and illiteracy are revealed.

The chart in Figure 8.1 can be adapted to record a character's development over time.

# Understanding the interaction between characters

Once students have explored individual characters and groups of characters and have a range of evidence and language at their disposal, they are ready to analyse how the characters interact with one another, with events and how they may change over time. The timelines suggested above may have already highlighted some key interactions and their effect on the protagonists.

In a lengthy and complex novel or play, sorting out the relationships between characters can also be a way of gaining clarity about the text. The simple **'dramatis personae'** exercise above could be a starting point for key relationships between the characters, but more complicated interactions will also need to be unravelled.

## *Sociograms*

Sociograms are a useful tool for charting the interrelationships between characters. They can provide students with a record of the characters and their emotional as well as more practical relationships. One possible starting point is to use mind mapping software (or simply pen and paper) and place a character in the middle of the page. The other significant characters are then added to the page. To encourage students to think about the relationship of the central protagonist with the other characters, various visual techniques can be used (the precise instructions can be adapted according to the text and what it is felt important to draw out from the students).

• Firstly, the characters who have the strongest **connection** (or most interactions) should be placed **nearer** to the main character, and the others further away.

• Characters which students feel have the greatest **impact** on the story (or the main character) can be **written** in a larger font.

• Lines can be drawn between the central character and the others. The colour of these lines could indicate positive (red) or negative (blue) relationships with thickness indicating the degree of warmth or dislike.

• Arrows can also indicate the direction of these feelings – so a line between characters A and B may be thick and red, whereas between B and A, the line may be much thinner and blue.

- An intermittent line of dots or dashes could also be used to show regularity of contact or any rupture in relations.

- Lines can also be drawn between the peripheral characters to show their interconnection in a similar way.

- Students can be encouraged to add additional visual information as they feel is relevant to the particular text.

If pairs of students are given large sheets of paper to work on, the results can be shared and discussed. Alternatively, one student or group could take one central character whilst another group focuses on a different protagonist and the results compared.

An additional dimension to this approach may emerge if the two sociograms are drawn from each individual protagonist's perspective. Their (differing) assessments of how close and how important other characters are to them, could illustrate interesting dynamics within the text and reveal hidden relationships and attachments. This also helps students to consider how characters are seen by other characters within the text. Ruiz Zafón's *La sombra del viento* or Lorca's *La casa de Bernarda Alba* work well with this activity.

## Influence and effect

The sociogram activity will have identified the relationships between characters. As students are encouraged to analyse these relationships, it is useful, firstly, to ask them to categorise each relationship using some appropriately chosen adjectives provided by the teacher. They can of course add to these themselves, but by supplying a core vocabulary the teacher ensures that all students have a basis for the subsequent discussion and written work e.g.

- positive: nurturing; loving; mutually beneficial;
- negative: controlling; destructive; manipulative; unhealthy; suffocating;
- surprising; understandable; inevitable.

The important second stage is to give a **reason** for the choice of adjective(s) which where possible is linked to **evidence** from the text.

The third stage is to examine the consequences of these dynamics. What happens because of a particular relationship? This leads students to begin to analyse what has caused protagonists to act as they do and to think about their **motivation**.

## *The first time I met … consequences*

Another way for students to explore the relationships between two characters is to imagine them looking back at their first meeting. This can again be orally or in letter format and addressed to the other person or to a third party. Some students may benefit from a writing frame to get them started. Possible prompts could include the following written as sentence starters in the target language. Students draw on details from the text as well as their imagination to complete the sentences. Of course, some first meetings may have happened long before the start of the narrative and may require significant imagination, but students should draw on clues in the text as a basis for their thoughts.

- The first time I met X, … ….
  - date or time; occasion; place and setting; description of place and atmosphere;
  - who else was present;
  - appearance and clothes;
  - feelings before the meeting;
  - first impressions;
  - hopes or fears caused by the encounter;
  - immediate actions after the meeting;
  - how the meeting changed me;
  - feelings now looking back.

- If this is set up carefully with simple sentence starters types on a vertical strip of paper, the game **consequences** can be played. Students sit in a circle and each start with a strip of prompts and complete the first sentence from the perspective of a particular character. They fold over their answer and pass the strip on to their neighbour on the right to complete the second prompt (they receive a new strip from the person on their left) and so on until all questions are answered. It is always fun to see how each strip has been completed as a team effort. More importantly, ideas are shared and agreeing on a finished 'best' version (and why) stimulates discussion of students' differing interpretations.

- In the persona of one character, students could describe in more detail how their life changed after meeting another. Michael in Schlink's *Der Vorleser* could for example write a letter to Hanna or Tita to John Brown in Esquivel's *Como agua para chocolate*.

## *Changing relationships*

The relationships between characters may change over time possibly in response to events and a character's own development as described above. In the examples of Thérèse and Anne in Mauriac's *Thérèse Desqueyroux* or Vinca and Phil in Colette's *Le blé en herbe*, this change is related to the arrival of a third character, Jean and Mme Dalleray respectively.

- Two accounts of the relationship can be drafted by students – one before and one after this disruption in their relations. This is an opportunity for the student to put him or herself into the mind of the characters and see it from their (perhaps differing) perspectives.
  - This can be done orally with the students 'in character' explaining their feelings as an internal monologue, or recounting them to another friend, interviewer or counsellor. It could be acted out as an exchange of views between the characters.
  - Alternatively, the characters may write down their thoughts in the form of a letter.
  - The voice of the 'disruptor' could also be explored.
- The change in relations may happen more gradually and once again a timeline will help to plot this and link it with other events. If two characters are shown on the same timeline, this may highlight interesting contrasts in fortune. In Kafka's *Die Verwandlung*, Gregor's relationship with his sister Grete gradually and symbolically deteriorates. However, as Gregor fades away, his sister's development blossoms.

## *Compare and contrast*

When contrasts between individual or groups of characters are clear within the text, then it is useful to prepare students to write a compare and contrast type essay.

- A simple way to do this which supports all students in the early stages of studying a text is to write a series of statements about the two characters or groups of characters on individual slips of paper.
  - Students then work together to separate these into categories describing character A and character B. Hugo and Hoederer from Sartre's *Les mains sales* would work well.
  - Complexity may be added by using ambiguous or shared traits or sentences which do not apply to either character. These can be discussed and students have a bank of statements to use to describe and compare the characters.

Work on phrases which can be used to compare, such as 'however', 'on one hand', 'in contrast' *etc*. can also be introduced and students asked to use these and the sentences to write up their thoughts.

It is important for students to discuss the **author's intention** when inviting readers or the audience to compare and contrast different characters or groups of characters. This will often lead back to the themes of the text and may offer alternative ways of seeing a situation or be intended to send a clear message about the author's views (see Chapter 9).

Relationships between groups of characters, *e.g.* between men and women, between different generations or between Jews and non-Jews, East and West Germans, Prussians and the French could also be fruitful areas to explore in some texts as discussed above.

## Understanding the interaction between character and events

Characters may be seen as a catalyst for events or reacting to them. Often it is a combination of both scenarios which drives the plot and the characterisation. As above, students can draw character profiles before and after a significant event, to see how an individual character has been affected.

### Flow charts

In order to consider the effect of an event on all the characters, it is useful to create a large diagram of its consequences.

- In the middle of a sheet of paper, place an event such as the death of Lou's baby sister in de Vigan's *No et moi* or Gregor's metamorphosis in Kafka's *Die Verwandlung*. Arrows flow outwards to each of the principal characters. Students note down how the character is affected by the event.
  - In stage two, students draw further arrows from each character showing what actions he or she took as a result of this effect.
- This approach can also be used to show how characters are affected by a particular **theme**, for example, money in Dürrenmatt's *Der Besuch der alten Dame* or food in Esquivel's *Como agua para chocolate*.

## Viewpoints

A question may focus on how a character sees the events which unfold in the narrative.

- One technique is to have different characters evaluate the ending of the novel or play. For example, in Colette's *Le blé en herbe*, how do Vinca, Phil and Mme Dalleray view their respective situations at the end of the narrative? Can they offer an alternative, more agreeable ending? This can be done in groups, with the perspectives shared or acted out in class.
- Students could write a summary of the whole story from a chosen character's viewpoint. Seeing the action through the character's eyes, students can imagine their inner thoughts and motivations. An interesting example is *Meursault, contre-enquête* (Daoud 2014) where the action of Camus's *L'étranger* is written from the viewpoint of the murdered Arab's brother. Another suitable text would be de Vigan's *No et moi* where No explains her point of view. Students could also consider the point of view of the policeman, Fumero, in Ruiz Zafón's *La sombra del viento*.
  - These can be compared with the students' own views of the action.

Such activities remind students of the layers of possible viewpoints and how the author has skilfully constructed them.

## Without me

To explore the importance of a character within the story, students could be challenged to think about how the action of the novel or play would change without him or her. Students can choose a character, write a brief 'alternative' synopsis without them and the rest of the class can guess whom they are talking about. This is a good opportunity to practise conditional sentences, for example.

## Balloon debate

Thinking what the story would be like without a character is another way of preparing for a 'balloon debate' amongst the characters. Here each student (or pair), representing a character from the story, must make the case for his or her continued presence in a sinking hot air balloon. Each character puts forward a reason why he or she is essential for the story and after everyone has spoken, the group votes and one character is thrown overboard. This continues until only one character remains in the balloon. Students should have time to prepare their arguments in advance, and that way can be encouraged to use particular structures such as *'il faut que … '* etc.

# Understanding motivation

Interpreting why characters behave in the way they do is an important aspect of the analysis of a text and trying to understand what lies behind a character's actions gives students the opportunity to explore motivation more generally.

## A personal perspective

One benefit of studying literature is that it can help us to understand ourselves. Therefore, when trying to understand characters, students may first relate their situations to their own lives and occasions when they acted in certain ways. A useful initial discussion could ask the questions:

* Why do we act in certain ways?
* What influences our judgements?

This offers the opportunity to teach a range of abstract emotions and factors, which can be introduced first if required: *e.g.*

* self-interest; selflessness; love; hatred; anger; jealousy; guilt; morality; tradition; upbringing; thoughtlessness; rashness; prejudice; loyalty; misunderstanding; pride; principles; pain; responsibility *etc.*

* Students could try to match the motivation with high profile figures from literature, history or public life (e.g. Othello; Romeo and Juliet; Napoléon).
* They could decide which motivations are most applicable to themselves (and then for various characters in the text).
* Students may be willing to share instances from their own lives when they acted because of a particular emotion (or just think about them privately).
* Students focus on incidents relevant to the character in the text and consider how they would act in the face of a betrayal (Vinca in Colette's *Le blé en herbe*) or a death threat (Ill in Dürrenmatt's *Der Besuch der alten Dame*).

## Internal or external

When discussing why characters act in certain ways in the text, students could share as many reasons as possible for a particular action or reaction (e.g. Hanna's suicide in Schlink's *Der Vorleser* or the Meursault's murder of the Arab in Camus'

*L'étranger*). They can then consider whether these reasons stem principally from the character's internal psychology or are due to specific external circumstances and other people. Often, the reality will be a combination of the two, but it does allow students to speculate further about the character's true nature, and to think about whether events were avoidable or inevitable. When attributing motivation to an event, students can draw a **pie chart** to indicate the percentages of the reasons which led to a character's choice of action.

## *Dramatising the text*

Drama can help students to understand characters and their motivation. Acting out key scenes in plays is, of course, a well-established way of students getting under the skin of the protagonists by speaking their words and enacting their gestures. This process can also be beneficial in looking more closely at characters from a novel.

### *Freeze frame*

Choose a key episode from the text. This may feature a pivotal revelation or clash between central characters. Students read the scene carefully, and then stage the action as if in a film. They imagine that the film is frozen at the critical point, and students must adopt the positions and expressions of their characters at that moment. What are their facial expressions and body language betraying about what they are thinking and feeling? Discussion about how to stage this tableau invites students to think about what drives the character in the scene.

### *Stage directions*

Taking staging a step further, teachers or students can identify key exchanges of dialogue in the novel (or this could be adapted for use with passages of indirect speech if necessary). Everything is stripped away other than the actual words spoken. Students then discuss the dialogue and consider who is speaking, the circumstances, what is happening and the emotional charge or impact of the situation on the characters. They then perform their interpretation, paying attention particularly to how the feelings of the characters are expressed through voice and gesture.

### *Stream of consciousness*

This type of improvisation highlights what is not voiced in the text, but which illuminates a character's inner thoughts and motivations.

- A good example might be Maupassant's *La mère sauvage*, in whose house four Prussian soldiers are billeted. One day the mother receives a letter informing her that her only son has been killed in battle. She makes a special meal, asks the soldiers for their names and addresses and tells them that they will sleep very well that night in her comfortable barn.

- Students could act out the meal scene, with one student behind the soldiers voicing their thoughts, while another voices the internal and rather more sinister thoughts of the mother.

- An alternative might be for the students to act out a scene after death where the mother and the young Prussians have an honest discussion about what has happened and one can explore her motivation and whether the soldiers understand her point of view.

*Interior monologue*

This technique of dramatising what the characters are thinking but not saying aloud in the text can be a powerful way of exploring motivation and latent feelings. It can also be used as a creative writing exercise, imagining adding this as an extra scene in a play where the character addresses the audience directly, or writing the description of his or her thoughts into the episode in the novel.

## Giving the character a voice

Following on from dramatising the text, scenarios can be set up in class where the students place the characters in situations where they must explain their emotions and justify their actions.

*On trial*

The character is on trial in a court of law, accused of a particular offence. Meursault in Camus' *L'étranger*, Thérèse in Mauriac's *Thérèse Desqueyroux* or Katharina in Böll's *Die verlorene Ehre der Katharina Blum* would all make good subjects.

- The activity can be set up as a 'live' trial with prosecutor and barrister asking the accused questions about what has happened and why. (Other students can be witnesses, judge and jury.)

- The character on trial may choose to make a statement, detailing his or her version of events and why they occurred.

- Alternatively, the scene can be between the two lawyers at sentencing, where one puts forward the case for the maximum penalty to be given whilst the other has to explain the character's behaviour and argue for mitigating circumstances. Here the students are arguing on behalf of the character in the third person.

- Most students will benefit from support in terms of some structure about the number of questions they should prepare and some phrases appropriate to the legal setting. They will need time to prepare (ideally in groups) before 'going to trial'. As with many drama and oral-based activities, including the Foreign Language Assistant is a great help in preparing students for their roles.

- Students could summarise the trial proceedings to practise reported speech and set out the positions for and against the character in written form.

## Interview practice

Another way of giving characters a voice is to interview them. This is a more straightforward question and answer format which can be made more dramatic with the inclusion of microphones and video recording if appropriate.

- This could be a studio or magazine interview where the character reflects at leisure. Here students could support one another by dividing into two groups. One group (A) decides upon the questions which will be asked by the interviewer whilst the other group (B) prepares answers for the likely questions for the interviewee. Depending upon the size of the class, these groups then split and pair up in as interviewer and interviewee (A and B) to conduct the interview. In this way all students are involved in the speaking activity and receive support in preparing their role.

- Alternatively, the character could face 'on the spot' type news reporting as a particular event unfurls. The choice of the exact format and point in the action will depend upon the text of course, but students could be encouraged to do both reporter-style interviews and then summarising pieces to camera to practise in the first, second and third person.

## Hotseating

This activity is both popular with students and encourages deep thinking about the text they are studying. As a drama technique, it could be used during the reading or after the book is finished. One student is chosen to represent a main character and sits at the front, facing the others. This character is cross-questioned about his or her actions and has to justify the behaviour. This might include questions such as 'Why?' and 'How did you feel?'.

This will work differently for a play and a novel, in that the novel has suppressed subtext, whereas a character's words in a play can be referred to. Cornudet in Maupassant's *Boule de Suif* or the mother in *La mère sauvage* would make a good hotseating subject, as would Tartuffe in Molière's play. Claire in Dürrenmatt's *Der Besuch der alten Dame* or Hanna and Michael in Schlink's *Der Vorleser* would be powerful subjects.

### Characters in conflict

The crux of a story often revolves around a central conflict for the main protagonist(s) e.g. should Hanna in Schlink's *Der Vorleser* take the blame for something she did not do or admit that she is illiterate at her trial? One voice could be the character's conscience, making all the arguments for one, (perhaps more noble), course of action whilst its less reputable counterpart could put forward reasons for acting differently (and perhaps less honourably). As students act out the dilemma in this way, it gives them an opportunity to practise persuasive language and to consider why the character acted the way he or she did.

### Regrets

In the character of the protagonist, students may consider what, with hindsight, he or she would have done differently. This offers many opportunities to practise more complex linguistic structures such as 'if I had known, I would have ....' (conditional perfect) or, in French, the subjunctive mood to describe wishing or regret. Students can be given a model structure to follow and asked to write, for example, six sentences describing what they regret and would have done differently.

### Creative writing

Another way of giving characters a written voice is through their imagined online life (social media, messaging, tweeting, blogposts) or perhaps less anachronistically for some characters, their diary entries for particular events. These are discussed in Chapter 11.

## Understanding the relationship between the author and the characters

The interplay between the author and the characters is explored in Chapter 9 in relation to any autobiographical elements, themes and the narrative voice within the story. Questions to raise with students about this relationship may include the following:

- Is the character the author? (not necessarily the main one)
- Is the character a representation of the author?
- Is a particular character used as a mouthpiece for the author?
- Is the character used to reflect a particular historical or social viewpoint?
- Does the author's sympathy appear to lie with a particular character?
- Is the character used as a negative example to the audience?
- Is the character intended to be realistic or just a 'type'?

# Conclusion

Ultimately, students' discussions should develop beyond a superficial level (either linguistically or conceptually), allowing them to form a judgement about the characters and the aspects of their role discussed above. These judgements will encompass the actions and characters of protagonists, but also what they represent and how realistic they are as people or how effective they are as symbols. Students should be encouraged to have a 360° view of the characters and be aware how they are seen by others within the text. They should seek to analyse their actions in terms of cause and effect and explore their interaction with external influences and internal motivations. Often characters will have a mixture of sometimes contradictory traits and students should be prepared to weigh up this (human) complexity to reach an overall assessment of them. Students can consider the characters' actions, emotions and motivations in the light of their own experiences and world view.

Students should practise identifying how their understanding of the characters will be beneficial in many essay questions which do not specifically ask for a character study. Answers to questions about the text's **themes**, for example, are often exemplified by reference to the characters. When asked to analyse the theme of friendship in de Vigan's *No et moi*, the student will look at the interaction of the main characters. Evaluating how realistically a theme is portrayed *e.g.* adolescence in Colette's *Le blé en herbe*, also depends upon an understanding of the characters. A text's imagery or symbolism could also be illustrated in part through the characters. Above all, students must be careful, however, to tailor their knowledge to the exact requirements of the question as discussed in Chapter 10.

# Implications for teaching

- Study the types of character questions used in the examination.
- Provide a range of exercises which enable students to develop the language necessary to discuss characterisation.

- Help students to understand and evaluate how characters are portrayed and their motivation.

- Discuss how characters interact with other characters and events and how they develop over time.

- Give students the opportunity to form opinions and to see the characters from different viewpoints.

- Plan activities which help students to 'get under the skin' of the characters and reflect upon their actions from a personal perspective.

# References

Daoud, K., 2014. *Meursault, contre-enquête*. Arles: Actes Sud. This has also been published in English (2015, translated by John Cullen) as *The Meursault Investigation* by Oneworld Publications.

Hares, R., 1984. *Compo Lit! French Literature Essay-Writing*. London: Hodder & Stoughton.

Hayhoe, M. and Parker, S., 1984. *Working with Fiction*. London: Edward Arnold.

Parkinson, B. and Reid Thomas, H., 2000. *Teaching Literature in a Second Language*. Edinburgh: Edinburgh University Press.

# 9 | Understanding themes, style and structure

## Introduction

Although characterisation will be a central element of understanding most novels and plays, in the A level examination, students can expect to have the choice of a second question which will probably ask them to consider the **themes** or the **style** and **structure** of the work. For students to earn high marks, they must answer these questions analytically rather than just descriptively. Therefore, students must explore the question of **why** the author has, from all the available options, made these particular choices about theme, style and structure.

- Why has the novel or play been written in this particular way?
- How do these decisions of style and structure contribute to the effectiveness of the piece?
- What may these choices suggest about the author's underlying intentions and preoccupations?

Here, we offer some suggestions for how these elements may be treated in class. They cannot be treated in isolation, however, and the ideas and approaches discussed in Chapters 6, 7, 8 and 9 necessarily overlap. Students should be guided to synthesise different features of their novel or play to draw conclusions and support their opinions with precise textual evidence.

## Themes

The themes explored in a text offer an insight into what interested the author and what he or she was trying to achieve. These themes may have a personal significance for the writer and be set in a particular time or place, but in order to give the work a wider appeal (especially to later generations and different cultures), the themes are often rooted in universal human emotions and dilemmas. Themes highlighted in early examinations include **justice** (Camus's *L'étranger* and Dürrenmatt's *Der Besuch der alten Dame*); **repression** (Lorca's *La casa de Bernarda Alba*); **guilt** (Frisch's *Andorra* and Schlink's *Der Vorleser*); **religion** (Brecht's *Der kaukasische Kreidekreis*) and loneliness (de Vigan's *No et moi* and Matute's *Primera memoria*).

When the teacher first reads the text, key themes will come to light and reading of contextual and biographical materials should provide further assistance. Useful information is now available on most examination board websites to support the teaching of individual prescribed texts e.g. the *Introducing Film and Literature Guides* which can be found on the Pearson qualifications website for Edexcel.

## Socio-historical context

Socio-historical context often provides an important framework for the principal themes within a text. This thematic content may be allowed to emerge gradually through reading and discussion of the text or may provide an entry point into it. Questions of pre-reading are discussed in Chapter 5, but it is worth reiterating the point here. **Social and cultural themes**, such as immigration or poverty (e.g. in Guène's *Kiffe Kiffe demain*; Etcherelli's *Elise ou la vraie vie*), can be linked with students' other language work and non-literary sources can provide useful background research about contemporary issues. Similarly, if the specific **historical context** of the work is important to understanding the themes, then prior research about the treatment of Jews during the Nazi occupation of France (Joffo's *Un sac de billes*) or the guilt felt by the post-War generation in Germany (Schlink's *Der Vorleser*) can make the whole text more accessible and meaningful from the start.

Where the work makes conscious **reference to another text**, such as Anouilh's retelling of the classical myth of Antigone, it is helpful for the students to be aware of the Greek tragedian Sophocles' rendering of the struggle between family and state in order to appreciate fully the thematic resonances of the play. In this instance, asking students to research the myth and perhaps draw up a family tree of Antigone and the Oedipus clan allows them to start to enter the world of the drama and understand why themes of family honour, internecine conflict, grief and justice matter so much to the main protagonist.

Another way to bring out the thematic importance of the contextual background is by using **visual stimuli** such as paintings, photographs, film stills or clips, newspaper headlines or articles relating to the particular period such as Algeria in the 1940s (Camus' *L'étranger*), or the fall of the Berlin Wall (Hensel's *Zonenkinder* or König's *Ich fühl mich so fifty-fifty*).

Caution is required at A level however. Although it may be important to understand the socio-historical context of the text and in some cases the philosophical stance of the author, these should not distract the student from discussing the *text itself*, unless this information is specifically asked for in the question.

## *Uncovering themes*

Students will need help to understand themes arising from an unfamiliar context, but they should be encouraged to uncover themes for themselves. In this way they are more likely to gain confidence in their own ability to interpret the text. Certain themes may emerge quickly, but support may also be needed. Asking students to look at the **title** (Sartre's *Les mains sales*; Böll's *Die verlorene Ehre der Katharina Blum*), the **historical and geographical setting** (König's *Ich fühl mich so fifty-fifty*) or the **central conflict** of the text is a good place for them to start to generate ideas.

- Students can be encouraged to debate the literal and possible metaphorical meanings of the **title**.
    - What does this tell us about the novel or play?
    - What feelings or expectations does it evoke in the reader or viewer?
    - Are these fulfilled in the actual text?
    - Is the title successful and in what way?
- When reading the text, students can be asked to look for specific examples of how **society** is depicted. These examples can then be categorised by students as ideas start to emerge *e.g.* relating to money, class, race.
- Themes may also be addressed through the **central oppositions** in the text. These may be exemplified within characters or more broadly in contrasting elements of the story. Seeking these oppositions within the text can help students to understand any contradictions within a theme. In Hensel's *Zonenkinder* and König's *Ich fühl mich so fifty-fifty* we see the actual contrasts between life in East and West Germany but come to understand that these contrasts can result in inner conflicts within the teenage citizens and themes of identity and liberty emerge. To focus students' attention on a particular area of contrast, ask them to look for particular contrasts and see what they deduce about the themes.
- With a group who are in the early stages of their A level course, it may be useful to introduce a range of **abstract nouns** (*e.g.* friendship; loneliness; wealth; poverty; identity; childhood; love; guilt; justice *etc.*).

- ○ These nouns can be written on cards so that they can be sorted and physically manipulated. Some cards will be relevant to the themes of the text, some less so.

- ○ Individually or in pairs, students can choose the 5 most relevant, the 5 least relevant and perhaps a middle category which have some relevance.

- ○ Students also have some blank cards onto which they can write any other themes which they feel have been missed. Their choices are then shared, explained and discussed.

- ○ As an extension or homework activity, students add at least one quotation or precise reference to the text which illustrates the theme. These can then be also shared.

## Exploring themes

Students need to use the text to gather evidence to support their discussion of the themes they have uncovered.

- • A **whole-class activity** could be used to capture a range of views on themes.

  - ○ Large sheets of paper are placed around the room with the theme written in the centre. Students circulate, adding any pertinent points from the text.

  - ○ The sheets are then divided between the class. The role of each group or individual is to think about their theme(s) more closely and to expand on (or dispute) the points already noted down (e.g. by looking for textual evidence) and to add any new ones they think of. (At this stage groups could be given some questions to guide their thinking).

  - ○ After a specified amount of time, the groups re-display their posters and students repeat stage one, adding anything which has occurred to them about the other themes during their own discussions and looking at what other groups have added. During this stage, students could pose questions about the themes on the posters, which the 'owners' of the poster then have to try to answer as an additional or homework activity.

  - ○ Posters could be swapped to continue the process or given to a different group to summarise the points made and share with the class.

  - ○ As a written exercise, students could be encouraged to write a paragraph (or more) starting: *The theme of X is important in Y because* …

- • **Mind maps** can be helpful in highlighting all references to a particular theme. It is useful to **categorise** how various aspects of the theme may be seen: in the characters; their situations; their relations with others; the action; the physical setting; the historical context, and also possibly in the symbolism, style and structure used. Using categories to organise the references can help to analyse **how** the author or dramatist uses and conveys the theme. Different groups could be given different categories to explore and report on.

- o Some pre-written sentences which fit into these categories could be given to students so that they have some core language from the start which they can then categorise and use as a model for writing their own additional sentences.

- It is important to consider the themes in relation to the **characters**. Each student is given a different character and asked to examine what role he or she plays in relation to the central theme.

  - o Do they embody it?
  - o Are they oppressed by it?
  - o Do they provide a contrast to it?
  - o What would the character say about the theme?
  - o Does it make them act in a certain way?
  - o How is this relationship described by the author?
  - o What influence does the character's portrayal have on the audience's under-standing of the theme?
  - o Can the student empathise with the character's position?

These questions can be adapted depending upon the nature of the theme.

- o An example could be the theme of loneliness in de Vigan's *No et moi*. Here the younger characters experience loneliness in different ways but it reveals some underlying similarities between their different family situations. Lou's parents also experience loneliness and this emotion can in part be said to drive every-one's actions. By looking at the theme in relation to each character in this way, new connections can be made between different aspects of the novel. Students can discuss their findings and any differences and similarities within the portrayals analysed.

- o Similarly, students could draw a mind map of the characters in Esquivel's *Como agua para chocolate*, with Tita in the centre and Pedro, Nacha, Mamá Elena, Gertrudis and Rosaura branching out from her. On each of the branches, the food-related incidents associated with each character could be marked, along with their consequences.

- o Written support can be offered by writing a couple of sentences about each character's situation in relation to the theme. Students then match these sentences with the relevant character and go on to extend the information given in a similar style.

- Initially it may be helpful to give students some **key passages** on which to base their discussions of a theme. Questions based on these passages can help to make a tricky theme seem more concrete. In König's *Ich fühl mich so fifty-fifty*, the themes of identity and personal liberty are central to the characters' dilemmas. Specific passages can support students to answer questions from different characters' perspective e.g. What does personal liberty mean? How important is personal liberty for happiness? Is family more important? What makes up your identity? Students can use textual evidence to answer in the persona of Thomas or Sabine. They can also offer their own **personal view** as they evaluate the characters' standpoints.

- A simple revision aid for students is to keep a **list of quotations** organised by theme.

- Students can also be encouraged to look at how **symbolism** (of place; language; action) reinforces particular themes.

## Making a judgement

Students may be asked to make a judgement about the author's portrayal of a particular theme. How convincing or how balanced does it appear? Some themes will be familiar to students, such as childhood, first love, loneliness, adolescence or friendship, whilst others may require them to think more deeply e.g. guilt, poverty, discrimination. Students should look closely at the text to find examples to support their judgement, and also, where possible, those which show the other side of the coin. These can be debated orally in class.

## Uncovering the message

Debate often surrounds what an author is trying to *say* to the audience.

- Why is this theme important?
- Is the author simply raising it or does he or she have a particular view that they are trying to convey?
- Is the author trying to change something or simply to reflect its existence?

Importantly, students should be careful not to claim too much. Their language should reflect that **interpretations** of an author's intentions or message are possibilities rather than statements of fact. This is a good opportunity to showcase the subjunctive mood! Of course, the author may simply be raising questions to provoke debate on an issue rather than offering solutions.

Clues to an author's views can be sought in **biographical** circumstances:

- There may be parallels with author's own life and upbringing (e.g. Joffo's *Un sac de billes*);
- The action may resonate with the author's contemporary context (e.g. Anouilh's *Antigone*).

There may also be some disagreement between the meanings ascribed to a work by others and those claimed or disclaimed by the author. Brecht's political beliefs on theatre are well documented (and he believed that theatre *can* change the world) and with modern authors, it is relatively easy to access interviews and commentaries by authors themselves. Some include commentaries with the book itself such as the *Nachwort* in Dürrenmatt's *Der Besuch der alten Dame* or Joffo's *Dialogue avec mes lecteurs* in *Un sac de billes*. In the former Dürrenmatt rejects any specific historical parallels or meanings with his work, despite interpretations to the contrary. Anouilh refused to comment on speculation that in *Antigone* (first performed in 1944), Créon represents the Nazis and Antigone the French Resistance. Of course, an author may hide or disclaim true meanings in a repressive or dangerous climate. For example, Lorca was killed by General Franco's regime in Spain shortly after finishing *La casa de Bernarda Alba*.

The author may signal his or her meaning include the **dramatic and stylistic techniques** used.

- The author or dramatist may *appear* to be speaking to the audience directly through the **narrator** or dramatic **Chorus.** This may also be artifice and should be analysed carefully.
- **Irony, parody and satire** are comic techniques used to expose human failings and wrong-doing. Brecht's theatrical *Verfremdungseffekt* is designed to make the audience critically engage with the atrocities of the actions on stage. Orgon is mocked for his slavish devotion to Molière's *Le Tartuffe*, leaving the audience in no doubt about its absurdity and Tartuffe's true hypocrisy. The damage that such folly can potentially wreak on the innocent is also spelled out beneath the humour.
- **Institutions** such as the popular press and the police in Böll's *Die verlorene Ehre der Katharina Blum* or the Church and Education in Dürrenmatt's *Der Besuch der alten Dame* may be criticised through their representation by weak or corrupt individuals.
- Characters may also appear to be the **author's mouthpiece** (e.g. Dorinne in *Le Tartuffe*). Students can be asked to decide who in a comedy is shown to be the voice of reason or good sense.

- Similarly, students can judge which characters are shown **sympathetically** or **critically**. Why is this? What do they represent?

- Once again, the key **oppositions** in the text bring to light the principal questions of the piece. In Schlink's *Der Vorleser*, Hanna and Michael's stories confront us with the tension between individual guilt during the Holocaust and the nation's collective responsibility for its horrors. In Hensel and König's works we see the contrast between life in East and West Germany and that the consequences of reunification may be problematic for teenagers from the East.

- **Symbolism** may be used to ascribe meaning and positive or negative views about characters and their conduct.

- How the play or novel **ends** may also indicate what the author wants the audience to reflect on. Are we left in hope or despair about the situation (and the world)? Are we satisfied that right has triumphed? Are we left with the sense that some problems are insoluble?

Students should evaluate how successful they feel the author has been in conveying a particular message.

## *Relevance and reception*

As part of their analysis, students can consider the relevance of the text and how it has been received and interpreted, both at the time of publication and today. These may be different, especially with works that were written in a different socio-historical context. In the 17th century, Molière's *Le Tartuffe* was banned by King Louis XIV for its critique of religious hypocrites. Sagan's *Bonjour tristesse* shocked its contemporary audience due to the overt sexuality of the teenage narrator (and the fact that the author herself was only 18) and spoke directly to the new social mores of the emerging post-war generation. French readers today would not experience the same shock at Cécile's exploits. In Ernaux's *La place*, one may ask if the resistance of Annie's father to education and social mobility still exists in some communities. Anouilh's *Antigone* (1944) debated loyalty to the state against individual morality during the Nazi occupation of France and Frisch's *Andorra* (1961) addresses antisemitism. Brecht's *Mutter Courage und ihre Kinder* is set during the 17th century but delivers a universal message against the horrors of war, inspired by the invasion of Poland at the beginning of World War II.

Students should evaluate how relevant the novel or play is today. Issues of adolescence, childhood, first love, heartbreak and loss are timeless and common to us all no matter the actual setting. Other topics may seem more remote, especially in unfamiliar settings. With a play, it is often possible to see a more contemporary production. For example, an English version of Molière's *Le Tartuffe* by Shakespeare at the Tobacco Factory in Bristol (Power and Hilton 2017) vividly transposed the play into a modern setting. If this is not possible, students can explore what could be changed to update a production and decide upon an appropriate modern day setting for *Antigone* or *Andorra*. Dürrenmatt's *Der Besuch der alten Dame* has the unspecified historical setting '*Gegenwart*' (the present) and an imaginary location. Students can give full rein to their imagination in the staging.

For novels, students may think of similar or parallel situations today.

- Are there settings where Jews are still persecuted or where minorities are discriminated against because of their faith? (Joffo's *Un sac de billes* where, tellingly, the plight of Joseph and Maurice replicates within the book the flight of their father from Russia a generation before.)
- How might it feel to live in a divided country such as North and South Korea? (König's *Ich fühl mich so fifty-fifty*).
- Are there societies today where women's roles are dictated by their position within the family and their marriage choices overruled by family considerations? (Esquivel's *Como agua para chocolate* and Lorca's *La casa de Bernarda Alba*.)
- What is it like to live in the inner-city immigrant communities in the UK and does the media fairly represent marginalised communities? (Guène's *Kiffe kiffe demain*; Begag's *Le Gone du Chaâba*.)

The reader's own interpretation of the text's themes and meaning should be discussed and may be required in the examination. The **reader-response approach** discussed in Chapter 2, shows us that meaning is ultimately co-constructed by the author and the reader. Students should be encouraged therefore to bring their own **personal meaning** to the text and be able to express this in writing. Indeed, if time allows, the question of personal relevance is an area which lends itself to the imaginative and creative responses discussed in Chapter 11.

Finally, the themes and meanings of a novel or play provide a rich area for **debate** (and may in some cases overlap with non-literary social and historical topics on the syllabus). Students might take two sides or aspects of the theme, such as the positive and negative consequences of love shown in Esquivel's *Como agua para chocolate* or the merits of life in the East versus life in the West in König's *Ich fühl mich so fifty-fifty*. The 'structured controversy' activity described in Chapter 4 could be used as preparation for a whole-class discussion or simulated 'Question Time' debate to ensure that all students have something to say.

# Style

When we think about the author's style, we are primarily asking students to analyse the decisions the author or playwright has made in order to achieve his or her purpose, and the desired (or perhaps unintended) effect on the reader or audience. Students may be encouraged to think about the creation of the novel or play as a series of decisions beginning with the very format in which to **tell the story**, how the telling of the story is **organised** and the **language** which is chosen to create the mood and texture of the narrative. By asking students to notice and discuss these choices, they can be guided towards a deeper understanding of the text and its intentions, and of the writer's craft. It also reinforces the appreciation that the novel or drama is a **construction** which, given different choices, could have taken on a different form.

## *Choosing the genre and setting the tone*

Sartre and Camus wrote both plays and novels. So why is *Les mains sales* a drama and *L'étranger* in prose? Similarly, why does the novelist Dürrenmatt write *Der Besuch der alten Dame* as a play? Could the same stories have been written in another form?

- Students could be challenged to imagine and sketch out how the novel or short story could be transposed for the theatre and *vice versa* (this process happens when books are made into films). If time allows, an interesting creative exercise can be undertaken where students choose either an act or scene or a passage or chapter and actually do this.

- In small groups, students could list the advantages and constraints of the existing format compared to those of the other medium. They may consider factors such as length, geographical and historical setting and staging, the nature of the story, its complexity and how to communicate it and the characters to the reader or audience. Which works best, description or direct portrayal?

- Ultimately students should be able to express **why** the author may have decided upon the particular format.

The author has also chosen to treat his or her theme or story in a particular way. He or she has **chosen** to write a tragedy, a comedy, a tragicomedy, a satire or parody, a romance, an autobiographical account or fiction.

- Once again, students consider if any other approach would have been possible and discuss **why** they feel this genre has been chosen. Molière's *Le Tartuffe* for example is a comedy which ends happily but could equally have been written as a tragedy had Tartuffe not been exposed as a charlatan.

Linked to genre, students can consider the overall **tone** of the studied work. Is it optimistic or pessimistic; joyful or sad; epic or small scale; local or universal; impersonal and detached or personal and involved? Does it represent a real world or a fantasy world? Do these different tones intermingle? (See Hares 1984.)

- Students may be asked to decide which adjectives best describe the tone (either from a set of cards or along a continuum from optimistic to pessimistic *etc.* as described in Chapter 8 *The character continuum*).

- They may identify passages or scenes where the tone changes (for example, between the comic and the tragic in Dürrenmatt's *Der Besuch der alten Dame* or between joy and sadness in Pagnol's *Le château de ma mère* or between the realistic and fantasy elements in Ruiz Zafón's *La sombra del viento*). This could be marked using a 'timeline' of scenes or chapters.

  ○ Students consider **why** these changes of tone occur and what effect they have on the reader or audience.

## Literary movement

The author may be writing within a particular literary tradition or school of thought. Examples may include magic realism of Allende in *La casa de los espíritus* or Esquivel's *Como agua para chocolate;* the *Verfremdunseffekt* of Brecht's epic theatre or the philosophical influences on Camus of Existentialism. When looking at drama this is often important, as Dürrenmatt's *Der Besuch der alten Dame* for example draws on epic theatre traditions, Brechtian principles and those of classical Greek tragedy. Lorca was part of the *Generación del 27* group of authors when writing *La casa de Bernarda Alba* and *Bodas de sangre*. It is important for students to know the basic precepts of any movement with which the author was aligned, but their focus should remain firmly on the text itself when answering examination questions.

- Once the principles have been explained, students can be helped to understand by being given selected passages to discuss. They can then identify examples from other passages and scenes and discuss how these have shaped the text.

  ○ What was the author trying to achieve by using this technique?

  ○ What effect does it have on the audience?

- If time allows, students could improvise a scene using the technique to achieve the same effect.

All these form part of the background to understanding the author's style. The author must then decide, influenced by these ideas, how to structure the story.

## Narrative voice

Students should understand that what they are reading or watching on stage has been shaped in a very particular way by the author. The events and characters may or may not be based on fact, but they are still presented via the lens of the author or dramatist. Additionally, in a novel, the narrator (if not the author) may add a second filter for the reader. Often this involves the audience being manipulated to respond in a particular way.

- A simple exercise can help to demonstrate to students how any account, even a factual one, is shaped by the teller. A version of an exercise carried out by Kramsch (1993) could be recreated by staging a simple interaction at the start of the lesson. A colleague enters the room, whispers something to the teacher, picks up some papers, drops one and leaves again. Students are given 5 minutes to write down what happened and then compare their accounts. (It may be worth doing this in English as the versions will differ more than if constrained by using the target language). Some students may have been purely factual in their reports, whilst others will have been more descriptive; some may have speculated about what was said or the purpose of the visit *etc.* No two accounts will be exactly the same and may give different impressions of the incident if recounted to someone who had not been present. Questions about what was prioritised and what was left out of the students' accounts start to show them that when we write, choices are always being made. This is a prelude to discussing **why** these decisions were made.
- Alternatively, students could also be asked to stage a scene from the novel or play for filming. Once they have to make directorial decisions about props and lighting, camera angles and close-ups *etc.*, they see how these choices can significantly influence how the scene (and its meaning) are conveyed to the audience.
  - Comparing a passage from a novel with how it is portrayed in film also illustrates this. Watching clips of the same scene from two different productions of a play has the same effect.

Students must analyse **how** their text is told and by whom. When dealing with a novel or short story the following questions are useful to explore with students.

- Who is telling the story?
- Is it the author, a character or a third person narrator?

- Is it always the same person or are there multiple narrators?
- Is it written in the first (I) or third (he/she) person?
- What **effect** is created by the chosen form of narration?

*First person narration*

Students should explore the significance and **effect** of a story which is told in the first person. Ideas to consider include the following.

- It may stress the autobiographical nature of the work (if the author is the narrating character as in Joffo's *Un sac de billes*);
- It may create empathy or closeness with the character and privilege his or her point of view as the action is seen through his or her eyes; (for example the continual interior monologue in Guène's *Kiffe kiffe demain* strengthens Doria's voice and opinions as she communicates directly with the reader);
- It may make the narrative seem more accessible (especially through the simpler, direct speech of a teenager in Guène's *Kiffe kiffe demain* or through the use of the present tense in de Vigan's *No et moi*);
- It may give the character-cum-narrator the opportunity to look back from a (wiser) standpoint as with Cécile in Sagan's *Bonjour tristesse*;
- It may be used to generalise beyond the character, for example, Jana Hensel uses the first person plural *'wir'* in the autobiographical *Zonenkinder*;
- Long monologues or direct asides to the audience may replicate some of the effects of first person narration in a drama and their purpose and effect can also be explored.

*Third person narration*

Similarly, students can consider the effect of third person narration. The narrator should not be immediately equated with the author's voice, for he or she is a device used by the author to tell the story. However, in some autobiographical novels, the narrator may represent the voice of the author in telling his or her own story.

- It may create (the illusion of) neutrality and objectivity in the account;
- It may create distance between the narrator and the characters and action;
- It may allow the author to pass comment on the action;

- In a classical play, the Chorus may take the role of the narrator and address the audience directly, often telling them what to think (for example the Chorus in Anouilh's *Antigone*) Students can consider the effect of addressing the audience directly.

Techniques such as the use of letters may create another type of narrative voice. In König's *Ich fühl mich so fifty-fifty*, Thomas and Sabine use letters to communicate once separated. This bypasses the narrator and allows the teenagers to narrate the historical events from a direct personal perspective.

## Trustworthiness

Students should also consider whether the narrator is reliable and trustworthy. An autobiographical author may be expected to recount events largely as seen from his or her perspective, but perhaps, like Hensel in *Zonenkinder*, he or she can also show some broader understanding from an adult perspective. An author may be very open about his or her (moral) stance or bias, or this bias may be hidden. The narrator in Böll's *Die verlorene Ehre der Katharina Blum* may claim impartiality but reveals bias in the way incidents and emotions are depicted. Michael, the first person narrator in Schlink's *Der Vorleser* does not confront many of the issues relating to his relationship with Hanna and her past. Of course, the narrator may not be in full possession of the facts or may have an interest in concealing or misrepresenting them. Students can consider whether the narrator has a reason to be biased.

Exploring these narrative styles can help students to focus on why the author has made certain narrative decisions and how these affect the audience.

- The effects of a first versus third person narrator on the reader can be demonstrated by taking a passage and rewriting it in the other mode. This also tests students' ability to manipulate verbs and pronouns. For example, the second paragraph of de Vigan's *No et moi* could be rewritten in the third person from when Lucas smiles at Lou.

- In a passage where the narrator is talking about a character, students could underline words and phrases in different colours to ascertain whether descriptions are positive, negative or unbiased.

- It is also interesting for students to consider who else could tell the story and what might change if a different character were the narrator.

## *Use of language*

Students should explore the **type** of language used by the author or dramatist. They should try to characterise the language as, for example,

- archaic or modern;
- detailed or impressionistic;
- simple or complex;
- formal or informal;
- erudite (often containing references to other literature) or down to earth.

As language can be seen as a way of reflecting identity, the way someone speaks can be a key part of their characterisation.

- Hensel (*Zonenkinder*) uses culturally specific language from her childhood in East Germany to stress her difference from the West and distance the reader.
- Regional variations can also be identified (e.g. Colombian Spanish in García Márquez's *El coronel no tiene quien le escriba* and Provençal accents in Pagnol's *Le château de ma mère*).
- The *verlan* in Guène's *Kiffe kiffe demain* captures Doria's voice and the idiom of teenagers in König's *Ich fühl mich so fifty-fifty* privileges their perspective, despite the third person narration.

Language can also be a way of confusing and distancing the audience, and alienation techniques can be seen in Dürrenmatt's *Der Besuch der alten Dame* which uses advertising clichés, antiquated vocabulary and strange repetitions of words to discomfort the audience. Brecht's use of songs (e.g. in *Mutter Courage und ihre Kinder*) can also be investigated.

- As a linguistic exercise, students could rewrite into formal French some of Doria's narration (Guène's *Kiffe kiffe demain*). This would give students the opportunity to focus on slang words and on how negative sentences are 'misformed' in colloquial speech.
- In Pagnol's *Le château de ma mère*, Lili's letter to Marcel (which emphasises his lack of formal education) could be corrected by students as a language exercise.

### *Language techniques*

Authors and dramatists use a range of stylistic devices in their writing. This area of language can be quite technical and it is generally not expected that students will

155

write at length on this subject. However, they can be aware of noteworthy aspects of the author's style. Teachers who wish to explore this in more depth can research the key stylistic features of the text and author studied (study guides will usually do this in ample detail) and then identify relevant extracts to use with students. In poetry, stylistic features are of greater importance and more specialist work here would be worthwhile (see Further reading).

Most importantly, students should be able to explain the **effect** created by a particular use of language and **why** it serves the writer's purpose. A clear **example** from the text is important to illustrate this in the examination. When asking students to look at style, simple **concrete** tasks can be the most effective (Hill 1986). This could be underlining words in a passage or counting features *e.g.* the number of adjectives as opposed to nouns, or words with three or more syllables.

- Students prepare a passage at home to focus on *language* use rather than content. Depending on the focus of the passage, students are asked to underline various features.

   o They use different colours to underline verbs and adjectives (or adverbs, pronouns, proper names *etc.*) This will help them to see if the paragraph is largely action or description.

   o In a descriptive passage, students underline the words which are strictly necessary for the story and then analyse those which remain. What is their purpose? What mood do they create? In short stories, students may note an author's economical or concise style, painting a picture in a few words.

   o In a poetic passage, students can underline all the figurative language and identify imagery, metaphors and similes. Are these effective in creating mood? Do they express an idea more powerfully, vividly or concisely? What effect do they have on the reader or audience? Do they unsettle or reassure the reader?

   o In a novel such as Pagnol's *Le château de ma mère*, where descriptions of the landscape are so important, students could choose their own favourite and then share the reasons for their choice with the class. This will encourage them to think about the effect of the language on them as the reader.

- In a novel or short story, the presentation of the **characters' speech** and thought affects the pace and rhythm of the narrative. The characters may speak directly in their own voice so that the text is broken up with dialogue in speech marks or their speech may be reported indirectly. This will make the characters seem more or less close to the reader. One may also note whether characterisation is mainly shown through characters' actions, their words or descriptions of them.

- o As a language exercise, students could transpose a short passage of indirect speech into direct speech to be read or acted out (or it could be written as speech bubbles!). Similarly, the opposite could be tried.
- o If students read aloud both versions, they may see the effect of direct versus indirect speech on the pace and energy of the passage.

- An audio version of a passage (or reading aloud) can also help students to understand the rhythm of the language and draw their attention to short and long sentences, short and long words, alliteration, assonance, repetition *etc.* What is the purpose of the effect? In plays students could decide how the form fits the content, for example using short lines to create a fast pace in a dramatic moment of activity or a long monologue to allow characters time for reflection.

- A gapped text or cloze exercise can be used to draw attention to a particular linguistic feature. Students try to replace the adjectives *etc.* either with or without the support of the original words initially. This is particularly useful with poetry or rhyme.

## *Symbolism*

Symbolism is an important feature which can be used to reveal hidden meanings and highlight the themes of the play or novel. It can also give the text a poetic quality. Symbolism (such as heat and cold, food as love and medicine in Esquivel's *Como agua para chocolate*; colours in Colette's *Le blé en herbe*) can provide cohesion within a text.
Symbolism may be found in many areas of the text.

- Titles (such as Colette's *Le blé en herbe* or Esquivel's *Como agua para chocolate*);
- Settings (Esquivel's *Como agua para chocolate* is set during the Mexican Revolution where the combatants are struggling for social change and freedom just as Tita is fighting against her mother's tyranny);
- Names (of the characters in Lorca's *La casa de Bernarda Alba*);
- Recurrent motifs of objects or actions (washing in Schlink's *Der Vorleser* and whitewashing in Frisch's *Andorra*);
- Characters themselves may be symbols or ciphers and simply represent institutions (e.g. Frisch's *Andorra* and Dürrenmatt's *Der Besuch der alten Dame*);
- Ideas may be used metaphorically as well as literally such as Michael's illness and Hanna's illiteracy in Schlink's *Der Vorleser* and Gregor's transformation into an insect in Kafka's *Die Verwandlung*.

- Groups of students can follow different images throughout the play or novel and then report back on their possible meaning and value within the narrative.

### Use of humour

The use of humour in plays (e.g. farce, satire, irony and parody) has been discussed in Chapter 7, but humour can also be present in novels. Satire can be used to show up hypocrisy and human failings and reinforce the theme of the novel (e.g. Voltaire's *Candide*).

Features which may indicate humour include paradox or irony, understatement or exaggeration, caricature and parody, slapstick and farce *etc*. The humour may be affectionate and gentle (e.g. Pagnol's childhood exploits with Lili in *Le château de ma mère*) or more vicious and dark (e.g. the wreaths which keep arriving to signal Ill's impending death in Dürrenmatt's *Der Besuch der alten Dame*). In *Zonenkinder*, Hensel's sense of humour may be used to offset the sadder elements she describes such as the loss of her homeland. Similarly, Doria in Guène's *Kiffe kiffe demain* and Josyane in Rochefort's *Les petits enfants du siècle* see humour in their difficult situations. Again, students need to consider **why** the author or dramatist may have decided to use humour and what it contributes to the play or novel and what the writer was trying to achieve, maybe in terms of theme, characterisation or appeal to the audience or reader.

# Structure

Students should be able to recall the events of the novel or play accurately and suggestions for helping students get to grips with the plot of the novel or play may be found in Chapters 6 and 7. When analysing a text however, students should also be aware that **how** the author or dramatist chooses to structure the telling of the story will significantly influence the nature and impact of the finished work. In this section, we focus on the techniques the author uses to organise the action and what effect these may be designed to create.

## Narrative structure

### Chapters and acts

Students should note how the author or playwright divides the action. This may be into traditional chapters in a novel or acts and scenes in a play. Deviations from the norm are interesting and prompt the question of what the author is trying to achieve. Questions for students to consider include:

- Are the chapters given titles and what effect does this have?

  In Esquivel's *Como agua para chocolate* each chapter bears the name of a month and is preceded by a recipe. This nomenclature subverts the actual timescale of the novel and the recipe emphasises the symbolic nature of food in the story.

- Are there sections which stand outside the main action of the book?

  For example, what is the purpose of the prologue or epilogue? In Pagnol's *Le château de ma mère*, the final pages are set fifteen years after the story of Marcel's childhood.

- Is the action unbroken?

  In Anouilh's *Antigone*, the usual structure of acts and scenes is ignored. The prologue stresses the inevitability of the action which follows.

## Classical unities

The classical unities of time, place and action suggest other ways of looking at text construction. The unities were in part derived from Aristotle's *Poetics*, but were developed by French neoclassical dramatists of the 17th century. Racine's tragedies and Molière's comedies tried to present action which unfurled within a period of 24 hours, in one place and avoiding plots which were subsidiary to the main dramatic action.

Students can think about the novel or play in terms of the **timespan** over which the action takes place, whether the **setting** is constrained or expansive and whether there is one dominant **plotline**. If there are many subplots, what is their effect on the novel or play? Lengthy novels such as Ruiz Zafón's *La sombra del viento* or Allende's *La casa de los espíritus* which also cover a span of history are in contrast to the effect created by the constrained world and focused plot of Sagan's *Bonjour tristesse* or Kafka's *Die Verwandlung*.

## Time

How the author uses time is of particular importance and students can consider the following questions.

- What timespan does the narrative cover?
- Are the events presented in chronological order?
- Does time progress consistently or does the action leap forward, leaving irregular gaps between episodes?
- If the events are not presented chronologically, what techniques are used and why?

In König's *Ich fühl mich so fifty-fifty* a **flashforward** (prolepsis) technique is used in the first chapter to the point of Sabine's later escape. In Anouilh's *Antigone*, the Chorus spells out for the audience how the drama will end. Does this heighten tension or diminish it?

Authors may also make use of **flashback** (analepsis), where preceding action is revealed, such as in Sartre's *Les mains sales*. Students can consider whether a non-linear narrative is confusing or informative for the reader e.g. García Márquez's *Crónica de una muerte anunciada*. In Esquivel's *Como agua para chocolate*, the monthly structure is subverted by the timescale of the events in each chapter.

Students can also note where the narrator stands in relation to the chronology of the action. In Sagan's *Bonjour tristesse*, Cécile is the narrator who at the beginning is looking back over the events of the summer. In *Zonenkinder*, Hensel is relating events of her life, which have a chronology of pre- and post- German reunification, but she chooses to organise the chapters and her memories thematically.

- In order to illustrate where events are not told chronologically, a **timeline** can prove helpful, both to clarify the plot and to illustrate the structure.

  o Key events are written on cards and students have two timelines of the action. On the first timeline (which is divided into chapters), the events are ordered as they are in the text. On the second timeline, time is marked chronologically and students arrange the events in the order they actually happened. Students consider why non-linear time has been chosen by the author and for what purpose?

## Beginnings and endings

Two important aspects of a text's structure are how it starts and how it finishes. Students can discuss the purpose of the introductory scene of a play or the start of a novel and how successful they judge the beginning of their text to be. Purposes may include:

- setting the scene;
- meeting the characters;
- creating interest in the story;
- setting the tone;
- preparing the readers or audience for what is to come.

Students can work in groups with their text to discuss:

- what the reader or audience is told;
- what they are not told;

- what questions are raised for the reader or audience;
- what expectations are established;
- how successful they consider the opening.

Where specific techniques are used such as the Prologue in Anouilh's *Antigone* where the plot is laid out in advance for the audience or when Molière delays *Le Tartuffe's* entrance on stage until the third act, students can discuss the reasons for this and the effect on the audience.

Students should also explore what they expect from the *dénouement* or ending of a story. Should it offer a tidy resolution of the action or is an open ending more interesting? Should good triumph and evil be defeated? Is a happy ending more satisfying or simply unrealistic? Does the author intend us to learn something (and if so what?)?

Students ask themselves how they would categorise the end of the novel or play they are studying and how it has made them feel. Once again, they may find it helpful to evaluate their response against pairs of adjectives *e.g.*

- realistic or unrealistic;
- ambiguous or clear;
- inevitable or avoidable;
- satisfying or unsatisfying;
- powerful or anticlimactic;
- shocking or unmoving;
- uplifting or depressing.

One aspect of the dramatic climax of a narrative is the point at which the ending becomes inevitable. Students can decide if this is so, and at what point that became the case. Tackling this question helps them to understand characters' motivations and the significance of events.

- Students could draw a flow diagram (or timeline) of the events (and protagonist's characteristics) which led to the final *dénouement*.
  - They discuss what was 'the point of no return' (if indeed the outcome was inevitable) and why.
  - Students list ways in which a different outcome could have been possible, *i.e.* which events would have needed to change. This works well for tragic outcomes *e.g.* Hanna's suicide in Schlink's *Der Vorleser;* Adela's suicide in Lorca's *La casa de Bernarda Alba;* the deaths of Hugo and Hoederer in Sartre's *Les mains sales* and of *Andri* in Frisch's *Andorra.*

    ○   As support, students could be given a list of statements to prioritise along the lines of 'Andri's death could have been avoided if, … [Der Lehrer had never said he was a Jew]' *etc.* (*cf.* Collie and Slater 1987). They could also write their own sentences based on a model.

### *Alternative scenarios*

- If time allows, students can be challenged to rewrite the ending of the novel or play (in the style of the author). This can be a free choice or alternatively they can each be given an adjective which must fit their ending e.g. 'comic'; 'tragic'; 'shocking'.

    ○   These can be read or enacted to the rest of the group and the preferred alternative ending chosen.

## *Plot arcs*

Teachers may find referring back to the discussion of dramatic structure in Chapter 7 useful. It is important for students to analyse the start of the text (the exposition or setting the scene) then to explore how the plot evolves, rising to a climax before the resolution or dénouement. The rise in tension in Molière's *Le Tartuffe* is dramatic and the dénouement comes about through the introduction of a *Deus ex machina*. In Böll's *Die verlorene Ehre der Katharina Blum*, tension is never far from the surface but the pressure on Katharina mounts to a climax when she confronts and shoots the journalist, Tötges, in her flat. Students can show the plot arc as a chart, with a timeline on which critical events are noted.

## Conclusion

The focus of this chapter has been quite wide, dealing with the themes, style and structure of the text. In suggesting ways of uncovering and exploring the main themes, both in themselves and in relation to the characters, we have tried to suggest ways of developing students' knowledge and sensitivities. Students have also been encouraged to uncover the author's message and to explore both the reception of the text when it was written and its relevance for today. Students should also have some appreciation of how the author has crafted the text and be able to identify and comment on some of the stylistic and structural devices used.

# Further reading

Teachers may also find the *Literature Glossary* available on the Edexcel A level Modern Languages website very useful for explaining **technical terms** for form, structure and style in English.

Maley and Duff (1989) and Duff and Maley (2007) have sections on exploiting various linguistic features of **poetry** with examples from the English second language teaching classroom. Paran and Robinson (2016) give examples of second language approaches (using English language poems) which could be adapted to a modern languages context.

Hares (1984) gives examples of **poetic style and devices** from French literature if teachers wish to look more deeply into technical aspects of verse form, rhyme, vocabulary and figures of speech.

# Implications for teaching

- Ensure that students can identify the key themes of the text and give clear examples to support this.
- Enable students to uncover the author's background and beliefs and the socio-historical context of the work.
- Encourage students to keep a list of quotations organised by theme.
- Discuss how themes are presented by the author and what he or she may be trying to convey.
- Promote collaborative learning and interactive exercises to help students share and develop their ideas and think about the themes from a personal perspective.
- Enable students to develop a good understanding of narrative voice.
- Focus time in class on discussing key passages and make use of available audio and video materials if appropriate.
- Allow students to consider the stylistic and structural choices made by the author and identify noteworthy examples.

# References

Collie, J. and Slater, S., 1987. *Literature in the Language Classroom: A Resource Book of Ideas and Activities*. Cambridge: Cambridge University Press.

Duff, A. and Maley, A., 2007. *Literature*. 2nd ed. Oxford: Oxford University Press.

Hares, R., 1984. *Compo Lit! French Literature Essay-Writing*. London: Hodder & Stoughton.

Hill, J., 1986. *Using Literature in Language Teaching*. London: Macmillan.

Kramsch, C., 1993. *Context and Culture in Language Teaching*. Oxford: Oxford University Press.

Maley, A. and Duff, A., 1989. *The Inward Ear: Poetry in the Language Classroom*. Cambridge: Cambridge University Press.

Paran, A. and Robinson, P., 2016. *Literature*. Oxford: Oxford University Press.

Power, D. and Hilton, A., 2017. *Tartuffe: After Molière*. 2nd revised edition. Bristol: Favell & Marsden, in association with Shakespeare at the Tobacco Factory.

# 10 Writing the examination essay

## Introduction

In one respect, the endpoint of the A level course is the examination essay when students are judged on their ability to **discuss and analyse** the text they have studied in the **target language**. By this stage they will:

- be familiar with the text and its meaning;
- be able to demonstrate their understanding of themes, characters and plot;
- present arguments which analyse, rather than simply describe these elements;
- respond critically to the text, and offer a personal perspective;
- support their arguments with concrete examples from the text;
- express themselves coherently and appropriately in the target language.

However, learning how to bring all the elements of their knowledge together whilst writing under examination conditions represents an important challenge for students.

This chapter looks at the specific requirements of the A level written examination and suggests activities which teachers can use to prepare students to meet these with confidence. It introduces ideas for the period of examination **revision** and for use by students in the **examination** itself. The longer-term process of **developing writing skills** throughout the A level course is also discussed.

## The examination essay: the specific requirements

When first preparing to teach the literature element of the course, teachers will familiarise themselves with the examination requirements. These will shape the teaching programme and should be shared with students early in the course. All examination boards make a significant amount of material available online before and after each examination session explaining what the examiners are looking for from candidates. Requirements do **change** and so checking communications from the Board and regularly online is essential. Signing up for **email alerts** and following the subject advisor on **social media** (e.g. on Twitter or blog) is a good way to keep up to date.

The following analysis of these requirements relates directly to the current A level syllabus used in England, but the broader principles discussed may be applied more generally to preparing students for literature examinations. Requirements are slightly different for candidates taking WJEC and CCEA examinations in Wales and Northern Ireland where currently one essay is written at AS (literature or film) and one at A2 (literature only).

- All examination boards offer a choice of two questions for each text studied.

- Teachers may opt for one literary text and one film, or two literary texts. (In the case of AS, just **one** text or film is required)

- Depending upon the Board, each essay should be between approximately 300 and 350 (AS 250–300) words in length.

## The mark scheme

The exact mark scheme at A level varies between Boards (AQA and Eduqas 40 marks; Edexcel 50 marks per essay as an additional 10 marks are awarded specifically for accuracy). Marks are awarded for language and content in line with the Assessment Objectives AO3 (Manipulate the language accurately, in written form, using a range of lexis and structure) and AO4 (Show knowledge and understanding of, and respond critically and analytically to, different aspects of the culture and society of countries/communities where the language is spoken). The respective mark schemes for AS and A level highlight the expectation of an **analytical** (as well as critical) response at the higher level (see Ofqual 2016 pp.12–14).

### Language

In relation to **language (AO3)**, the various examination boards differ slightly, but consider essays broadly against the following criteria:

- **complexity of grammatical structure** (including length of sentence and use of idiom);

- **range of vocabulary** (high frequency words and phrases will score less well).

Further exemplified are:

- use of appropriate **literary terminology**;
- **fluency** of writing (on a scale from stilted to articulate);
- use of appropriate **style and register**.

The most successful students will therefore be consistent in their ability to write articulately, showing a range of expression. They demonstrate that they can manipulate the language in order to express themselves clearly and develop cogent arguments.

**Accuracy** is an interesting element. For Edexcel, a separate mark grid assesses accuracy along a scale of **coherence** and **clarity of communication**. The essay must read well and be unambiguous in the *message* it communicates. Errors are categorised in terms of those which do not hinder clarity (*e.g.* gender and agreements), those which do hinder clarity (*i.e.* where the reader has to work out exactly what is being said) and those which prevent the understanding of the intended message. This last category can be caused by incorrect verb agreement or tense or may be due to interference from English words and structures. For the Eduqas and AQA boards, errors are considered more in terms of both **frequency** and **seriousness**. However, which errors are deemed serious does vary between boards and so it is wise to study these closely. The same applies to what constitutes articulate or complex language according to the chosen board.

In preparing candidates for success in the examination therefore, teachers will wish to focus attention on:

- avoiding serious grammatical errors *and*
- correctly using complex constructions.

Where the balance between the two lies will depend on individual students but helping students to **write clearly** is of great importance: within the mark scheme, significant marks are lost when grammatical errors obscure meaning. This can arise when students attempt constructions which are overly complex or, when they translate their thoughts directly and inappropriately, from English into the foreign language.

# Grammar

To avoid serious errors, students should pay attention to the following:

- correct verb forms (especially irregular ones);
- correct use of pronouns;
- correct use of prepositions following verbs;

- correct agreement of adjectives or past participles (especially where meaning is altered);
- correct use of common idiomatic expressions;
- correct use of case endings (German);
- correct word order in main and subordinate clauses (German).

Within each language there will be particular areas of focus to work on.

# Complex language

Complex language includes tenses such as the pluperfect and future perfect, the passive voice, the subjunctive mood, the use of relative pronouns and the use of conjunctions and pronouns in sentences to express abstract ideas or build complex reasoned arguments. Candidates are also rewarded for avoiding repetition by using synonyms and a range of expressions.

Elements of complex language to focus on therefore include:

- the use of all types of pronouns;
- tenses which suggest conceptual complexity;
- connectives which support a range of subordinate clauses, including those requiring the subjunctive;
- constructions involving the correct preposition for verbs and verbs followed by the infinitive;
- present and past participles.

## *Content*

In terms of **critical and analytical response (AO4)**, marks here are awarded according to the essay's:

- **relevance** to the question;
- reference to the **social context, issues and themes** of the work studied;
- demonstration of **logical argument linked to conclusions**;
- selection of **appropriate evidence** from the text to support arguments;
- overall **critical interpretation** and **evaluation**, offering **points of view** rather than simple description.

High scoring essays are those which offer a **logical argument** which answers the **precise question** set and which use **detailed evidence** from the text to support the points made. Essays which are simply discussions of the text in general or which rely on story-telling rather than analysis will be heavily penalised. Candidates must demonstrate these additional skills in order to do themselves and their ideas justice.

# Developing writing throughout the teaching programme: principles and practice

Before looking at specific examination practice exercises, it is helpful to consider how post-GCSE students develop their writing abilities earlier in the A level course. Much of Year 12 teaching is concerned with bridging the gap between students' GCSE knowledge and the demands of A level. Typically, the starting points of individual students can be very different in terms of their grammatical understanding, range of vocabulary and general confidence in writing. These elements must be built up gradually alongside the ability to develop opinions about a work of literature, or a film, and express these in the target language using the appropriate register.

It is worth noting that the 'critical and analytical' writing required in the A level examination is the most difficult type of writing for students (in both their first and second languages). **Descriptive** and **narrative** writing will have been reasonably familiar to students at GCSE, but '*expository* writing' (that which is explanatory or argumentative) is both new and significantly more challenging (Macaro 2003 p.225). Understanding this progression allows teachers to design writing tasks which gradually increase in difficulty. This additional challenge can be offset by the **support** given to students. For example, the quality of students' responses to a written task has been shown to improve if they are given suggestions for *vocabulary* along with the title, and to improve still further if they are given an *exemplar* to act as a model (Macaro 2003). This is useful to bear in mind when first introducing students to essay writing, and when considering differentiation for individual students. AS level examination papers follow this pattern by offering bullet points of suggested content for the essays.

Experience of working with effective writers can also offer basic principles to support students in developing their writing generally, before tackling the specific demands of the examination situation.

## *Write from the start*

Research shows that starting to write early is important (e.g. Macaro 2003; Gordon 2008). It is not advisable to wait until they have read the full text before expecting students to write about it. Suggestions in previous chapters identify **short and**

**regular, ongoing writing tasks** such as snowball synopses and character studies through which students become accustomed to putting their thoughts about the text down on paper. Writing can in fact be satisfying as it helps students to develop and organise their thoughts about what they are reading. These supported and short-term goals all build students' confidence with writing and can gradually reduce students' fear of the examination essay.

Starting with **familiar types of tasks** (e.g. letters, character profiles) can also build confidence. Graham (1997) suggests leaving writing full essays until much later in the course for the additional reason that this is more likely to discourage the tendency of learners to try to simply translate what they want to say word for word from English. **Creative or imaginative tasks** also have a role to play in getting students writing (see Chapter 11 for suggestions).

Encouraging students to write about the text from the **perspective of their own experience** can help to make the task less daunting. Through this approach, students develop their relationship with the text and are reassured of the validity of their own points of view (Chambers 1991).

Harnessing students' **IT and media skills** may prove motivating and reassuring. For example, using Microsoft Publisher or other desktop publishing packages to create leaflets or posters about an author or aspect of a text or its background, exploits a familiar method of composition for many students. Editing is also easier on an electronic document.

**Open-ended and optional tasks** can help to stretch the most able candidates as studies identify that effective writers are those who look for opportunities to practise their writing outside the classroom in order to develop their range of vocabulary and use of structures (Gordon 2008). The principle of increased support for more challenging tasks is worth remembering here.

## Speak first

As identified in previous chapters, **oral discussions** can be an important precursor to writing. Interactive activities which allow students to practise the language of argumentation and persuasion can help students to write as ideas have already been formulated and road tested.

## Develop vocabulary

This is not only important in the A level mark scheme, but for students' writing development overall. Research indicates that vocabulary knowledge correlates with the quality to writing produced (Macaro 2003) and that effective writers also read widely (Gordon 2008). The process of **reading** the text itself should be instrumental in developing students' vocabulary (and it is important that teachers ensure that students actively work on this throughout the course).

Additionally, reading in the target language around the text (**articles, reviews** etc.) should be encouraged for students aiming to maximise their grades. Some students may wish to set up Google alerts for relevant new articles and teachers and students could use a tool such as **Pinterest** to post useful additional reading within the group. Pinterest or other such tools could also act as an electronic, personalised scrapbook for a student's own reading.

Guidance on how to use the more advanced functions of a bilingual (and/or monolingual) **dictionary** during this reading can reinforce the value for students of a dictionary as a support for their own writing. Ideas for developing vocabulary more systematically, with emphasis on register and literary terminology, may be found later in this chapter.

## *Share the secret*

Finding out how students tackle the various stages of (essay) writing is an important element of strategy training and can offer pointers for how they can be helped to improve. Simply encouraging students to think about their own writing habits can be beneficial and discussion of *learners'* **experiences and practices** can help both teacher and students to see different, and perhaps more effective, ways to write.

Most students will also benefit from having *clear and specific guidance* from the teacher about how to write the essay. This is a feature of the **genre approach** to teaching writing (Gordon 2008). This approach emphasises the importance of understanding the purpose and context of a type of written task and its necessary linguistic features (e.g. register) and structure. A model or 'expert' text (*i.e.* a sample essay) is first discussed and dissected by students. The teacher then explains the conventions which underpin its construction and supports students to replicate this themselves. (The **process approach** to writing stresses the importance of learning to write through a recursive cycle of drafting and review following feedback. Both techniques can successfully combine to help inexperienced writers understand what they are aiming for and how to get there when faced with unfamiliar tasks.)

Studies have consistently highlighted however, that students may not have been **explicitly taught** effective ways to approach writing an essay. It is probable that they have actually covered this in English lessons but may not transfer this knowledge to the second language context. This may be particularly true of students who have not continued with essay-based subjects at A level. It is also important to remember that ways of working must be modelled and reinforced **over a period of time** before they become embedded into a student's practice.

An effective strategy for explaining and reinforcing all aspects of the writing process is undoubtedly **teacher guided shared writing.** In this whole class activity the teacher starts to compose on the whiteboard whilst explaining aloud his or her thought processes. In this way, students are shown the decisions that an 'expert' writer makes about how content and language are used to complete the task. After several sentences, the teacher then acts as a scribe whilst students offer suggestions for continuing the composition. The think-aloud discussion continues as the suggestions are reviewed and refined collectively. Students can then go on to complete the task in smaller groups and eventually, individually. This type of group composition can build confidence and support less experienced writers by demystifying the writing process. **Collaborative writing** is indeed generally recognised as an important tool in developing students' individual writing (see Hedge 2000; Adams with Panter 2001) and suggestions for other exercises based on this principle are included later in the chapter.

## Be strategic

In Chapter 6 the value of teaching reading strategies throughout the course was discussed. Strategy training also plays an important role in developing students' written skills (e.g. Harris 1997; Graham and Macaro 2007). Useful strategies may focus on how to organise the writing process, how to deal with linguistic difficulties and how to monitor, evaluate and ultimately improve what has been written. In order to develop independence therefore, students need to be *taught* both cognitive and metacognitive skills.

Graham's work with Year 12 A level students (Graham 1997; Graham and Macaro 2007) investigated their approach to written tasks and identifies the following areas where strategic behaviour can lead to better writing outcomes which we shall now consider:

- planning;
- formulating new sentences;
- editing and drafting;
- monitoring and checking.

### Planning

Planning is important and has been linked to the so-called 'formulation stage' of students' writing. Graham and Macaro (2007) found that how A level students planned their writing affected not simply the essay structure, but also the linguistic quality of what they wrote. These researchers taught students in their study the planning technique of **'mind mapping'** after discovering that it was largely absent from the students' writing toolkit. Whilst it is likely that learners are familiar with the technique nowadays, teachers may find it helpful to investigate whether or not their students actually *use* it when approaching an extended written task. This type of planning is useful not only for **structuring** thoughts and the content of the essay, but the authors also found that the process was important **linguistically** for retrieving the language the students needed for the task. This allowed them to review what they were able to say and identify where they could not confidently express their ideas.

The question of which **language** to use when planning is also worth discussing with students. In order to assist the subsequent 'formulation stage', students should ideally write down as much in the **target language** as possible. In class, group planning may help with this (Graham 1997) and when it comes to the examination, it is important that the plan is written in the target language. However, studies show that effective learners *do* use their mother tongue to organise and generate their ideas, and to evaluate their writing strategies (Macaro 2003). Students will inevitably think in their mother tongue at this strategic or metacognitive level, and so teachers should help students to avoid the pitfalls of 'thinking' in English in terms of their actual writing. The real danger here lies in verbatim translation from English, as students focus more on what they want to say, rather than what they are able to say in the target language. A common complaint from examiner reports highlights how anglicisms, *faux amis* and even invented words obscure meaning and significantly reduce the candidate's overall mark for the literature essay. If students can use planning to think about their *language* as well as content as they practise essays in class, this should deliver benefits.

- For classwork and homework, **mind mapping software** (if the school subscribes) can be particularly useful as it enables changes to be made easily and colours and font size to be deployed to show hierarchy and categorisation.

- Asking students to attach a mind map or other **evidence of planning** when they hand in work to be assessed will reinforce the importance of planning, ensure that students practise the skill and also allow teacher feedback on how they go about this. These steps will prepare students for planning in the examination.

*Formulating new sentences*

As students are planning how they will answer the essay question in terms of content, the key task is to 'evaluate the gap' (Graham and Macaro 2007 p.160) between what they know how to say and what they wish to say. Students will come to the examination prepared with well-drilled phrases (and opinions). However, in order to respond properly to an unseen question and to attain higher marks, students must be able to formulate previously untested sentences.

It is worth teachers spending time on helping students to develop strategies to cope when they encounter such difficulties in the examination as this will increase their overall linguistic independence. Students could explicitly practise the following strategies during shared writing sessions so that they regard them as an integrated element of the planning, drafting, editing and checking cycle.

**Combination and restructuring:** Here students think about what they *do* know how to say and then adapt the known phrase, perhaps by combining it with parts of another familiar expression *or* by substituting different vocabulary. This approach can be encouraged by teachers routinely challenging students to reuse existing knowledge in a new way, especially during guided shared writing sessions. With practice, students' confidence, and hopefully their language repertoire, will improve.

**Generating new sentences:** Here students draw on their grammatical knowledge to construct a new sentence from scratch.

**Paraphrase or avoidance:** How to paraphrase to get the message across is a skill which is often focused on more in oral lessons (Graham 1997). However, students can be encouraged to employ similar methods in order to express their ideas when writing. As a last resort, leaving out a particular point can be a legitimate strategy to avoid penalties for unclear meaning or anglicisms.

**Simple starter activities** which challenge students to rewrite useful sentences in different ways, or express a given point in the target language, without reference materials, can get them used to thinking on their feet. Working in pairs to do this could help students to explain their thought process and evaluate their eventual solution.

### Drafting and editing

As well as planning, students should understand from early in the course that drafting and editing are routine stages of their formal writing. After all, in English language lessons, the process of drafting and reworking compositions is well established with drafting books and formative feedback at interim stages in the writing process. Changes can be made quickly, repeatedly and tracked thanks to word-processors. Adams (with Panter 2001) points out that ideally students will have become accustomed to drafting and editing earlier down the school. This may involve identifying common errors and 'star sentences' through class and pair discussion. Adams also suggests displaying editing conventions on the wall so that students see editing and redrafting as a natural part of writing, rather than associated with error.

Used in combination with feedback, this approach can support students in the writing process, and encourage them to be proactive in improving their own work, perhaps drawing on **checklists**.

## Monitoring and checking

Acting on teacher feedback is undoubtedly important, but ultimately, students must be able to monitor the quality and accuracy of their *own* writing. In the examination, failure to spot avoidable grammatical errors, for example, will reduce their overall mark. 'Checking' is typically done at the end of the essay and is often, but not exclusively, linked with linguistic accuracy. Frustratingly, simply imploring students to 'check their work' does not always bear fruit, often because students do not know what they are looking for or because they have difficulty spotting their own mistakes (Carduner 2007)!

A **checklist** can be a helpful tool in combatting difficulties with checking and instilling good habits and attention to detail. It can also help students to see the connection between what they are learning in 'grammar lessons' and their own written work. There are several ways of approaching this. A purely grammatical checklist may list features to review such as:

* spelling and genders;
* verb/subject agreement;
* verb endings;
* tense use/sequence of tenses;
* adjectival/past participle agreements;
* use of case and correct endings;
* word order (especially in problem areas of compound tenses with negation or pronouns in French, or subordinating conjunctions in German).

It is useful for teachers to identify common errors mentioned in examiners' reports, and make sure that these are part of the checklists until the errors are expunged! This can also apply to common vocabulary errors and anglicisms. These errors can be placed into a grid which students can refer to.

The usefulness of checklists may be maximised in the following ways.

* Students can be asked to complete the checklist grid and submit it with each piece of writing to act as a reminder.

- A 'teacher' column can be used to highlight errors (or omissions) in each category.

- If items are numbered, these numbers can be used on the student's work to identify the type of error to be corrected.

- Checklists can be personalised and act as a dynamic part of the formative feedback loop: students will have their own specific difficulties which need attention.

- Similarly, the checklist should evolve alongside a student's grammatical competence and some items dropped.

- Checklists for editing can incorporate content and language as well as grammatical accuracy.

- Some students may find it reassuring to jot down their own (brief) checklist at the start of the examination as a reminder.

- A mnemonic or key for specific difficulties could also be considered.

In order for checklists to be effective, it is important that:

- the teacher models how to use the checklist in class – perhaps on a sample paragraph or essay;

- students understand the difference between reading and grammatical *proof-reading*: here they are reading for a very specific purpose and for *detail* rather than overall meaning;

- lists are not too long or they can become counterproductive and hamper the writing process;

- lists focus on errors which are either easily corrected or serious enough to obscure meaning (Carduner 2007);

- students take responsibility for monitoring their own accuracy.

It is a delicate balance however between checking and the danger of **disrupting the writer's flow**. Research by both Hedge (2000) and Graham (1997) indicates that successful writers organise their ideas first and let the essay take shape before checking for grammatical accuracy. Other studies (e.g. Macaro 2003) have found that GCSE learners, on the contrary, were more effective when they checked their work as they went along. Here there is room for individual preference, but in the exam situation especially, students should not be diverted by a grammatical query. They should put a mark in the margin and return to the problem later, by which time the answer may have become clear!

A checklist acts as reminder of what to check (which may in itself be all that is needed), but it cannot give the student the correct answer. Helpfully, Macaro (2003) distinguishes between **checking** where the student makes use of *external* materials such as grammar notes and dictionaries to verify what is needed, and **monitoring** where the student draws on their own *internal* knowledge of the language alone. This is of course the situation in the examination.

**Monitoring strategies** which can be used to self-evaluate written work, without access to external tools, can be practised with students (Harris 1997; Adams with Panter 2001).

- **Auditory monitoring** (when read aloud, does it sound right?): This strategy relies on exposure to lots of target language discussion around the topic, and understanding of the phoneme/grapheme correspondence in the language. This strategy may be less effective with less capable students however as they may not know what sounds right (Graham 1997).

- **Visual monitoring** (does it look right?): This strategy can be very effective, especially if students have been trained to pay attention to the written form.

- **Backtranslating** (does it make sense when I translate it back into English?) was an effective strategy used by students in Graham and Macaro's study (2007) and can help students to spot mistakes of meaning and grammar.

- **Patterns and rules** (have I applied the rules?). Students actively judge what they have written against the grammar they have learnt.

In shared guided writing, teachers can encourage students to think aloud and describe the monitoring mechanisms they are using. **Self-assessment** by students when submitting practice essays can be an important element in developing their ability to monitor their work and autonomy in their writing. Field (1999) suggests that in between the first and second readings of a student's own draft, he or she reads that of a friend. Obviously not possible in the examination, but this may be a useful part of a formative approach, testing the idea that it is often easier to spot errors in other people's work.

## *Focus on feedback*

Teachers and students are very familiar with the feedback principles of assessment for learning (e.g. Black and Wiliam 1998), which have been used in their earlier language lessons and remain an essential part of the teaching and learning process. This is time-consuming for the teacher however, and only effective if students *use* it to improve their writing. Disappointingly, this may not always be the case, especially if students do not always understand how to engage and act on the feedback given (Macaro 2003).

## Teacher feedback

In order to be effective, feedback should:

- comment not only on grammatical accuracy but also on **quality of expression and content** (in line with the mark scheme). As students write longer pieces, the relevant examination mark scheme can be used so that students know what they are aiming for. In order not to hamper students' written flow, initial feedback should perhaps prioritise content, with the focus on form coming later (Gordon 2008);
- indicate how clearly the student has got his/her **meaning** across (rather than just focussing on surface accuracy);
- comment on a **student's ideas** and how they are **organised**;
- require students to **revise their own work** rather than simply relying on the teacher to improve their writing. (If the teacher simply corrects the mistakes, there is the danger that students may not understand what was wrong or just file away the best copy.) To do this, teachers may:
  - ○ indicate errors by using a code (e.g. sp = spelling) or numbers linked to a checklist;
  - ○ ask for a reordered plan taking into consideration the feedback given;
  - ○ select a paragraph to be rewritten using more sophisticated language or making the meaning clearer.
- highlight **areas for attention** which can then be added to checklists for specific focus in the next essay;
- be a part of a **recursive (continuous) editing process**. Written work submitted **electronically** has many advantages such as the use of colour; underlining and highlighting; the track changes and comment box tools. Passages can be copied and pasted for specific attention.

## Peer feedback

Reports of the effectiveness of peer feedback are mixed. However, researchers (cited in Macaro 2003) observe that getting learners to comment on one another's work can encourage collaborative learning. The peer reviewer is able to point out where he or she does not understand the writer's meaning (this could be related to language or content), the writer can explain what he or she was trying to say and then together they can improve the passage. Interestingly, students here also reported an increased sense of ownership of their text as they could decide whether to take up their (peer) reviewer's comments or not. Above all, an important aspect of both teacher and peer feedback is encouraging students to **reflect** on the process of writing and how to improve. This should pay dividends when they are 'flying solo' in the examination.

## *Talk about it*

In guided shared writing the teacher describes his or her thought processes to the students and in written feedback comments on those of the student. If students are having particular problems with composition, however, then another technique which Hedge (2000 pp.299–302) calls *conferencing*, may prove useful. The teacher sits with the student who 'thinks aloud' whilst writing, describing what he or she wants to express and where the difficulties or uncertainties lie. These may involve language or structure and content. Whilst time-consuming, small classes and 'writing' or carousel lessons may allow this type of intervention. This insight into where the students face problems (and how they go about solving them), can also be tried in a written form. Students annotate their essays where problems occur (stating what they do not understand or why they have opted for a particular form of words) and the teacher can then better understand their misconceptions and target feedback and practice accordingly (Macaro 2003).

# Writing for the examination

As the examination approaches, teachers will want to practise more specifically those areas which correspond to the A level mark scheme. Writing for the examination is a new skill and students need plenty of practice in the different steps which make up writing a successful essay. The following activities are organised in line with the foci of the mark scheme and can also be used to target specific difficulties seen in particular student essays.

* AO3: language skills;
* AO4: critical and analytical response to the question.

In addition, it is important to read the **examiners' reports** after each assessment session and identify any areas which have been highlighted as **best practice** from successful candidates *and* those noted as **common weaknesses** which have lost candidates marks. This information can form the basis of specific examination preparation. In addition to providing past essay titles, some boards publish **indicative content** for the questions to illustrate how the question could have been answered well. When the following exercises suggest working with exemplar essays or excerpts, using this content is a good starting point for teachers to write their own plans and answers for exploitation in class. The annotated examples of candidates' answers which are published may also be useful for work with students in the ways described below. Anonymised former students' essays (used with permission) can also be useful for analysis, correction *etc.*

## *Language skills (AO3)*

The majority of these skills will be worked on in other non-literature lessons, but specific preparation for the literature essay could include the following areas.

- Learn the appropriate **terminology** for discussing technical aspects of the novel or play (see Appendix 2).

  o A **memrise** (www.memrise.com) or **quizlet** (www.quizlet.com) vocabulary test can be set up by teachers or students to practise this vocabulary in the same way as other sets of words or phrases.

  o Using familiar vocabulary games can help to fix this more unusual vocabulary. These can take the form of 5 minute activities on the interactive whiteboard or even games such as 'Hangman'.

- Similarly, learn expressions and sentence structures which allow students to discuss the question in the appropriate **register and style**. Students should see examples in essays and be challenged to include a selection in their own writing. Vocabulary games can also be used with these phrases.

- Students should use a **range of** (more sophisticated) **vocabulary** and this can be encouraged in a variety of ways.

  o Students can use **reading logs** to record (and learn) new expressions and incorporate them into their own writing. It is helpful if they identify their own words and phrases in addition to those highlighted by the teacher.

  o **Synonym sheets** which list alternatives to common words are useful. Target high frequency verbs particularly (*e.g.* to have; to be; to go; to say (when reporting speech); to think) or common adjectives for physical or psychological character description (beautiful; tall; angry). **Word mats** can be produced and points scored for using the vocabulary in all lessons.

  o Give the class a **basic passage** and challenge them (perhaps in teams) to change as many words as they can to improve it. Students can also work on longer model answers, transforming a *version de base* into a *version de luxe!*

- o **Dictionary exercises** (looking for all words and phrases derived from a keyword or a synonym hunt) can enlarge vocabulary and help students to get a feel for how the language 'works', using suffixes and prefixes to indicate different parts of speech. This may help them to make educated guesses and avoid confusion between, for example, adjectives and adverbs in French or verbs with the same root but different prefixes in German.

- o Language which conveys **doubt or possibility** is useful for showing nuance and the subjunctive mood is helpful for offering opinions and tentative conclusions.

- o Word and sentence level **games** can be used to practise conjunctions, opinions, quantifiers *etc.*

- o Students should also be alerted to particular difficulties such as the *faux amis* and anglicisms noted in examiner reports and words which are easily confused such as *raconteur/rencontrer, personnage/caractère; improvar* for *mejorar; überall* for *im Großen und Ganzen* and *bekommen* and *werden.*

- Using sophisticated phrases and vocabulary correctly can also enhance **fluency**. This is often shown by logical linking of sentences and the argument.

  - o Linking phrases can also be practised as items of vocabulary and having a range of these will avoid repetition.

  - o Students can also be given a list of sentences which they have to link together using the conjunctions and phrases they have learnt.

  - o It is helpful for students to have **key sentences** which use these expressions correctly, as this provides a base which they can adapt to their own meaning. Simply regurgitating them verbatim in the examination however, is likely to weaken the essay's overall fluency and relevance to the title.

*Further practice activities*

- A PowerPoint of a short text is made by the teacher, in which the first screen shows the first word of a sentence and subsequent slides reveal one word at a time until the whole text is shown. Students gain points by predicting the next word in the sentence until they have guessed the whole text. The group is then given 30 seconds to memorise the text, after which they work in pairs to write it accurately from memory. This prediction activity is beneficial for checking students' grammatical knowledge.

- A student, or the teacher, begins a sentence with a phrase and others continue the sentence in turns until it is complete. The class can then continue to devise complex sentences by linking students' individual contributions.

- Individually or in pairs, students are given a list of 'essay' phrases by the teacher. They must then write a continuous piece of prose which incorporates them all.

## Content: critical and analytical response to the question (AO4)

### Relevance to the question

Students must practise how to **interpret the question** to ensure that their essay answers the question asked. Examiner reports stress how important this is and an irrelevant answer will gain no marks at all. This is not just a danger for candidates with a weak knowledge of the text. It is natural for students who know a lot about a text to want to display all their knowledge, but if they write too broadly about the text they will be penalised for irrelevancies and may run out of time before being able to make enough fully relevant points. Although detailed work on this is easier when the text has been read, practice in how to interpret titles (in the target language) can begin early in the course. (Practice questions can be drawn from exemplar and past papers and it is also useful to mine questions about other texts to find further examples of how questions are phrased.)

### Understanding the question

It is important to ensure that all students are familiar with the meaning of keywords in order to assess correctly what the question is asking for. Figures 10.1, 10.2 and 10.3 contain a selection of keywords to practise.

In preparation, students should practise the following approaches:

- learn the **verbs** and **quantifiers** which frequently arise (these can be incorporated in oral and short written exercises straightaway);
- **copy out** the exam question (allowing time to think and connect with the words);
- **underline** the key words in the question to identify the focus: theme, style, characters *etc.*;
- identify whether the question has **multiple parts**;
- in the case of short stories or poetry, confirm **how many** must be referred to in the answer;
- identify the **type of question** and what it requires, *e.g.* a comparison; a character study (this will help them to decide on the best structure). Sometimes it is also helpful to identify what is **not** required;
- notice if the question asks specifically for a **personal opinion** or an **explicit judgement** (often triggered by phrases such as 'to what extent …?');

| Understanding essay titles: French | | | |
|---|---|---|---|
| **Verb** | **Keyword** | **Focus** | |
| **Examinez** | *comment*<br>*pourquoi*<br>*pour quelles raisons* | *ces thèmes* | *influencent* |
| **Expliquez (AS)** | *la façon dont …* | | *affectent* |
| **Evaluez** | *ce qui signifie …*<br>*la signification de …*<br>*l'importance de …* | *(les) techniques*<br>*(les) effets*<br>*(les) aspects*<br>*(le) rôle* | |
| **Analysez** | *l'impact de …*<br>*les attitudes envers*<br>*les rapports entre*<br>*le contraste entre*<br>*la réaction de* | *(les) personnages* | |
| **Discutez et justifiez** | votre réponse; vos raisons | | |
| | | **Opinion**<br>jusqu'à quel point<br>dans quelle mesure?<br>à votre avis? | êtes-vous d'accord? |

*Figure 10.1* Understanding French essay titles.

- remember that if the question starts with a quotation, they should evaluate the viewpoint expressed. (This will often require them to say **to what extent** they agree and is an opportunity for them to examine two sides of the issue before concluding with their personal stance.)

### *Reference to social context, issues and themes*

A key part of understanding what the question requires involves making sure that the answer includes relevant contextual information. Students should develop a clear mental list of the **themes and issues** for each text. When they are deciding what is relevant to the question, working down this list can help to ensure that the wider context is considered. Too much scene-setting about the author or the wider

| Understanding essay titles: German | | |
|---|---|---|
| **Verb** | **Keyword** | **Focus** |
| **Untersuchen Sie** | *ob* | |
| | *wie* | *ändert sich …* |
| | *warum* | *entwickelt sich …* |
| | *die These, dass* | |
| **Analysieren Sie** | *die Absichten ….* | |
| | *die Parallelen* | |
| | *zwischen* | |
| | *die Beziehung* | |
| | *zwischen* | |
| | *die Rolle bei …* | |
| | *die Wichtigkeit* | |
| | *die Wirkung* | *(auf als Zuschauer)* |
| | *die Konsequenzen* | |
| | *der Vergleich mit …* | |
| | *der Kontrast* | *zeigt* |
| | *die Entwicklung* | |
| **Beurteilen Sie** | | |
| **Kommentieren Sie** | *inwiefern gilt* | |
| | *X als … ….* | |
| **Vergleichen Sie** | | |
| **Questions** Wie gelingt es? Wie und mit welchem Erfolg? Inwiefern gilt es ….? | | **Opinion** Wie denken Sie darüber? Inwiefern sind Sie auch dieser Meinung? Inwiefern stimmen Sie mit dieser Meinung überein? |
| **Wie bewerten Sie** | *die Motive?* | Warum sind Sie dieser Meinung? Stimmt es …? Für oder gegen sprechen |

*Figure 10.2* Understanding German essay titles.

philosophy (e.g. Existentialism) is often superfluous however, and it is important to practise in class ways of referencing the context succinctly where relevant to the question asked.

Practice activities

- A technique for explaining or reinforcing '**relevance**' with students is to give them a title and a dozen (or more) bullet points (or sentences) about the text.

| Understanding essay titles: Spanish | | |
|---|---|---|
| **Verb** | **Keyword** | **Focus** |
| **Examina (AS)** **Explica (AS)** **Comenta (AS)** **Analiza** | *cómo* el tema de el *impacto* de | e.g. las técnicas de narración; la técnica narrativa; el estilo narrativo; las técnicas estilísticas; el uso de … (del lenguaje); la forma; la estructura |
| **Evalúa si** **Justifia** | la *evolución* de la *relación* entre el *efecto* de la *importancia* de tu respuesta | |
| | | **Opinion** ¿Estás de acuerdo? ¿Piensas que …? ¿Por qué ….? ¿Hasta qué punto ….? En tu opinión … |

*Figure 10.3* Understanding Spanish essay titles.

Students have to categorise them by relevance *e.g.* into highly relevant, partially relevant, irrelevant and then explain their choices. This could lead to class discussion highlighting discrepancies. Follow-up activities could include suggesting how to improve the partially relevant sentences or suggesting a title for which the other sentences *would* be relevant.

- A **diamond ranking** activity could also be used to prioritise the sentence in order of relevance to the essay. In terms of differentiation this is also a valuable exercise in giving students who may need it a firm base of model sentences for adaptation and reuse.

- As the exam draws nearer, as a starter or plenary activity, challenge students in pairs or as individuals to analyse and **summarise** what a title requires (and perhaps what it does not) in 10 minutes. Stress here the importance of relevance. This activity can be extended to include bullet points of what could be included.

*The structure of the essay: a logical argument linked to conclusions*

The next stage is **structuring** the essay. Points relevant to the title must be made in a **logical order**, leading to a **clear conclusion**. Taking time to plan will hopefully **avoid repetition** and allow the greatest number of salient ideas to be expressed within the time allowed. Students will be familiar with the introduction, development and conclusion format of essays. Some focused work on how to maximise the impact of their argument is still helpful however and contributes to the development of **transferable skills** through MFL.

## Introduction

The introduction sets the scene concisely. It should focus immediately on the precise question asked and not divert into either a repetition of the title or a generalised background to the author or text. Within the word count, there is only room for a short introduction of two or three sentences to show that the issue has been understood and outline the scope of the answer. Points made here should not be repeated later in the essay.

- When the text has been studied, give students a possible essay title and get them used to writing a succinct introduction, tailored to the title, as a regular **starter activity** to a lesson. These can then be shared and critiqued.

## Development

For AS candidates, it is useful to practise using the format of **prompts** which appear in the examination paper. Whilst using these is not obligatory in the examination, these points do help candidates with both relevance and structure and can also be used as support in the early stage of A level preparation. Students can practise writing short paragraphs about a variety of relevant prompts.

It is helpful to think about the type of question and therefore the most appropriate **structure** for the answer. The simplest approach for many essay types is to divide the main body of the essay into **two sections**. The first section will deal with one side of the argument, whilst the second puts forward the opposing viewpoint. This works well with the type of question which asks for a judgement about a statement *e.g.* 'how far do you agree with ...?'; 'to what extent is ...?'. The argument in the second section will usually be the one which carries most weight as the writer can refute points made in the first section and lead strongly into the concluding judgement. This is also an approach which can be used for a '**compare and contrast**' type essay, where for example, character A is discussed in the first section and then character B in the second. It is important to make sure that the same issues are covered in relation to both characters however, in order to establish the comparisons strongly. Alternatively, a more sophisticated approach would be to discuss a particular issue or trait in relation to characters A and B in one paragraph and then move on to a second point of comparison between them in the next paragraph and so on until all comparisons have been exhausted. If the essay asks for the **development** of the story or character over time, then it is best to make the points **chronologically** in successive paragraphs. Students should practise identifying which type of structure is most appropriate for various essay titles, allowing them to make their points in a logical order, without the need for repetition and to finish on a strong conclusion which addresses the question asked.

## Practice activities

- An exercise in which **paragraphs** have to be **reordered** can be useful for practising transition phrases. Students read an extended piece of text, in which the paragraphs have been mixed up. Clues are often in the linking phrases at the start of sections and students have to re-order the text in order for the ideas to flow naturally. In doing so, they gain practice in writing sequentially. Typical linking phrases can be found in Appendix 2.

- Students can also learn about logical structure by writing a plan of an exemplar essay. Before doing so, they can underline all the words which give the essay coherence and structure, for example:

  - words which **order** the points e.g. firstly, secondly, primarily, most importantly;
  - words which indicate **consequence** e.g. therefore, because, due to, in order to;
  - words which signal **balance or juxtaposition** of ideas e.g. however, on the one hand, on the other, not only but also.

  Understanding a good range of **conjunctions** (and their word order rules in German) is important here (Adams with Panter 2001).

## Conclusion

Students should bring their essay to a tidy end which answers the question directly. It should not repeat what has already been said earlier in the essay.

## Practice activities

- Students can **practise essay plans** under exam conditions and then **peer review** them.
- **Writing frames** can be very supportive in structuring the essay. The headings can be completed in note form, perhaps as a **jigsaw activity** (with different groups writing different sections and then reforming to collectively complete the whole

frame) and then finished individually as homework. Students could also be assigned different roles to check the final version (*i.e.* for quality of language used, for grammatical accuracy, for development of the argument, for use of evidence).

Students could use the indicative content from the board mark schemes as a guide and groups could also peer assess one another's essays. A *consequences-type* rotation of the writing frames between groups, could also lead to interesting results. Above all, getting students to share and review their ideas with one another can be very beneficial.


## Using evidence

Demonstrating a sound knowledge of the novel or play is necessary to access the higher bands of the mark scheme. Close reference to **specific episodes and events** provides evidence to support a candidate's argument. **Quotations** from the text can also lend an air of authority when used correctly, but students do need some guidelines to work from to avoid spoiling the effect.

* Use quotations only when they are relevant to the title and the argument. Irrelevant quotations will harm rather than enhance the essay.

* Use a quotation to express an idea, character or theme succinctly and perhaps more elegantly than a long-winded explanation. Avoid quotations which are overly long or lack impact.

* Use a quotation to illustrate an author's style or use of language.

* Use quotations which are accurately written and attributed to the correct character and event in the narrative. If unsure of the exact quotation, it is better to make the point in reported speech.

* Use quotations in context, as part of the argument. Avoid stand-alone quotations whose purpose is unclear.

* Use short quotations for greatest impact. This also avoids breaking the flow of the students' own writing.

Students should also be taught how to integrate quotations correctly into the essay and be confident with the use of quotation marks in the relevant language. Longer quotations will require a separate line and indentation, but it is better to reduce quotes by inserting an ellipsis … to indicate where text has been omitted. It is an effective strategy to learn quotations which are concise and which can be used to illustrate multiple points. A well-kept file of quotations can also help to recall points about the text. Quotations are not always essential however, and a precise reference to the scene or conversation can be equally useful.

## Practice activities

- Activities and games that are used to practise vocabulary and phrases can also be adapted to practise quotations (e.g. www.memrise.com; hangman with words instead of letters).

- Writing the individual words of quotations on different cards which then have to be put back together in the correct order can force students to focus on learning the quotation accurately. It becomes more challenging if several quotations are mixed up together. Team races can add some excitement to this! Similarly, this type of **re-ordering** can take place on the interactive whiteboard (against the clock, perhaps).

- Teams of students try to catch one another out by taking it in turns to read out quotations whilst their opponents try to **guess who said them** and at what point in the text.

- Students can also be challenged (individually or in groups) to order a set of key quotations in the **order** they appear in the text and match them to the speaker. Bonus points can be gained for additional information e.g. who the speaker was addressing at the time, who was the comment about, what happened next, why is the quotation important etc.?

- Students can also practise quotations using the **running dictation** technique.

### Encourage analysis

At A level, the mark schemes specify that candidate essays should **analyse** rather than simply **describe**. It can be difficult for students however to distinguish between the two. The language used in the essay question should help to remind students what is required e.g. analyse, explain, justify your opinion etc.

In earlier chapters, the analysis of characters, plot, themes and style have been discussed and students should bring this knowledge to their examination essays. A simple formula used widely in other subjects, such as PEA (**Point, evidence, analysis**), can provide students with a handy aide-mémoire to avoid description without evidence and explanation. As they work on this in their own writing, students benefit from seeing this in practice in sample essays.

- As introduction to analysis, students highlight on an exemplar essay or extract, in two different colours, sentences which are purely descriptive and those which are analytical. Discussion of their decisions help to develop their understanding of the difference and can lead to drawing out the **vocabulary and phrases** which indicate **analysis**.

- The same process can be used to identify **evidence** and **opinions** and lead to a discussion on how one is used to support the other. This can be done as a **peer** feedback exercise (grammar and structure are not the focus here) or by students on their own writing. This visual feedback can give an immediate picture of how much analysis has been included.

- Giving **opinions** is also an important aspect of analysis and the use of oral activities which encourage students to express a variety of opinions fluently is a good precursor to writing.

  - The teacher makes a set of cards with different phrases expressing opinions. The letters on each card represent the first letter of each word in the phrase (e.g. *I_ m_ s_ _ _ _ _ q_ _ = Il me semble que; P_ _ _ _ _ q_ _ = Pienso que*).

  - Themes from the text are written on the whiteboard and students then take it in turns to choose a card from the pile of cards which are face down on the table and give an opinion.

  - Qualifiers can be used to extend students' opinions for additional challenge and points.

## Examination technique

Students should practise how to organise their time during the examination itself. A focus on the following key areas can help them to become normal practice.

### *Examination routine*

- They should take time to read **all** relevant questions carefully before selecting which to answer (this allows the brain to be 'background' processing the second essay whilst writing the first).
- Students should clearly identify which question has been answered.
- Writing out the question can help to spark ideas and allow time to concentrate on exactly *what* the question requires. Underlining key words is important.
- A brief plan should be written (in the target language) before starting to write.
- The plan may have five or six points for paragraphs with evidence and justification.
- The plan should show how the key words of the title are addressed.
- It may help to write on alternate lines in case words need to be changed or added. *Legibility is important!*
- Students should delete any drafts which should not be marked.
- They should leave time at the end for proofreading and checking, focussing on language, content and accuracy.

- Student may wish to construct an **aide-mémoire** where they can tick off that they have read the questions, planned and structured the essay, included examples from the text, kept it relevant, answered the question, avoided repetition, included formal essay structures and vocabulary and proofread carefully for grammatical errors.

## *Practice in class*

- Students should practise writing essays within the **time allowed** in class and at home.

- Although all that is written will be marked, it is advisable that students become accustomed to (and comfortable with) writing essays of the **correct length** (and they know how this looks on the handwritten page). Examiners' reports suggest that students suffer when they write too much: they lose focus and make a greater number of errors.

- To help students whose writing is wordy and vague, the teacher might ask the class to **reduce** a rambling sample piece of writing to half the number of words, while retaining the content.

- Students should learn to **divide their time** between the two essays evenly.

- If they are having difficulty with the planning and checking, try dividing the allowed time into **planning, writing and checking slots**. They can replicate this at home and indicate time spent on each section when handing in the essay for marking. (Do not accept essays without a plan and evidence of checking!).

# Revision

Students will benefit from reminders throughout the course to keep **notes** and quotations organised by topic or character and thorough plot summaries. They should also use the **dictionary** properly to note full grammatical information on nouns, verbs *etc.* and to **learn** appropriate vocabulary and phrases on a weekly basis. In addition to the more formal examination practice, using games and quick starters and plenaries to practise the content and language they need and how to interpret the question are equally useful.

Figure 10.4 suggests some **questions** which can be translated into the target language and adapted to fit a particular text. These can be used in a variety of ways as revision by trying to get students used to expressing their opinions orally, and in a game format. Mini-whiteboards could also be used for quick written answers.

| | | |
|---|---|---|
| Describe a principal character. | How does the author create suspense/ interest? | Give two reasons for reading the book/seeing the play. |
| Describe a secondary character and his or her importance to the plot. | Do we care about the characters and why? | Give a less successful aspect of the book/play. |
| Why does character A act in the way s/he does? | Analyse the author's narrative style | In what way is the book relevant to today? |
| How does character A develop during the novel/ play? | Explain the importance of event X in the novel/ play. | What is the most important event of the book and why? |
| Contrast characters A and B. Which is more important to the plot and why? | Why does the novel/ play end in this way? | How could the book be improved? |
| To what extent do you agree with the statement … … …? | What is the author trying to tell us? | Ask the person opposite a question about the book/play. |
| What are the most important themes of the book/play? Why is this? | Has the author's life influenced the book/ play? | Talk for 2 minutes on your choice of topic. |

*Figure 10.4* Revision questions.

- These can be used as random 'pop ups' on the interactive whiteboard or on cards for students to work in pairs or small groups to answer as they turn them over.

- They can be numerically graded in groups 1–6 according to difficulty or topic area. Students could then throw a die and answer a corresponding question. Or students could choose 'harder' graded cards in order to score more points!

- The activity can be made more difficult by imposing a time limit (60 seconds) for which students must speak or other criteria, such as 3 sentences or including a particular phrase, also uncovered at random.

- Students must give at least one piece of evidence from the text to support their claims and start each answer with an opinion phrase.

- The questions could also be hidden on the interactive whiteboard behind a noughts and crosses board which students have to answer to gain the square.

- Alternatively, the questions could be copied onto a simple board game format (e.g. snakes and ladders) where students land on squares and have to answer the question in order to progress.

- The questions could be changed to become sentence starters which students then have to complete.
- Answers can be expanded on and written up at home.

# Conclusion

Preparing students thoroughly for the examination offers them the opportunity to do justice to the work they have done in reading, appreciating and analysing the text. This is best achieved by demystifying what is required and allowing plenty of graded practice across the course. Writing strategies and examination technique gradually become embedded and students gain the fluency and insight to answer a range of questions about the text, confident in their ability to achieve A level success.

# Further reading

For a more detailed account of how to investigate and develop **strategy use** with students see Graham and Macaro (2007) and a fuller discussion of the difficulties of **student self-monitoring** may be found in Graham (1997 pp.164–166).

# Implications for teaching

- Study the assessment criteria and ensure that students are aware of how to achieve the highest bands in both language and content.
- Plan graded writing tasks from the start of the course and provide opportunities to write in different forms to maintain interest.
- Support written tasks by providing models, writing frames and initial opportunities for oral practice in pairs and groups.
- Show students how to plan, structure and write an essay for the examination, including how to interpret the question.
- Teach students strategies and tools for checking the accuracy, content and language of their writing.
- Ensure that feedback mechanisms are effective and require students to act on improving their work.
- Be aware of what examiners' reports have signalled as good practice and common pitfalls in examinations and then work on these in class.
- Boost students' confidence with lots of practice and revision activities.

# References

Adams, J. with Panter, S.A., 2001. *Just Write! Pathfinder 40*. London: CILT.

Black, P. and Wiliam, D., 1998. *Inside the Black Box: Raising Standards through Classroom Assessment*. London: School of Education, King's College London.

Carduner, J., 2007. Teaching proofreading skills as a means of reducing composition errors. *Language Learning Journal*, 35(2), pp.283–295.

Chambers, G., 1991. Suggested approaches to A-level literature. *Language Learning Journal*, 4, pp.5–9.

Field, K., 1999. GCSE and A/AS level teaching and learning: similarities and differences. In: N. Pachler, ed. *Teaching Modern Foreign Languages at Advanced Level*. London: Routledge, pp.33–59.

Gordon, L., 2008. Writing and good language learners. In: C. Griffiths, ed. *Lessons from Good Language Learners*. Cambridge: Cambridge University Press, pp.244–254.

Graham, S., 1997. *Effective Language Learning*. Clevedon: Multilingual Matters.

Graham, S. and Macaro, E., 2007. Designing year 12 strategy training in listening and writing: from theory to practice. *The Language Learning Journal*, 35(2), pp.153–173.

Harris, V., 1997. *Teaching Learners How to Learn. Strategy Training in the Modern Languages Classroom*. London: CILT.

Hedge, T., 2000. *Teaching and Learning in the Language Classroom*. Oxford: Oxford University Press.

Macaro, E., 2003. *Teaching and Learning a Second Language. A Guide to Recent Research and Its Applications*. London: Continuum.

Ofqual, 2016. *GCE Subject Level Guidance for Modern Foreign Languages*. Accessed January 2019 https://assets.publishing.service.gov.uk/government/uploads/system/uploads/attachment_data/file/517343/gce-subject-level-guidance-for-modern-foreign-languages.pdf.

# Sparking creative language use

## Before and beyond the set text

## Introduction

We have focussed so far on the specific demands of preparing students for their A level examination. However, as discussed in Chapter 2, the benefits of studying literature in a foreign language extend beyond this single goal. The opportunities for linguistic, cultural and personal development which literature offers to advanced students can also be enjoyed by **younger learners** and prepare them for their later literature study (Chambers 1991). Indeed, the study of authentic and literary texts is currently an important part of the primary curriculum for modern languages, and teachers at Key Stages 3 and 4 (of students aged 11–14 and 15–16 respectively) also draw on excerpts from literary texts in preparation for the GCSE examination.

The National Curriculum states that Key Stage 3 students should be taught to 'read literary texts in the language [such as stories, songs, poems and letters] to stimulate ideas, develop creative expression and expand understanding of the language and culture' (DfE 2013 p.2). This use of literature to spark the imagination and students' **creativity** is a strong rationale for using literature both before and beyond the A level set text. Creative projects are an excellent tool for engaging learners and supporting differentiation at all stages, as long as an appropriate level of support is included in the task.

In this concluding chapter, we shall offer suggestions of texts which can be used to develop students' familiarity with literature prior to A level, and then consider the types of activities which use their reading as a springboard for students' own creativity in speech and writing (Duff and Maley 2007).

# Materials which can support students' reading

Reading texts in French, German or Spanish below A level will enable students to expand their vocabulary, consolidate knowledge of grammar and explore the culture of the target language country. This is beneficial to all students and becoming sensitised to the power of language and emotions by reading shorter texts will greatly help those who go on to study at a deeper level. Significantly, reading widely, even with simpler texts, is perhaps the key to reading successfully (and with enjoyment) at A level (Brumfit 1985).

## *Graded readers*

In the 1990s schools were encouraged to make use of a wide range of reading materials in the language classroom, and many schools had reading schemes. While some have kept this feature, many departments feel that it is difficult to set up and maintain in an already crowded languages curriculum and reading often remains the neglected skill. However, if books are available to students, either in the school library or as part of a collection which can be lent to students in plastic wallets, then independent homework study time can be used for reading (for ideas, see Swarbrick 1998).

European Schoolbooks (www.eurobooks.co.uk) offer readers which appeal to adolescents such as the graded *Teen ELI readers* in French and German: level 1 books are based on a vocabulary of 600 words, level 2 800 words and level 3 1,000 words. They include some classic stories and have activities and a glossary. *Young adult ELI readers* in French and German includes audio material and may suit higher attainers at Key Stage 4. There is also the *Lire en français facile* series at four levels, based on different themes: Real life; Science fiction; Fantasy; Detective and Adventure. The *Lire et s'entraîner* series includes audio material and the *Collection 24 heures* takes the reader through the francophone world, providing rich cultural references. Similarly, *die DaF Bibliothek* has books based on different towns or regions of Germany.

For Spanish, there are graded readers in the series *Un día en …* with stories touching on love, tourism and gastronomy in Spain, Cuba, Mallorca, Mexico and Argentina. They highlight the culture and traditions of each setting. The readers include free online access to the audio content, a visual dictionary, cultural notes and exercises to aid understanding.

The Easy Readers series, available from European Schoolbooks and other publishers, are also graded in difficulty and include many of the more popular classics, including some on the A level syllabus. (It may be better to avoid reading specific titles which might be studied at A level, in that the element of surprise would no longer be there.) French titles include Voltaire's *Candide*, Molière's *Le Tartuffe*, Mauriac's *Thérèse Desqueyroux* and Pagnol's *Le château de ma mère*. *Les contes de la bécasse* might provide good prior experience of Maupassant's writing if *Boule de Suif* were being studied at A level. The series contains a glossary and could be used at either Key Stage 3 or 4. There are some German and Spanish titles, although fewer than for French.

Mary Glasgow Publications also has audio materials and videos online for adapted classic literature, such as Goscinny and Sempé's *Le Petit Nicolas* (www.maryglasgowplus.com). MGP magazines are also a very useful source of graded reading in French, Spanish and German. *Le petit quotidien* (www.playbacpresse.fr) is an excellent production focussing on up-to-date issues in science and nature, with historical articles too. *Les docs de l'actu*, available from the same site might suit higher attainers at Key Stage 4.

A **link school abroad**, organised through the British Council, or a school exchange can also provide a good way of obtaining reading materials at little or no cost. Teachers can organise a book and magazine swap with the partner school but it is important to specify suitable titles. The partner school is asked to collect second-hand books and magazines from the list; these can be brought back to the UK after a school visit. Key series are '*J'aime lire*' or *Collection Rose* and *Collection Verte*, both of which often have easy versions of classic stories.

### Reading logs

It is useful for students to record their opinions on the books they read and we have included suggestions for reading logs in French, German and Spanish in Appendix 3. These can easily be simplified for younger learners, by simply reducing the 'free text' and including boxes which can be ticked to record how the book made them feel and their overall appreciation.

## Children's literature

An obvious source of literature for use in school is children's literature: nursery rhymes, fairy tales and fables where the story may already be familiar and where the (repetitive) nature of the text is designed to be accessible and easily remembered. The simple patterns can reinforce grammar points very successfully. An interesting Norwegian study (Birketveit and Rimmereide 2017) has also demonstrated that young students who were allowed to **choose** from a wide variety of authentic picture books to read saw a subsequent improvement in their own second language writing in the genre.

The universal nature of **fairytales** compensates for the lack of cultural references specific to the country whose language is being studied (although Perrault and the

Brüder Grimm can be discussed e.g. *Die Bremer Stadtmusikanten*). The '*J'aime lire*' series, features *Cendrillon* and *La Belle et la Bête* and favourites in all three languages include *Little Red Riding Hood, Tom Thumb, Jack and the Beanstalk, Snow White and the Seven Dwarfs, Sleeping Beauty, The Princess and the Pea*. For French, the websites http://litteratureprimaire/eklablog.com/and http://iletaitunehistoire.com offer stories, *contes* and legends, fables and poems, *comptines* and songs. Sources for these in German and Spanish are listed in the sections which follow.

As the stories are familiar, lots of exploitation can be done in terms of ordering and matching sentences and gap-filling. The picture stories provide a good model for students and older students can also rewrite a modern version of the stories, for example, in Snow White, the mirror on the wall might be a laptop or tablet and the poisoned apple a different fruit.

In a similar vein, **fables** are also often well known to students and can be found online. There are often videos, too, on YouTube and audio versions which can be downloaded. A favourite is *Le Lion et la Souris* (www.appuiseries.fr). This is in the form of an appealing video at www.youtube.com/watch?v=8lkPUEP0ZQ0. Other classic fables enjoyed by students might be: *La Cigale et la Fourmi; Le Corbeau et le Renard; La Cigogne et le Loup*. As extension work, gifted students could write a modern version of the fable, using the moral as guidance, or indeed invent their own.

Other children's favourites in French include the (culturally relevant) **bandes dessinées** e.g. Goscinny and Underzo's *Astérix*, Hergé's *Les aventures de Tintin* and Peyo's *Les Schtroumpfs*.

## *Literary extracts*

Literature can be used to supplement non-fiction reading by the use of short authentic extracts which can boost students' confidence and allow them to experience a range of styles and authors (Brumfit 1985). Some extracts from literary sources can be used at Key Stage 3, although Key Stage 4 is probably more appropriate for texts at this level. These extracts can be chosen **thematically** to supplement factual writing on topics such as poverty, history or geography. They can also be used as part of cultural projects often conducted about different regions of France, Germany or Spain. Descriptions by Pagnol, for example, can evoke the countryside of Provence.

Extracts can be helpful in giving students practice in handling synonyms, gap-fill and true or false questions and in recognising the *passé simple*, thus building up passive knowledge of verb forms which will be more prevalent at A level. Literary extracts can also show different forms of writing, *e.g.* descriptions, journal type entries, letters, messages and also ways of speaking. Written dialogue and plays can demonstrate formal, informal, comic or dramatic ways of speaking, arguments and courtship as a prelude to students' own composition. The following types of passages could be marked by teachers as useful to exploit with GCSE learners.

- descriptions of different characters (from a range of foreign texts) which can be read, compared and used as a springboard to enrich students' own character descriptions;

- dialogues from literature can act as the spark for students' own writing with a twist, e.g. the diagnosis scene in Molière's *Le malade imaginaire* (Acte III, Scène X) can be studied for its comic effect and provide students with a model to write (and act) a similar comic dialogue whilst practising the topic of illness;

- descriptions of landscape or weather can enrich students' own work and an extension exercise could be to turn the model on its head and write a contradictory description;

- descriptions of daily routine in the present or the past which could act as a model for students;

- extracts which deal with themes such as friendship, family, love or conflict.

Figure 11.1 contains suggestions from a variety of French books and are listed in order of linguistic difficulty to enable teachers to select appropriate texts for students in Key Stages 3 and 4. Authors such as Sagan, Pagnol, Ionesco and Maupassant could also be considered.

# Poetry

Poetry is one of the most accessible and rewarding ways of introducing adult literature to younger learners. An introduction to poetry at Key Stages 3 or 4 can sensitise students to this form of writing and help them develop a personal response to the work of a range of poets. For all learners, poetry provides an excellent springboard for their own **creativity**. Poetry allows students to experience different figures of speech, the sounds and rhythms of the language, and presents the opportunity of exploring different forms (*e.g.* rhymes, epic and concrete poems and ballads) and themes such as love, hate, loss *etc.* In contrast to novels, poems promote **close, intensive** reading of a text.

Children are introduced to poetry very early in primary school and are able to appreciate and write poems and join in the oral aspect of poetry reading. Poems appeal to many children in that they

- present manageable chunks of language;

- often use unusual words to paint a picture;

- are rhythmic and often have repeated grammatical patterns;

| Le petit prince | Antoine de Saint-Exupéry | the passage where the little Prince asks for a drawing of a sheep | |
|---|---|---|---|
| La maison de papier | Françoise Mallet-Joris | Daniel's childhood, adolescence and travels | |
| Djinn | Alain Robbe-Grillet | Editions de Minuit ch. 2 pp.26–28 | the passage where the hero takes an ill-fated shortcut to meet a stranger at the Gare du Nord. |
| | | Editions de Minuit ch. 4 pp.51–54 | the passage where Marie asks the narrator for a story. Excellent for introducing the passé simple to a class. |
| Voyage autour du monde | Louis-Antoine de Bougainville | chapter 9 lines 1–34 | similarities with Candide's journey to Eldorado |
| L'étranger | Albert Camus | the passage where Meursault visits the beach and everything conspires to lead him to stabbing the Arab | |
| L'assommoir | Emile Zola | the passage where the zinc worker is singing on the roof before his accident | |

Figure 11.1 Suggestions of French literary extracts for use before A level.

- give freedom to experiment with language;
- allow the use of rhyme or free verse.

Having experimented with simple poetry at Key Stage 2, students' skills are more developed by the time they reach the secondary school. For students at Key Stage 3 traditional **comptines**, which are rhythmic and very memorable, could be learnt and performed by students. In German, Busch's Max und Moritz combines rhyme with a much-loved children's story which could be exploited with teacher support.

Figure 11.2 lists additional poems which are accessible from Year 9 onwards and selected poems by **Maurice Carême** which are beautifully written and simple enough to be studied by students below A level.

Learners need a model in order to write their own poetry and these can be found from various sources including poems that older students have written and

| | | Maurice Carême | |
|---|---|---|---|
| **Luc Bérimont** | *Je donne* | *Liberté* | *La colère* |
| **Jacques Charpentreau** | *L'embouteillage* | *Si seul* | *La liberté* |
| **Paul Eluard** | *Liberté* | *La Tour Eiffel* | *Merlin* |
| **Jacques Prévert** | *Le déjeuner du matin* | *L'or* | *Si tu étais. je serais* |
| | *Page d'écriture* | *L'artiste* | *L'homme* |
| | *Pour faire le portrait d'un oiseau* | *Ponctuation* | |
| | *Paroles* | *Pourquoi faire?* | |

The **ALL Literature Project**, (http://all-literature.wikidot.com) to which teachers contribute, has some excellent resources for using texts linked to *Le message, Le déjeuner du matin* and *Le cancre* (Jacques Prévert). There is also a link to a very clear video from Francine Christophe, htpps://www.viralviralvideos.com/2016/01/02/woman-tells-powerful-story-about-a-kind-act-during-the-holocaust. For more poems and songs, the teacher could consult the national education website www.pass-education.fr An example of a good poem to exploit on this website is Prévert's *Les animaux ont du souci.*

*Figure 11.2* Suggestions of French poems from Year 9 onwards.

anthologies of children's poetry. A **poetry competition** could be a good focus for students' writing.

- Students can be inspired to write their own **shape poems** through studying Apollinaire's **Calligrammes** at Key Stage 3, where the language is made more memorable through its visual representation. The most famous *calligrammes*, which can be found online, include *Il pleut* and poems in the shape of the lady in a hat, the Eiffel Tower and the cat.

Other forms of poems which students could write are:

- **Haiku** (three line poems with 5–7–5 syllables in respective lines).

- **Elfchen** poems, with 11 words in any arrangement, for example, 1–2–3–4–1 words in 5 lines.

- **Lunes** poems; these are arranged as 3–5–3 words in three lines, with a surprise or shock in the third line.

Poetry can also be used as a creative response to a different stimulus or a text that is being studied.

- In Chapter 8 we discuss using a *portrait chinois* (a form of poetry) to capture a character and this can be used for any real or imaginary figure.
- The familiar *Bonjour, Au revoir; Hallo, Auf Wiedersehen* form of poetry can also be applied to a literary stimulus (perhaps to encapsulate the plot of a novel or play) or used to respond to a theme such as homelessness. Perhaps No's story in de Vigan's *No et moi* could be expressed in this way as people and places come and go from her life.

There are many ideas for encouraging students to work with poems, *e.g.*

- Lines from a poem can be cut up and jumbled; students are then asked to reconstitute the original (*e.g.* Jacques Prévert's *Le déjeuner du matin* works well);
- A 'running' dictation could also be used to build the poem by a pair or group;
- Students can be asked to fill the gaps in lines of a poem; they could be given a selection of words to fill the gaps, or alternatively choose their own words to complete the poem. In either case, it can be interesting for them to compare their new version with the original poem;
- Students could produce a picture, or a story or take a photo inspired by a poem;
- Alternatively, music or art could act as the stimulus for a poem (Morgan 1994);
- A poem could provide a way into a social or historical period;
- Students could write a (simple) poem to evoke the setting of a novel or its atmosphere or one inspired by a character or the book's theme.

Hearing poetry **read aloud** is very important in terms of appreciating rhythm and rhyme in a foreign language. Many sites online facilitate this including www.lyrikline.org/en/home/where poets read their work in many languages alongside the written text. Duff and Maley (2007 pp.86–88) have an interesting group activity called 'verbal tapestry' in which groups of students listen to a poem read aloud, then each choose a fragment to practise and finally perform together to create a tapestry of sounds. Other forms of meaningful repetition are also explored in order to help students to develop both a sense of the poetry and pronunciation.

## Songs

Using songs is a powerful way of internalising grammar ahead of time and of enriching vocabulary. Involuntary Musical Imagery (INMI) is more commonly known as earworms, tunes that stay in the head long after they are heard (Jakubowski *et al.* 2017). For specific French songs which enable students to develop their language and cultural background, teachers may consider: Boris Vian – *Le Déserteur*; Julien Clerc – various; Jean Ferrat – *La Montagne*; Maxime le Forestier – *Mon frère*; and Joe Dassin – *Champs-Elysées*.

## Letters

The letter is a further type of authentic text which can be exploited in the classroom.

- A resource on the ALL Literature Project http://all-literature.wikidot.com (*Lettre de Georges Gallois*, 1915) is a letter during World War I posted by Sarah Brough and Bernard Clark. Teachers of French piloting a literature activity might find this an appropriate text for exploitation.

- In Pagnol's *Le château de ma mère*, Marcel writes a goodbye letter to his parents as he plans to become a hermit. Later in the book, Marcel's friend, Lili, writes a long letter to him. It might be possible for higher attainers at Key Stage 4 to work in pairs correcting Lili's letter.

- *Une si longue lettre* by Mariama Bâ, also on the syllabus, is written as a series of letters between the main character Ramatoulaye Fall and her best friend Aissatou after the sudden death of Ramatoulaye's husband Modou from a heart attack. Again, this might be appropriate for some higher attainers at Key Stage 4.

## German materials

- The **ALL Literature Project** http://all-literature.wikidot.com has very good German materials, from fairytales and stories to poems. *Fairytales from the Brothers Grimm* are particularly useful. Märchen from the Goethe Institut include: *Aschenputtel; der Froschkönig; Dornröschen; Hansel und Gretel; Rotkäppchen; Rumpelstilz-chen; Schneewittchen*. There are also resources associated with the Brecht poem *Wenn die Möpse Schnapse trinken* and traditional songs such as *O Tannenbaum* and *Alles was ich wünsche*. Resources such as *Der Ball der Tiere* and the short film *Yoko-manche Freunde sind cooler als andere* are also useful.

- The **childrenslibrary.org** website has some stories which could be used at Key Stage 4: they can be downloaded free. Stories such as *Finbo, Wenn ich dich nicht hätte* and *Lügen haben kurze Beine* could easily be used. The **Gutenberg.org** website has a fairytale section.

## Spanish materials

- The **ALL Literature Project** http://all-literature.wikidot.com has some excellent Spanish resources, including two poems by Gloria Fuentes, *Los Reyes* and *Todo está en su sitio*. There are numerous *Cuentos infantiles*, some with pictograms and other poems such as *Un hombre sin cabeza* and *Tu Cristo es judío*.

- On YouTube, video versions of fairytales may be found, for example *Ali Baba y los 40 ladrones, Los Zapatos Rojos, La Principesa y el guisante, Hansel y Gretel* and *La Bella addormentada*. Some have English sub-titles, which is a good aid to learning. Students might watch a fairytale as part of their homework and the teacher can check whether it has been done by getting their students to write twenty phrases from the story as they watch for a second time.

- www.childrensbooksforever.com has illustrated children's stories, which can be shown on Smartboards.

- https://cuentosinfantiles.net – an excellent site for children's stories.

- www.hablacultura.com is a very useful website containing texts and videos on Spanish culture and customs. Texts are categorised according to level (A1, A2, B1).

- www.gloriafuertes.org has information about children's poetry and story books and memorable poems.

- www.rinconcastellano.com has a good collection of classical children's stories as free e-books.

- www.mafalda.net/index.php/ES/has the background to the Mafalda books and suggests where titles can be obtained.

## Bridging the gap

As there is usually a long gap between the end of the GCSE exams in Year 11 and the start of Year 12, the teacher may decide to set up a summer programme for future AS and A level students where they extend their reading and which involves practice in all four skills. The short story, *Mateo Falcone* by Prosper Mérimée, is gripping and will hopefully engage students in their work. The story is set in Corsica and involves themes of family, hospitality and honour; it is readily available online. A series of tasks based on the story can be found in Appendix 4.

## Creative activities sparked by literature

The set text and other works of literature provide a rich source of stimuli for students' own creative output in both speaking and writing. The following suggestions could all be used alongside the study of the literature text at A level as time permits. The advantages of asking students to work creatively include:

- opportunities for personalisation which also give learners different ways to excel;

- creative tasks which have a role to play in developing students' overall writing and speaking;

- encouragement of collaborative working where different students can bring their strengths to bear;

- a sense of audience for either a poem, comic strip, poster, song, play, video or audio recording;

- practice of all four skills;

- development of skills of team working and project organisation;

- opportunities to exploit a variety of written and spoken forms *e.g.* letters, dialogues *etc.*

- ways of integrating literature into the wider curriculum;

- tasks which can be for groups or individuals and completed at home or in class;

- utilisation of students' considerable ability with modern media.

In order to be successful, creative activities should highlight the **audience** for the finished product, so that students feel that their creation has a purpose in the same way that the original authors wanted to have their work read or performed. Students also need a **model** to work from (less confident linguists will stick closely to this and more confident students will develop a more individualised response). The more structured the model, the easier the linguistic task and some of the following activities can be achieved with relatively little language. Adding a **humorous** (or fantastical) dimension to the task often works well in stimulating students' imaginations and a feeling of freedom in the task. Students do not need to have read the whole work in order to complete some of these activities and may be given a brief summary of the plot in order to then focus on a **particular extract** for a specific reason. Giving students **choice** about the activities they undertake and giving them the opportunity to create their **own response** to the text can also be powerful ways to motivate engagement and can lead to some excellent results. The suggested activities are divided into categories and most can be completed either orally (which can be recorded) or in writing.

## The literature classroom

(Where the culture of reading is promoted in school and via the **Faculty blog**).

- Students write a **book review** of a favourite book or film or a book (in Chapter 4).

- Students write a **biography** of a particular author to be shared with other students, displayed or added to the Faculty blog.

- Students could research and review another book by the same author or from the same period.

- Students could **write to a living author** (via publisher or website) asking questions about their life and work.

205

- Students could create a **literature link** with a foreign partner school, sharing projects and acting as an audience for some of the following activities.

## Thematic project work

- The specific background to the set text can be used as a springboard for a **cultural project** linked to a historical period or geographical region. This can be presented in various ways (perhaps of each group's choosing, as long as certain pre-determined criteria are fulfilled) such as in film, a presentation or a magazine-type feature. **Cross-curricular projects** could also be planned here.

- **Extracts of literature** (not necessarily from a set text) can be **combined** with factual newspaper articles or a problem page to spark class research on a particular social or cultural theme: e.g. immigration into France, homelessness, social exclusion; the position of women or on a particular period of history (aspects of World War II or German reunification or Franco's Spain) or of a geographical region (Barcelona, Provence etc.). This can be presented in class (in groups) or as a class magazine for sharing with another class or an exchange school.

- Students can **compare different poems** on a particular theme and display these along with a commentary (e.g. of the context in which each was written, what the author was trying to say) and perhaps their own version of a poem on the theme for modern-day Britain. A link with the English Department could perhaps supply relevant anglophone work for comparison.

## Pre-reading

- The **treasure box** activity aims to stimulate students' interest by prompting a creative and oral response to some of the main objects in the play. The teacher presents students with a treasure box. Inside have been placed clues about the characters or plot of the text. These might include small pictures or artefacts which are key to the text, a torn paper with part of a note from one character to another, a comment about a character. The objects could be revealed one by one and the group asked to build up the story around them. This could take the form of a game where everyone takes turns to continue the story, including the items in a believable way. When all the contents of the treasure chest have been revealed, the class could be asked if they wish to revise their opinion in any way. A good homework exercise would be for them to write their own version of the story. As they start to read the original text, they will be interested and amused to see if they chanced on accurate facts. Ultimately, students could construct their own treasure box for a particular character.

- A variation of this could be devised using a **dustbin**. Here the students speculate about characters and plot based on what they have thrown away.

- Give students the **opening sentence** (or a first paragraph or longer) of a short story or novel and organise the class into groups to discuss **what might happen next**. Students could take particular responsibilities to decide on the context and setting, the characters and the plot. The end product could be a plan or synopsis of their imagined story, a short drama based on the scenario or a poem which continues the tale. Groups can present their work and the class could vote for the most interesting (or comic, or realistic or surreal!). If the groups are given a further few lines from later in the story, this can guide the students to a version which may be closer to the original. Some groups could be given one, two or three lines to work with and see how the versions alter.

## Plot summaries

- Retelling the story in various forms e.g.
  - as a **comic strip** (specify number of frames) or a **photo story;**
  - as a series of **mimed tableaux** (specify number again);
  - as a **5-minute play** (along the lines of the Reduced Shakespeare Company!);
  - as a **radio play**;
  - in a **certain number of words;**
  - as a **poem**;
  - **tweeting** the plot in a certain number of characters or per chapter/act;
  - a **news broadcast** or **newspaper article**;
  - as a series of **diary entries** for a main character;
  - adapt a scene or episode for **filming**.

- Students could enact a conversation between a character and a **fortune teller** who, in response to questions, predicts what is about to happen. Students could be guided with categories to prepare such as romance, travel, loss, career, surprise *etc*. This could be framed either with the future tense or as possibilities in the subjunctive mood.

- Students could produce **promotional material**, film clips, trailers, poster, book jackets for a text.

- Students could be asked to rewrite the story for a **younger audience**, *i.e.* in a picture book format or with a simplified plot or cartoons.

- The story could also be retold from a different **character's** or different ideological **perspective**, for example, that of the Arab in Camus' *L'étranger*. Another suitable text would be de Vigan's *No et moi* where No explains her point of view.

## Plot scenarios

- Imagining (in drama or dialogue, or prose or verse) episodes **before** the action of the story e.g. Doria's life before her father left in Guène's *Kiffe kiffe demain*.

- Episodes can also be created (in dialogue or prose) detailing a **continuation** of the story. This could be a prison visit between Katharina Blum and Gotten in Böll's story. Writing an extra **episode** would give students an excellent opportunity to study and try to replicate the author's style.

- Students could imagine 'the sequel' (in the form of a synopsis, an opening paragraph, or a film trailer). This could follow the further adventures of No in de Vigan's *No et moi*, for example.

- Students make one change about the plot and write the revised (and very different) synopsis.

- An alternative ending could also be written for a novel or play, changing it from tragic to happy, or where a key character lives rather than dies or does find romantic happiness.

- Dramatising gaps in the narrative (e.g. Pagnol's *Le château de ma mère* between the summer and Marcel's mother's death or in Schlink's *Der Vorleser*, episodes of Michael's life after Hanna has left). Similarly, students may dramatise what characters may have said to one another 'off-stage'.

## Characters

Students may write *about* the characters.

- Writing a *portrait chinois* as discussed in Chapter 8.
- Designing a **horoscope**. This activity is intended to provide students with an introduction to characterisation and a variety of expressions and vocabulary to allow them to communicate their views. Using exemplar horoscopes from target language magazines gives the students interesting vocabulary and phrases to adapt.
- Writing an **obituary**. This is a formal and rather solemn summary of a character's life. It can be made more fun by asking for a satirical or negative obituary for an ill-liked character. This also offers an opportunity to write and research the back story of a character such as Fumero or Fermín in Ruiz Zafón's

*La sombra del viento*. The obituary could be written from both positive and negative perspectives.

Characters may represent *themselves*

- Writing a **blog** (complete with interesting hashtags!).
- As **interviewees** on a TV chat show, news broadcast or magazine article (Chapter 8).
- Writing to a **problem page** with their dilemma and then receiving a response. Many characters from the set texts are candidates for this *e.g.* Lou's mother after her bereavement in de Vigan's *No et moi*.
- Writing an **article or letter to the press** on a topic relevant to the book, *e.g.* Lou might write on homelessness following her encounter with No in de Vigan's *No et moi*.
- Students can also take the role of characters in **hotseating** or **characters in conflict** as described in Chapter 8.
- Students can also write brief, but telling, **messages** between characters. One can imagine the daughters in Lorca's *La casa de Bernarda Alba* resorting to a few insults in the way they communicate. Equally, No might be messaged by her friend Lou when she is worried about her in de Vigan's *No et moi*. König's *Ich fühl mich so fifty-fifty* would be an ideal novel for messaging thoughts and reactions.
- Writing a character's **social media page** would be a valuable activity for students to engage in, as it involves in-depth knowledge of the character and creativity but restricted language. The activity may seem anachronistic for most older books, however, with artistic licence, this can work really well. While some characters like Meursault in Camus's *L'étranger*, would certainly not have a social media page, others like Cunégonde in Voltaire's *Candide* or Josyane in Rochefort's *Les petits enfants du siècle* would make good subjects. To choose a strapline for a character would be interesting and students would enjoy the 'about me' section, where they write what others think about them. A possible template is shown in Figure 11.3 which can be translated into the desired language.

## *Other types of writing*

- The **recipes** in Esquivel's *Como agua para chocolate* provide a model for actual and metaphorical recipes for students to copy (and practise particular verb forms).
- **Letters** in literature are a good starting point for student replies. Additionally, the letter format can offer a different way of allowing students to imagine how one character may express his or her feelings about a person or an event, either informally (a kind of interior monologue) or formally, as in a letter of complaint, of apology or to a newspaper. Different styles of writing can be explored.

| Social media page for | |
|---|---|
| *Message/strapline:* | |
| **Name** | |
| **Birthday** | |
| **Education** | |
| **Single/married** | |
| **Family members** | |
| **Job** | |
| **Religious views** | |
| **About me** | |
| **Friends** | |
| **Photos** | |
| **Favourite books** | |
| **Favourite films** | |
| **Interests** | |
| **Likes** | |
| **Dislikes** | |

*Figure 11.3* Suggested outline for social media page (translate as required).

- Writing a **letter** from one character to another can be a powerful way for students to empathise with the characters and deepen their understanding. Good examples might include the niece to Werner von Ebrennac in Vercors' *Le silence de la mer*, Pedro to Tita in Esquivel's *Como agua para chocolate* after his marriage to Rosaura, Tita's sister.

- A character may also write a letter to his or her **younger self** e.g. Joseph in Joffo's *Un sac de billes*, Candide in Voltaire's work or Michael in Schlink's *Der Vorleser*.

- **Speeches** can also be constructed (and delivered) where characters argue their point of view on a topic close to their heart.

- For homework, students **draw a scene** from the text or choose photos to represent characters and locations on a **mood board**. They could comment orally or in writing on their work (Paran and Robinson 2016). Examples could include the beach scene with the Arab in Camus' *L'étranger*, or the route for the shortcut in Pagnol's *Le château de ma mère*, where the family is caught trespassing.

- Students may create a **game** based on the story to practise language skills and revise content. This could replicate Joseph's adventures and journey through France in Joffo's *Un sac de billes* or be based around the recipes in Esquivel's

*Como agua para chocolate*. Students could use digital media to add interactivity and graphics and really let their imagination run free.

## *Group activities*

Whilst the previous activities could be undertaken in pairs or groups, there are some orally-based activities which require collaboration. If any group activity is being filmed, it is important to have clearly defined roles for students to allow them to play to their different strengths. It is useful to impose time limits and to have a 'director' or manager within the group to supervise progress.

- Students can develop **dialogues** and **mini-plays** based on the characters, setting or themes of the text.
- Issues in the play or novel can act as a catalyst for a polemical **debate**.
- Students could stage a **trial** or a **balloon debate** as described in Chapter 8.
- Groups plan a **fantasy dinner party** with the guest list (and justification for each guest), the menu, the seating arrangements and the appearance and character of each person. As well as social niceties, certain topics of conversation can be chosen for discussion. Groups can simply write up an account of the dinner, to be presented alongside the other information or, it is more fun is to enact the dinner in the role of the chosen guests. It is a good way of imagining themselves into the characters and thinking about their relationships with the other guests and how they would react to certain topics and in certain circumstances.

## Conclusions

The purpose of the book is to support teachers who are new to literature teaching to navigate the demands of the A level syllabus. We have not focussed on how to teach specific texts but explored an approach which values the benefits for students in terms of their linguistic, cultural and personal development. Literature offers a rich source of language practice, cultural awareness and close critical reading. It can also spark readers' emotions, empathy and imagination. It is on this note of creativity which we end. We hope that teachers will continue to read in their chosen languages for pleasure and that they will share that pleasure with their students. After all, preparation for the A level study of literature takes place, often in a variety of small ways, in the preceding years of language learning.

# Further reading

Parkinson and Reid Thomas (2000) include a section on studying **poetry**. Duff and Maley (2007) have many engaging graded activities for using literature, particularly poetry, to teach English as a second language, many of which are adaptable to MFL. Paran and Robinson (2016) also provide a good introduction to poetry in the English-teaching context. Kramsch (1993 pp.156–171) stresses three approaches in **teaching poetry**: celebrating poetry (its physical form and sounds through performance); understanding through multiple meanings and perspectives and thirdly, experimenting with form and meaning and is interesting if teachers wish to think more deeply about this.

# Implications for teaching

- Investigate resources websites, some of which have been suggested here, and invite students to find other suitable resources for the class as a homework task.

- Consider incorporating reading homework for some classes which encourage younger learners to become familiar with fairy tales, fables, songs and *comptines*.

- Use literary extracts to supplement other areas of language learning (grammatically, linguistically and culturally).

- Plan how to use extracts from longer texts which will enable students to show a personal and creative response.

- Read some poetry and encourage students to write their own based on a model.

- Think about giving students who are between GCSE and the start of the A level course an interesting summer task based on a short story.

- Allow students to enjoy the creative possibilities which literature and their imaginations can bring to their language learning.

# References

Birketveit, A. and Rimmereide, H.E., 2017. Using authentic picture books and illustrated books to improve L2 writing among 11-year-olds. *The Language Learning Journal*, 45(1), pp.100–116.

Brumfit, C., 1985. *Language and Literature Teaching: From Practice to Principle*. Oxford: Pergamon.

Chambers, G., 1991. Suggested approaches to A-level literature. *Language Learning Journal*, 4, pp.5–9.

Department for Education (DfE), 2013. Languages programmes of study: key stage 3. National Curriculum in England. Accessed January 2019 https://assets.publishing. service.gov.uk/government/uploads/system/uploads/attachment_data/file/239083/ SECONDARY_national_curriculum_-_Languages.pdf

Duff, A. and Maley, A., 2007. *Literature*. 2nd ed. Oxford: Oxford University Press.

Jakubowski, K., Finkel, S., Stewart, L. and Mullensiefen, D., 2017. Dissecting an Earworm: melodic features and song popularity predict involuntary musical imagery. *Psychology of Aesthetics, Creativity and the Arts*, 1(2), pp.122–135.

Kramsch, C., 1993. *Context and Culture in Language Teaching*. Oxford: Oxford University Press.

Morgan, C., 1994. Creative writing in foreign language teaching. *Language Learning Journal*, 10, pp.44–47.

Paran, A. and Robinson, P., 2016. *Literature*. Oxford: Oxford University Press.

Parkinson, B. and Reid Thomas, H., 2000. *Teaching Literature in a Second Language*. Edinburgh: Edinburgh University Press.

Swarbrick, A., 1998. *More Reading for Pleasure in a Foreign Language*. London: CILT publications.

# Appendix 1
# Sources of information
# for teachers

## Examination boards

- The most important source of information for teachers can be obtained online from the examination boards. The list of set texts, examination requirements, assessment criteria, specimen and past papers, annotated scripts, marking schemes and examiners' reports should all be downloaded and studied carefully when preparing to teach the syllabus of the chosen board.

- Other examination boards may also use the same texts. Looking at their examination material can provide additional insights and be useful in setting practice essays and answers (see Chapter 10).

- The examination boards which set literature as part of the AS/A level syllabus are Assessment and Qualifications Alliance (AQA); Edexcel (Pearson); Eduqas (England) and WJEC (Wales); Council for the Curriculum, Examinations and Assessment (Northern Ireland).

## Purpose made resources for A level set texts

- Examination boards have produced free online materials for the texts on their syllabus, some designed for teachers and others for students. Depending on the particular board these include PowerPoint resources, interactive online activities, summaries and more general information on approaching the literature paper in the examination. Once again, popular texts are often set by more than one examination board and resources may be found via the board websites.
  *e.g.* Eduqas Digital Educational Resources: http://resources.eduqas.co.uk/

- A series of student study guides, written expressly for individual set texts and the AS/A level examination have been produced for purchase.
  *e.g.* Oxford Literature Companions (Oxford University Press)

Modern Languages Study Guides (Hodder Education)
'Getting to Know' Series (ZigZag Education)

- If studying a play (*e.g.* Brecht or Anouilh), this may appear on the A level Drama and Theatre Studies syllabus of some examination boards, and although studied in English, the support materials can provide useful background information.

- It is useful to find an edition of the text (for the teacher) which includes student notes. When foreign languages literature used to be taught in English at A level, series such as Harrap Modern World Literature and Methuen's 20th Century Texts provided a lot of useful support for the reader. Many can still be bought from online second-hand sellers.

## Online teacher resources and vocabulary sites

- Teachers are now sharing literature resources quite extensively and sites such as Tes.com (resources) and Teachitlanguages.co.uk can be searched to find a range of materials on popular texts.

- Languagesresources.co.uk have a range of free resources for French and Spanish A level texts including Maupassant, Molière, Sagan, Voltaire and Esquivel.

- Dolanguages.com have a range of film and literature resources in French, German and Spanish to purchase.

- Online vocabulary sites such as memrise.com and quizlet.com also have interactive exercises shared by teachers and students.

- Neil Jones' site has resources and ideas for students at all levels. The KS5 Spanish section includes background materials on Mexico in preparation for a class studying Esquivel's *Como agua para chocolate*. https://neiljones.org/.

- Rachel Hawkes' website includes her teaching materials for Lorca's *Bodas de Sangre*. These deal with the historical background, character analysis, the examination of imagery and symbolism, recurrent themes, preparation for an essay on a protagonist, Lorcian use of imagery, colours and stage directions and questions for individual students on the work and their feelings and reactions to it. www.rachelhawkes.com

  N.B. With freely shared and unedited content, it is important to check for the grammatical accuracy of the materials, as well as the suitability for a particular class.

## Student guides from universities

- It is useful to look out for any school study days run by your local University MFL Department.

- The University of Leeds has produced freely available resources for teaching texts and films on the new A level syllabus in French, German and Spanish. Search Language Teachers Resources at https://artsoutreach.leeds.ac.uk/whats-on-offer/for-teachers/.

- The University of Cambridge Language Centre has free online materials for Spanish (Lorca and Esquivel) and French (poetry) literature. Search in Open Courseware: www.langcen.cam.ac.uk/opencourseware/opencourseware-index.html.

- MOOC online courses are made available internationally and teachers can sign up to learn more about literature *e.g.* FutureLearn has hosted two courses on Gabriel García Márquez and continues to run other free, literature-related programmes.

- Villiers Park Educational charity has free online extension resources in French, German and Spanish for students who may wish to broaden their literature reading independently.

# Study guides

- Student study guides for native speakers are available for the majority of texts. These may be more useful for the teacher than students directly, but do provide background information, plot summaries, character profiles and stylistic notes which teachers can adapt for use in class. Vocabulary which is non-standard should be explained in the notes. The guides also provide teachers with a useful model of language for discussing literature.

   *e.g.* French: Profil Littéraire (analyse d'oeuvre) editions and Le PetitLittéraire. fr which has a large number of *fiches de lecture* to purchase online.

   *e.g.* Spanish: Resumenexpress.com have a similar range of Spanish *guía de lectura*

   *e.g.* German: Königs Erläuterungen.de study notes.

- Grant and Cutler Critical Guides (in English) cover texts by Pagnol, Sagan, Lorca, Sender, Allende, García Márquez and Esquivel.

# Social media platforms

- Pinterest allows teachers to collect, store and share visual materials such as photos, book jackets and quotations. Many existing boards relating to literature can be 'pinned' but should be edited and checked for accuracy.

- YouTube is a rich source of trailers and clips of productions of plays and film versions of novels and plays. Interviews with authors, sometimes reading their own works (*e.g.* Camus), can provide excellent background material and a sense of authenticity. Clips can also be very effective in bringing the socio-historical context of the text to life for students.

- Many modern authors also have their own websites and blogs which students can use for background research.

- Book club podcasts offer interesting discussions. *e.g.* BBC World Service *World Book Club* has episodes with authors Isabel Allende and Carlos Ruiz Zafón.

- Although in English, the BBC Radio 4 podcast *In Our Time* has discussed Sartre, Camus and Voltaire.

# Online resources from international websites

- Encourage students to use French, German and Spanish language search engines for *.fr; .de; .es.*

- National cultural and educational sites designed for native language speakers offer a wealth of free material on classic texts (some examples follow).

- It is also useful to look up the equivalent of 'English as a second language' resources but for French (FLE – *français comme langue étrangère*), German (DaF – *Deutsch als Fremdsprache*) or Spanish (ELE – *español como lengua extranjera*). There are a lot of creative resources to help students learn, including simplified literature texts.

### French

- La Bibliothèque Nationale de France has a wealth of online resources for certain authors *e.g.*
  **Jean-Paul Sartre** http://expositions.bnf.fr/sartre/
  A special exhibition contains a huge amount of visual material (theatre posters and stills, manuscripts, photos, newspaper cuttings), audio material (interviews with contemporaries and commentators about aspects of his life and works), synopses of all works, an illustrated timeline of his life and links to other authors of note and essays on aspects of his thinking.

  **Voltaire** https://candide.bnf.fr
  This is a remarkable resource with strong visual images, chapter summaries, interactive maps of Candide's journey, a glossed text, extensive background information about, for example, the contemporary slave trade, women in the 18th century, accompanied by other literary extracts on the theme up to the present day. There are also audio recordings of chapter summaries in clear French.

  It is worth exploring the school-based resources http://classes.bnf.fr/index.php. As an introduction to literature, there are resources on **La Fontaine** featuring vivid illustrations, the background to the genre and extracts from *Les Fables* http://gallica. bnf.fr/essentiels/fontaine/fables.

  For literary and historical background, there is also a free app on Louis XIV http://classes.bnf.fr/essentiels/albums/versailles/index.htm

Children's literature and *bandes dessinées* for younger students are also available.

- *Éduthèque* and *Éduscol* are professional sites for teachers in France with downloadable resources, videos and images about works of literature. www.edutheque.fr/accueil.html http://eduscol.education.fr

- Sites are often dedicated to individual writers such as Maupassant. This site contains all his works, translations, commentaries, synopses, journal articles http://maupassant.free.fr/. Audio readings of Maupassant's short stories with the text and with translations of key words can be found at www.languageguide.org/french/readings/.

- *La Page des Lettres* from the Académie Versailles has teaching resources for literature century by century. There are full programmes for teaching various texts in French schools. Some of the information may be useful for teachers. https://lettres.ac-versailles.fr

- *Le Point du fle* is for teaching French as a second language and has suggestions based on a wide range of other literature. The collection of *fiches pédagogiques* on literature include general activities and more specific worksheets with links to relevant material on other sites. Worksheets include Goscinny and Sempé; Saint-Exupéry, la Fontaine, Prévert, Molière, Hugo, Camus, Apollinaire (*Calligrammes*) and poetry. These are often just extracts with media links and worksheets and could be helpful for building younger students' literary awareness and language www.lepointdufle.net.

- *Franc-parler* is a useful site focussing on wider francophone literature. The *Anthologies des littératures francophones* has suggestions for reading www.francparler-oif.org/la-litterature-doutre-mer/.

- *Culturthèque* from the *Institut français* gives access to many free books to borrow including easy readers, children's books and collection of *bandes dessinées*. Digital books may be borrowed for 30 days (log in needed) *www.culturethèque.com*.

- TV5monde has free downloadable versions of French classics. These may be difficult but there are short fact sheets on the authors which may be useful for display or project work on authors. There are also *fiches pédagogiques* with certain texts, including Maupassant, La Fontaine, Mérimée and Baudelaire, Gaston Leroux. http://bibliothequenumerique.tv5monde.com. The *en scène* collection has materials on *Le Tartuffe* and background looking at Molière's oeuvre and universe plus recordings of theatre productions.

- Useful sites bring together different sources of information and provide accompanying worksheets! The *réseau-canopé* has dossiers of literature materials for FLE teachers at all levels *e.g.* search for Camus. It also lists sites where free downloads of classic texts are available. www.reseau-canope.fr/langues-en-ligne/francais-langue-seconde-langue-etrangere.html

### German

- Fluter.de is a current affairs magazine site in accessible language with lots of topical articles and videos and a section 'Buch' which students could use to read reviews and get a wider understanding of the literary scene in Germany. www.fluter.de/buch

- Broadcasters have videos and materials on historical topics, especially linked to Reunification and aspects of World War II e.g. ARD Mediathek and ZDF www.zdf.de/doku-wissen and Arte www.arte.tv/de/videos/geschichte/
  Planet-wissen.de (from ARD) is accessible and explains history and culture.

- Vorleser has short audio books in German which are free to download www.vorleser.net/.

- Der Spiegel's Gutenberg Project makes a vast range of German literature freely available which can be read online, with accompanying author profiles http://gutenberg.spiegel.de/
  Zeno is another similar site www.zeno.org/Literatur/.

- Annotext is a resource from Dartmouth College which allows students to read German literary texts online and to see a translation of any words they don't understand by clicking on them. This can speed up reading time for texts where students are preparing passages at home. https://annotext.dartmouth.edu/

### Spanish

- La Biblioteca Nacional de España has a range of digital works, including Lorca's *Bodas de Sangre* and *La casa de Bernarda Alba*. http://bne.es.

- The *Literatura* section of La Biblioteca Virtual Miguel de Cervantes has biographical information on Lorca, with digital texts, photos and links to other institutions www.cervantesvirtual.com/portales/literatura.

- The *Literatura* section of Hablacultura.com has an audio version of the article *Lorca e il mito gitano* and of his poem *Il romancero gitano* (the first poem is about the moon). Under 'cine y guerra civil española', there is an interesting article about the civil war and Spanish cinema http://hablacultura.com.

- *La Consejería de Educación* website has materials for A level themes, such as *la guerra civil española* www.mecd.gob.es/reinounido.

- La Real Academia Española has a range of monolingual dictionaries (under *recursos*) www.rae.es.

# Appendix 2(a) Literary phrases in French

| La production littéraire | |
|---|---|
| l'écrivain | writer |
| l'auteur | author |
| l'ouvrage | work |
| le romancier/la romancière | novelist |
| le roman | novel |
| le roman de mœurs | novel depicting aspects of society |
| le roman à thèse | novel with philosophical message |
| le récit/le conte | short story |
| le/la dramaturge | playwright |
| la pièce de théâtre | play |
| une satire | satire |
| l'ironie | irony |
| **Le contenu** | |
| le narrateur/la narratrice | narrator |
| le cadre | setting |
| le scénario | situation |
| la mise en scène | staging |
| les personnages | characters |
| les personnages secondaires | secondary characters |
| le personnage | character (individual) |
| le caractère | character/personality |

*(Continued)*

(*Cont.*)

| le protagoniste | protagonist |
|---|---|
| la représentation, caractérisation | characterisation |
| la relation | relationship |
| un thème (récurrent) | theme (recurrent) |
| cela traite (du thème) de … | it's about … |
| l'action/l'intrigue se déroule | the plot unfolds |
| l'intrigue secondaire | secondary plot |
| la péripétie | twist in the plot |
| l'apogée, le point culminant | the climax |
| le dénouement | outcome |
| décrire | to describe |
| représenter avec exactitude | to portray accurately |
| la description détaillée | detailed description |
| raconter en détail | to recount (in detail) |
| le réalisme | realism |
| peindre d'après nature | to depict life as it is |
| l'âpre vérité | the harsh truth |
| didactique | didactic, having a message |
| la signification | meaning, significance |
| signifier | to mean |
| un dialogue | dialogue |
| un monologue (intérieur) | a(n) (interior) monologue |
| avoir un impact sur | to have an effect on |
| symboliser | to symbolise |
| le symbole | symbol |
| refléter | to reflect |
| développer | to develop |
| dépayser les lecteurs | to transport the readers to another world |
| idéaliser | to idealise |
| imaginaire | imaginary |
| évoquer | to evoke |
| chimérique | fanciful |

(*Continued*)

(*Cont.*)

| la fantaisie | fantasy |
|---|---|
| le rêve | dream |
| la nostalgie | nostalgia |
| éclaircir | to explain |
| l'éclaircissement | explanation, clarification |
| évaluer | to evaluate |
| dégager l'idée principale | bring out the main idea |
| ce que veut dire l'auteur ici, c'est… | the author wants to tells us that |
| citer | to quote |
| la citation | quotation |
| porter un jugement sur… | to make a judgment on |
| une œuvre couronnée de succès | a successful work |
| retirer un grand profit de | to gain much from |
| s'identifier avec les personnages | to identify with the characters |

**Le style**

| *le style est* | sobre | *the style is* | controlled |
|---|---|---|---|
| | net/clair | | clear |
| | soigné | | careful |
| | imagé | | full of imagery |
| | raffiné | | sophisticated |
| | piquant | | entertaining, racy |
| | concis | | concise |
| | recherché | | refined |

**La réaction du lecteur**

| le chef d'œuvre | masterpiece |
|---|---|
| une œuvre de génie | a work of genius |
| une œuvre d'une grande portée | a highly significant work |
| l'auteur a de l'esprit | the author is witty |
| l'auteur s'exprime avec netteté | the author writes with precision |
| l'auteur enrichit son récit de … | the author enriches the story with … |
| l'auteur traduit clairement ses idées | the author conveys ideas clearly |

(*Continued*)

(*Cont.*)

| j'admire, on admire | | We can admire | |
|---|---|---|---|
| la puissance d'imagination | | the imaginative power | |
| la puissance du raisonnement | | the power of reasoning | |
| le foisonnement d'idées | | the wealth of ideas | |
| la profondeur des sentiments | | the depth of feeling | |
| la lucidité de la pensée | | the clarity of thought | |
| le récit saisissant | | the striking narrative | |
| les descriptions vives | | the vivid descriptions | |
| l'ironie mordante | | the biting irony | |
| l'esprit railleur | | the mocking wit | |
| *le livre* | passionne | *the book* | thrills |
| | tient en haleine | | grips |
| | suscite l'admiration | | arouses admiration |
| | suscite la réflexion | | is thought-provoking |
| | déborde d'humour | | overflows with humour |
| | est émouvant | | is moving |
| | est déroutant | | is disturbing |
| | est triste à pleurer | | moves you to tears |
| je ne suis tout à fait pas d'accord | | I don't entirely agree | |
| je ne suis pas du tout d'accord | | I don't agree at all | |
| en ce qui me concerne | | as far as I am concerned/for my part | |
| je suis persuadé que … | | I am persuaded that | |
| il va sans dire que … | | it goes without saying that<br>it is obvious that | |
| selon moi | | in my opinion | |
| d'un côté, de l'autre | | on the one hand, on the other | |
| le revers de la médaille, c'est … | | there is another side to the coin | |
| par contraste | | by contrast | |
| néanmoins | | nevertheless | |
| en tout cas | | in any case | |
| pourtant | | however | |
| malgré cela | | in spite of that | |
| malgré | | in spite of | |
| ou …, ou …/soit …, soit … | | either … or … | |

(*Continued*)

*(Cont.)*

| en ce qui concerne | as regards |
|---|---|
| dans une certaine mesure | to some extent |
| d'une façon ou d'une autre | one way or another |
| en conclusion, je constate que … | in conclusion, I should like to say that |
| en fin de compte | when all is said and done |
| **Des phrases utiles** ||
| par rapport à | with respect to, regarding |
| tout d'abord | first and foremost |
| à notre époque moderne | in our modern age |
| pour le moment | for the moment |
| de nos jours | nowadays |
| par le passé | in times past |
| à maintes reprises | time and again |
| de temps en temps | from time to time |
| de temps à autre | now and again |
| bien sûr | of course |
| dans l'ensemble | on the whole |
| en général | in general |
| **Procédés dramaturgiques** ||
| antagoniste (m) adversaire (m) | antagonist/foil |
| (dire quelque chose) en aparté (m) | an aside |
| catharsis (f.) | catharsis |
| apogée (m)/point culminant (m.) | climax |
| choeur (m) | chorus |
| notes d'humour (f.pl.) | comic relief |
| conflit (m) | conflict |
| dénouement(m.) | dénouement |
| Deus ex machina | Deus ex machina |
| ironie (f) dramatique | dramatic irony |
| personnages complexes | dynamic characters |
| flash-back (m), retour en arrière (m) | flashbacks |
| personnages (m.pl.) plats | flat/static characters |
| présage (m.)/préfiguration (f.) | foreshadowing |
| orgueil démesuré (m) | hubris |

*(Continued)*

*(Cont.)*

| monologue (m.) | monologue |
|---|---|
| accessoires (m.pl.) | props |
| déroulement/développement (m) de l'action | rising action |
| satire (f) | satire |
| personnages (m.pl.) secondaires | secondary characters |
| soliloque (m) | soliloquy |
| tragédie (f) | tragedy |
| erreur (f) fatale/erreur tragique | tragic flaw |
| unités (f) de temps/de lieu/d'action | unities of time/place/action |

# Appendix 2(b)
# Literary phrases in German

| Literarische Produktion | |
|---|---|
| der Schriftsteller (-in) | writer |
| der Autor | author |
| das Werk/ein literarisches Werk | work |
| der Romanschriftsteller (-in)/der Romancier | novelist |
| der Roman | novel |
| ein Roman, der gesellschaftliche Aspekte schildert | novel depicting aspects of society |
| ein Roman mit einer philosophischen Aussage | novel with philosophical message |
| die Kurzgeschichte | short story |
| der Dramatiker (-in) | playwright |
| das Theaterstück | play |
| die Satire | a satire |
| die Ironie | irony |
| **Der Inhalt** | |
| der Erzähler (-in) | narrator |
| der Handlungsort | setting |
| die Situation | situation |
| die Inszenierung | staging |
| die Figuren | characters |

(Continued)

(*Cont.*)

| die Nebenfigur | secondary character |
|---|---|
| der Charakter | character (individual) |
| die Persönlichkeit | character/personality |
| der Protagonist (-in) | protagonist |
| die Darstellung | characterisation |
| das Verhältnis | relationship |
| das Leitmotiv | theme (recurrent) |
| es handelt sich um | it's about |
| die Handlung entwickelt | the plot unfolds |
| die sekundäre Handlung | secondary plot |
| eine überraschende Wendung in der Handlung | twist in the plot |
| der Höhepunkt | the climax |
| das Ergebnis | outcome |
| beschreiben | to describe |
| genau schildern | to portray accurately |
| die detaillierte Schilderung | detailed description |
| bis ins Detail/in allen Einzelheiten erzählen | to recount (in detail) |
| der Realismus | realism |
| das Leben, so wie es ist, beschreiben | to depict life as it is |
| die harte Wahrheit | the harsh truth |
| didaktisch | didactic, having a message |
| die Bedeutung | meaning, significance |
| bedeuten | to mean |
| der Dialog | dialogue |
| der innere Monolog | (interior) monologue |
| sich auf etwas auswirken | to have an effect on |
| symbolisieren | to symbolise |
| das Symbol | symbol |
| denken/nachdenken/reflektieren | to reflect |
| entwickeln | to develop |
| ermöglicht es dem Leser, in eine andere Welt einzutauchen | enables the reader to be transported to another world |
| idealisieren | to idealise |

(*Continued*)

(*Cont.*)

| | |
|---|---|
| imaginär/scheinbar | imaginary |
| hervorrufen | to evoke |
| fantasiereich | fanciful |
| die Phantasie/Fantasie | fantasy |
| der Traum | dream |
| die Nostalgie | nostalgia |
| erklären | to explain |
| die Erklärung | explanation, clarification |
| einschätzen/beurteilen | to evaluate |
| die Hauptidee ausbringen | bring out the main idea |
| der Autor will damit sagen, dass | the author wants to tell us |
| zitieren | to quote |
| das Zitat | quotation |
| beurteilen/urteilen über (acc) | to make a judgment on |
| ein erfolgreiches Werk | a successful work |
| profitieren von | to gain much from |
| sich mit dem Charakter identifizieren | to identify with the characters |
| **Die Reaktion des Lesers** | |
| das Meisterstück/Meisterwerk | masterpiece |
| ein geniales Werk/eine geniale Leistung | a work of genius |
| ein hoch bedeutendes/wichtiges Werk | a highly significant work |
| der Autor ist witzig | the author is witty |
| der Autor schreibt mit Präzision/ Genauigkeit | the author writes with precision |
| der Autor bereichert das Werk mit … | the author enriches the story with. |
| der Autor vermittelt Ideen deutlich | the author conveys ideas clearly |
| *Man kann … … … … … … … … … …* *bewundern* die phantasievolle Macht den Scharfsinn den Gedankenreichtum die Empfindungstiefe die gedankliche Klarheit die bemerkenswerte Schilderung die bildhaften Beschreibungen die scharfe Ironie den spöttischen Geist | *We can admire* the imaginative power the power of reasoning the wealth of ideas the depth of feeling the clarity of thought the striking narrative the vivid descriptions the biting irony the mocking wit |

(*Continued*)

(*Cont.*)

| das Buch | begeistert/ fasziniert | the book | thrills |
|---|---|---|---|
| | fesselt | | grips |
| | erregt Bewunderung | | arouses admiration |
| | regt zum Nach-denken an | | is thought-provoking |
| | sprudelt über vor Humor | | overflows with humour |
| | ist herzergreifend | | is deeply moving |
| | ist beunruhigend | | is disturbing |
| | rührt einen zu Tränen | | moves you to tears |
| ich bin nicht ganz der Meinung | | I don't entirely agree | |
| ich bin absolut nicht der Meinung | | I don't agree at all | |
| was mich betrifft | | as far as I am concerned/for my part | |
| ich bin überzeugt, dass | | I am persuaded that | |
| es versteht sich von selbst, dass | | it goes without saying that | |
| es ist mir klar, dass | | it is obvious that | |
| meiner Meinung nach | | in my opinion | |
| es gibt dafür und dagegen | | there is for and against | |
| einerseits … andererseits | | on the one hand, on the other | |
| es gibt die Kehrseite der Medaille | | there is another side to the coin | |
| im Gegensatz dazu/dagegen | | by contrast | |
| trotzdem/dennoch | | nevertheless | |
| jedenfalls | | in any case | |
| jedoch | | however | |
| trotzdem | | in spite of that | |
| trotz (+gen) | | in spite of | |
| entweder …, oder | | either …, or | |
| was … betrifft | | as regards | |
| bis zu einem gewissen Grad | | to some extent | |
| auf seine Weise/auf die eine oder andere Art | | one way or another | |
| zum Schluss | | in conclusion, I should like to say that | |

(*Continued*)

(*Cont.*)

| wenn alles vorüber ist/schließlich und endlich | | when all is said and done | |
|---|---|---|---|
| **Der Styl** | | | |
| *Der Styl ist* | kontrolliert/ beherrscht | *the style is* | controlled |
| | klar | | clear |
| | sorgfältig | | careful |
| | voller Bildersymbolik | | full of visual imagery |
| | raffiniert | | refined |
| | schwungvoll/ feurig | | entertaining, racy |
| | präzise/kurzgefasst | | concise |
| | anspruchsvoll | | sophisticated |
| **Sinnvolle Sätze** | | | |
| in Bezug auf (+acc) | | with respect to, regarding | |
| zunächst/vor allem | | first and foremost | |
| außerdem | | furthermore | |
| als Beispiel | | by way of example | |
| in der Moderne | | in our modern age | |
| im Augenblick | | for the moment | |
| heutzutage | | nowadays | |
| in früheren/vergangenen Zeiten | | in times past | |
| immer wieder | | time and again | |
| von Zeit zu Zeit | | from time to time | |
| gelegentlich/ab und zu | | now and again | |
| natürlich/selbstverständlich | | of course | |
| im Großen und Ganzen/alles in allem | | on the whole | |
| im Allgemeinen | | in general | |
| **Dramaturgische Mittel** | | | |
| der/die Protagonist/in (der Hauptdarsteller, die Hauptfigur) | | protagonist | |
| der/die Antagonist/in (der Gegenspieler zum Protagonisten) | | antagonist/foil | |

(*Continued*)

*(Cont.)*

| | |
|---|---|
| etwas *beiseite* sprechen (nur das Publikum kann es hören) | an aside |
| die Katharsis, die Läuterung | catharsis |
| der Höhepunkt | climax |
| der Chor | chorus |
| die befreiende Komik (Stilmittel) | comic relief |
| der Konflikt | conflict |
| der Dénouement, die Auflösung | dénouement |
| ein Deus ex machina (m) (überraschendes Eingreifen einer göttlichen Macht) | Deus ex machina |
| die dramatische Ironie | dramatic irony |
| dynamische Figuren | dynamic characters |
| Rückblenden (f.pl.) | flashbacks |
| statische Figuren (f.pl.) | flat/static characters |
| die (epische) Vorausdeutung | foreshadowing |
| die Hybris/die Anmaßung/die Arroganz | hubris |
| der Monolog | monologue |
| die Requisiten | props |
| das Ansteigen der Handlung | rising action |
| die Satire | satire |
| die Nebenfiguren | secondary characters |
| der Monolog/das Selbstgespräch | soliloquy |
| die Tragödie/das Trauerspiel | tragedy |
| der tragische Fehler | fatal flaw |
| Einheiten (f.pl.) von Zeit(f.)/Ort (m.)/Handlung (f.) | unities of time/manner/place |

# Appendix 2(c)
# Literary phrases in
# Spanish

| La producción literaria | |
|---|---|
| el escritor | writer |
| el autor | author |
| la obra | work |
| el novelista | novelist |
| una novela | novel |
| una novela que representa aspectos de la sociedad | a novel depicting aspects of society |
| una novela con mensaje filosófico | a novel with philosophical message |
| un cuento | short story |
| el dramaturgo | playwright |
| la obra | play |
| una sátira | satire |
| la ironía | irony |
| **El contenido** | |
| el narrador | narrator |
| el escenario | setting |
| la situación | situation |
| la puesta en escena | staging |
| los personajes | characters |
| los personajes secundarios | secondary characters |

(*Continued*)

*(Cont.)*

| | |
|---|---|
| el personaje | character (individual) |
| el carácter | character/personality |
| el/la protagonista | protagonist |
| la caracterización | characterisation |
| la relación | relationship |
| un tema (recurrente) | theme (recurrent) |
| trata de | it's about |
| la trama se desarrolla | the plot unfolds |
| la trama secundaria | secondary plot |
| una torcedura en la trama | twist in the plot |
| tensión dramática creciente | rising action |
| el clímax | the climax |
| el resultado | outcome |
| describir | to describe |
| retratar con precisión | to portray accurately |
| una descripción detallada | detailed description |
| relatar | to recount (in detail) |
| el realismo | realism |
| representar la vida con realismo | to depict life as it is |
| la cruda verdad | the harsh truth |
| didáctico, moralizador | didactic, having a message |
| el significado | meaning, significance |
| significar | to mean |
| el diálogo | dialogue |
| el monólogo (interior) | (interior) monologue |
| tener un efecto en | have an effect on |
| simbolizar | symbolise |
| el símbolo | symbol |
| reflejar | reflect |
| desarrollar | develop |
| transportar a los lectores a otro mundo | transport readers to another world |
| idealizar | idealise |
| imaginario | imaginary |

*(Continued)*

(*Cont.*)

| | |
|---|---|
| evocar | evoke |
| fantástico | fanciful |
| la fantasía | fantasy |
| el sueño | dream |
| la nostalgia | nostalgia |
| explicar | explain |
| una explicación, una aclaración | an explanation, clarification |
| evaluar | evaluate |
| para sacar la idea principal | bring out the main idea |
| el autor quiere decirnos | the author wants to tell us |
| citar | quote |
| una cita | a quotation |
| hacer un juicio sobre | make a judgment on |
| una obra exitosa | a successful work |
| ganar mucho de | gain much from |
| identificarse con los personajes | identify with the characters |
| **La reacción del lector** | |
| una obra maestra | masterpiece |
| una obra de genio | a work of genius |
| una obra muy significativa | a highly significant work |
| el autor es ingenioso | the author is witty |
| el autor escribe con precisión | the author writes with precision |
| el autor enriquece la historia con. | the author enriches the story with. |
| el autor transmite ideas claramente | the author conveys ideas clearly |
| *podemos admirar*<br>el poder imaginativo<br>el poder de razonamiento<br>la riqueza de ideas<br>la profundidad de sentimiento<br>la claridad del pensamiento<br>la narrativa impresionante<br>las descripciones vívidas<br>la ironía mordaz<br>el ingenio burlón | *We can admire*<br>the imaginative power<br>the power of reasoning<br>the wealth of ideas<br>the depth of feeling<br>the clarity of thought<br>the striking narrative<br>the vivid descriptions<br>the biting irony<br>the mocking wit |

(*Continued*)

(*Cont.*)

| *el libro* | es emocionante | *the book* | thrills |
|------------|----------------|------------|---------|
| | agarra | | grips |
| | incita admiración | | arouses admiration |
| | es estimulante | | is thought-provoking |
| | desborda con sentido del humor | | is full of humour |
| | es inquietante | | is disturbing |
| | te mueve al llanto | | moves you to tears |

| | |
|---|---|
| no estoy completamente de acuerdo | I don't entirely agree |
| no estoy nada de acuerdo | I don't agree at all |
| para mí | as far as I am concerned |
| estoy convencido de que | I am persuaded that |
| no hace falta decir/es evidente que | it goes without saying that |
| es obvio que | it is obvious that |
| en mi opinión | in my opinion |
| hay argumentos a favor y en contra | there are pros and cons |
| por un lado ..., por otro (lado) | on the one hand, on the other |
| hay otra cara de la moneda | there is another side to the coin |
| en cambio | by contrast |
| sin embargo | nevertheless |
| de todos modos | in any case |
| sin embargo | however |
| a pesar de eso | in spite of that |
| a pesar de | in spite of |
| o ..., o ... | either ..., or |
| en lo que respecta, respecto a | as regards |
| hasta cierto punto | to some extent |
| de un modo u otro | one way or another |
| para concluir, en resumen | in conclusion |
| al fin y al cabo | in the end, ultimately |

(*Continued*)

(*Cont.*)

| El estilo | | | |
|---|---|---|---|
| *el estilo es* | controlado | *the style is* | controlled |
| | claro | | clear |
| | cuidadoso | | thorough/ detailed |
| | lleno de imágenes | | full of imagery |
| | elegante | | refined |
| | divertido | | entertaining/ racy |
| | conciso | | concise |
| | sofisticado | | sophisticated |
| **Términos generales** | | | |
| con relación a | | with respect to, regarding | |
| ante todo | | first and foremost | |
| además | | furthermore | |
| a modo de ejemplo | | by way of example | |
| en nuestra edad moderna | | in our modern age | |
| de momento | | for the moment | |
| hoy en día | | nowadays | |
| en tiempos pasados | | in times past | |
| una y otra vez | | time and again | |
| de vez en cuando | | from time to time, now and again | |
| por supuesto | | of course | |
| en general | | on the whole | |
| por lo general | | in general | |
| **Técnicas dramáticas** | | | |
| protagonista (m/f) | | protagonist | |
| antagonista (m/f) | | antagonist/foil | |
| un aparte (de teatro) | | an aside | |
| catharsis (f.) | | catharsis | |
| climax (m.) | | climax | |
| coro (m.) | | chorus | |
| toque cómico/interludio humorístico (m.) | | comic relief | |

(*Continued*)

(*Cont.*)

| | |
|---|---|
| conflicto (m.) | conflict |
| desenlace (m.) | denouement |
| Deus ex machina | Deus ex machina |
| ironía dramática (f.) | dramatic irony |
| personajes dinámicos (m.pl.) | dynamic characters |
| flashback (m.) | flashback |
| personajes que no evolucionan | flat/static characters |
| presagio (m) | foreshadowing |
| orgullo desmesurado (m.) | hubris |
| monólogo (m.) | monologue |
| accesorios (m.pl.)/utillaje (m.) | props |
| sátira (f.) | satire |
| personajes secundarios (m.pl.) | secondary characters |
| soliloquio (m.) | soliloquy |
| tragedia (f.) | tragedy |
| error/fallo trágico | tragic flaw |
| unidades de tiempo/lugar/acción | unities of time/place/action |

# Appendix 3
# Individual student
# reading logs

| Ma bibliothèque personnelle | | | |
|---|---|---|---|
| Auteur: | Titre: | | Publié en |
| Genre: | | | |
| L'action se déroule: | Quand? | | |
| | Où? | | |
| Les personnages principaux: | | | |
| Nom | Age | Occupation/ Fonction | Caractère |
| Résumé: | | | |
| Appréciation: | | | |

| ✓ | Quelle est l'intention de l'auteur? |
|---|---|
| | faire oublier la réalité |
| | troubler |
| | faire penser |
| | intriguer |
| | rendre triste |
| | choquer |
| | rendre conscient |
| | faire rire |
| | influencer sur le plan politique |
| | éveiller les émotions |
| | persuader |
| | faire agir |
| | stimuler |
| | distraire |

| Le style | | | | | | |
|---|---|---|---|---|---|---|
| | 1 | 2 | 3 | 4 | 5 | |
| peu intéressant | | | | | | très intéressant |
| difficile à lire | | | | | | facile à lire |
| difficile à comprendre | | | | | | facile à comprendre |
| style familier | | | | | | style soutenu |
| action compliquée | | | | | | action simple |
| action lente | | | | | | action rapide |
| introduction accrocheuse | | | | | | introduction plate |
| personnages invraisemblables | | | | | | personnages vraisemblables |
| personnages antipathiques | | | | | | personnages sympathiques |
| lecteur tenu à distance | | | | | | lecteur engagé |
| dénouement attendu | | | | | | dénouement inattendu |
| dénouement décevant | | | | | | dénouement convaincant |

| A mon avis | ✓ | |
|---|---|---|
| conseillé aux autres | | |
| déconseillé aux autres | | |

| Meine persönliche Bücherei | | | |
|---|---|---|---|
| Autor: | Titel | | Wann wurde es herausgebracht? |
| Genre: | | | |
| Die Handlung findet statt: | Wann? | | |
| | Wo? | | |
| Die Hauptcharaktere: | | | |
| Name: | Alter: | Beruf/Funktion: | Persönlichkeit: |
| Résumé: | | | |
| Beurteilung: | | | |

| ✓ | Welche Absicht hat der Autor? | | | | | | |
|---|---|---|---|---|---|---|---|
| | die Realität vergessen zu lassen | | | | | | |
| | dir Angst zu machen | | | | | | |
| | dich zum denken anzuregen | | | | | | |
| | dich zu faszinieren | | | | | | |
| | dich traurig zu stimmen | | | | | | |
| | dich auf etwas aufmerksam zu machen | | | | | | |
| | dich zu amüsieren | | | | | | |
| | dich politisch zu beeinflussen | | | | | | |
| | dich zum Handeln zu bringen | | | | | | |
| | dich zu stimulieren | | | | | | |
| | dich zu schockieren | | | | | | |
| | dich zu beunruhigen | | | | | | |
| | dich zu Träumen zu bringen | | | | | | |
| | dich zum Lachen zu bringen | | | | | | |
| **Der Stil** | | | | | | | |
| | | 1 | 2 | 3 | 4 | 5 | |
| nicht sehr interessant | | | | | | | sehr interessant |
| schwer zu lesen | | | | | | | einfach zu lesen |
| schwer zu verstehen | | | | | | | leicht zu verstehen |
| nicht literarisches Stil | | | | | | | literarisches Stil |
| komplizierte Handlung | | | | | | | einfache Handlung |
| langsame Handlung | | | | | | | schnelle Handlung |
| spannende Einleitung | | | | | | | langweilige Einleitung |
| unglaubwürdige Charaktere | | | | | | | glaubwürdige Charaktere |
| unfreundliche Charaktere | | | | | | | freundliche Charaktere |
| Leser wird auf Distanz gehalten | | | | | | | Leser wird miteinbezogen |
| erwartetes Ende | | | | | | | unerwartetes Ende |
| enttäuschendes Ende | | | | | | | überzeugendes Ende |
| **Meine Meinung** | ✓ | | | | | | |
| empfehlenswert | | | | | | | |
| nicht empfehlenswert | | | | | | | |

| Mi Biblioteca Personal | | | |
|---|---|---|---|
| Autor: | Título | | ¿Cúando fue publicado? |
| Género: | | | |
| La acción tiene lugar | ¿Cúando? | | |
| | ¿Dónde? | | |
| Los Personajes Principales | | | |
| Nombre | Edad | Trabajo/Función | Personalidad |
| Resumen | | | |
| Evaluación | | | |
| Desenlace convincente | | | |
| Desenlace decepcionante | | | |

| ✓ | ¿Cuál es el propósito del autor? |
|---|---|
| | Hacer que el lector olvide la realidad |
| | Hacer que el lector se preocupe |
| | Hacer pensar al lector |
| | Hacer que el lector esté fascinado por la novela |
| | Entristecer al lector |
| | Asombrar al lector |
| | Llamar la attención del lector |
| | Hacer reír al lector |
| | Influenciar al lector políticamente |
| | Divertir al lector |
| | Hacer que el lector se deshaga en lágrimas |
| | Persuadir al lector |

### El Estilo

| | 1 | 2 | 3 | 4 | 5 | |
|---|---|---|---|---|---|---|
| No muy interesante | | | | | | Muy interesante |
| Difícil de leer | | | | | | Fácil de leer |
| Difícil de entender | | | | | | Fácil de entender |
| Argumento complicado | | | | | | Argumento sencillo |
| Estilo no literario | | | | | | Estilo literario |
| Argumento se desarrolla despacio | | | | | | Argumento se desarrolla a un ritmo normal |
| Emocionante | | | | | | Aburrido |
| Personajes increíbles | | | | | | Personajes creíbles |
| El autor guarda las distancias con el lector | | | | | | El lector conecta con los personajes |
| El desenlace está previsto | | | | | | El desenlace no está previsto |

| Mi opinión | ✓ |
|---|---|
| Recomendado | |
| No se recomienda | |

# Appendix 4
# Bridging the gap

Activities for *Mateo Falcone* by Prosper Mérimée

A. Lisez le premier paragraphe et trouvez dans le texte la phrase ou le mot qui correspond:

1. de petits chemins

2. bloqués

3. terrain couvert d'un mélange d'arbres et d'arbrisseaux

4. ne pas avoir à

5. partie d'un arbre qui est sous la terre

6. un petit arbre

7. animal qui a de grosses cornes

B. Dessinez la scène que vous pensez voir après avoir lu le premier paragraphe.

C. Choisissez des mots descriptifs qui aident le lecteur à apprécier les difficultés du terrain.

D. Donnez les informations suivantes au sujet de Mateo Falcone:

| Taille | Signes distinctifs | Capacités |
|--------|--------------------|-----------| 
|        |                    |           |

E. Cherchez les qualités – et parfois les défauts – de Fortunato. Montrez comment il se débrouille avec le bandit, en se montrant:

| | |
|---|---|
| ingénieux | |
| prudent | |
| rusé | |
| bon acteur | |
| méprisant | |
| courageux | |
| faible | |
| fort | |

F. Cherchez les termes qu'emploie Gamba lorsqu'il s'adresse à Fortunato.

… … … … … … … … … … … … … … … … … … … … … … … … … … … … … …
… … … … … … … … … … … … … … … … … … … … … … … … … … … … … …
… … … … … … … … … … … … … … … … … … … … … … … … … … … … … …
… … … … … … … … … … … … … … … … … … … … … … … … … … … … … …
… … … … … … … … … … … … … … … … … … … … … … … … … … … … … …
… … … … … … … … … … … … … … … … … … … … … … … … … … … … … …
… … … … … … … … … … … … … … … … … … … … … … … … … … … … … …

G. Voici les gros titres d'un journal qui parle de l'histoire. Remettez-les en ordre:

1. Le retour des parents

2. Des soldats trouvent un dangereux bandit

3. Un bandit blessé cherche un abri

4. Justice en Corse

5. Tenté par une montre en or

6. L'astuce d'un jeune garçon

H. Citez des exemples du style concis de Mérimée.

… … … … … … … … … … … … … … … … … … … … … … … … … … … … … .
… … … … … … … … … … … … … … … … … … … … … … … … … … … … … .
… … … … … … … … … … … … … … … … … … … … … … … … … … … … … .
… … … … … … … … … … … … … … … … … … … … … … … … … … … … … .
… … … … … … … … … … … … … … … … … … … … … … … … … … … … … .
… … … … … … … … … … … … … … … … … … … … … … … … … … … … … .
… … … … … … … … … … … … … … … … … … … … … … … … … … … … … .
… … … … … … … … … … … … … … … … … … … … … … … … … … … … … .

I. Trouvez des exemples de coûtumes et d'habitudes corses.

J. Que savez-vous de la vie d'un paysan corse? Cherchez des détails dans le texte.

K. Trouvez des mots associés aux armes.

L. Trouvez des exemples de comparaisons dans l'histoire.

..........................................................................................................................

..........................................................................................................................

..........................................................................................................................

..........................................................................................................................

..........................................................................................................................

..........................................................................................................................

..........................................................................................................................

..........................................................................................................................

..........................................................................................................................

M. Trouvez dans le texte des exemples où le narrateur parle au lecteur

..........................................................................................................................

..........................................................................................................................

..........................................................................................................................

N. Vous êtes reporter pour un journal corse. Vous réussissez à interviewer Gamba et Fortunato (soit ensemble, soit séparément). Racontez l'histoire de leur point de vue.

O. Deux ans après, vous rencontrez Mateo Falcone dans le maquis. Il vous raconte la pire journée de sa vie.

P. A votre avis, quelles sont les phrases les plus dramatiques de l'histoire?

Q. Vous êtes artiste. On vous demande d'illustrer l'histoire. Réalisez un ou plusieurs dessins. Vous pouvez écrire un poème si vous préférez.

R. Que pensez-vous de l'histoire? Rédigez votre critique (100 mots au minimum) *et justifiez votre opinion.*

# List of set texts mentioned in the book

## French

# German

Böll, H., *Die verlorene Ehre der Katharina Blum* 56, 136, 143, 147, 154, 162, 208
Brecht, B., *Der kaukasische Kreidekreis* 95, 142, 147, 151
Brecht, B., *Mutter Courage und ihre Kinder* 27, 95, 103, 111, 147, 148, 151, 155
Dürrenmatt, F., *Der Besuch der alten Dame* 56, 94, 97, 99, 102, 105, 106, 115, 132, 134, 138, 142, 147, 149, 150, 151, 155, 157
Frisch, M., *Andorra* 99, 103, 105, 142, 148, 149, 157, 161, 162
Hensel, J., *Zonenkinder* 31, 53, 61, 142, 143, 148, 153, 154, 155, 160
Kafka, F., *Die Verwandlung* 27, 127, 131, 132, 157, 159
König, K., *Ich fühl mich so fifty-fifty* 19, 29, 31, 53, 61, 142, 143, 146, 148, 149, 154, 155, 160, 209
Mann, T., *Tonio Kröger* 115
Schlink, B., *Der Vorlese* 127, 130, 134, 142, 148, 154, 157, 161, 208, 210

# Spanish

Allende, I., *La casa de los espíritus* 151, 159
Esquivel, L., *Como agua para chocolate* 30, 56, 62, 74, 116, 127, 130, 132, 145, 149, 151, 157, 159, 160, 209, 210, 215
García Márquez, G., *Crónica de una muerte anunciada* 160
García Márquez, G., *El coronel no tiene quien le escriba* 31, 115, 155
García Lorca, F., *Bodas de sangre* 102, 151, 215, 219
García Lorca, F., *La casa de Bernarda Alba* 27, 56, 102, 104, 105, 108, 111, 115, 116, 129, 142, 147, 149, 151, 157, 161, 209, 219
Matute, A. M., *Prima memoria* 142
Ruiz Zafón, C., *La sombra del viento* 30, 53, 61, 127, 129, 133, 151, 159, 208

# Index

Printed in Great Britain
by Amazon

68305331R00147